THE EUROPEAN UNION SERIES

General Editors: Neill Nugent, Willia ͟ ͟

The European Union series provides an
ranging from general introductory texts  and
actors, issues, policies and policy proces:

Books in the series are written by leading ͟ up-
to-date research and debate. Particular at ͟ ͟y and clear
presentation for a wide audience of studen ͟ ͟s, and interested general readers.

The series editors are **Neill Nugent**, Professor of Politics and Jean Monnet Professor of
European Integration, Manchester Metropolitan University, and **William E. Paterson**,
Director of the Institute of German Studies, University of Birmingham.

Their co-editor until his death in July 1999, **Vincent Wright**, was a Fellow of Nuffield
College, Oxford University. He played an immensely valuable role in the founding and
development of *The European Union Series* and is greatly missed.

Feedback on the series and book proposals are always welcome and should be sent to
Steven Kennedy, Palgrave Macmillan, Houndmills, Basingstoke, Hampshire RG21 6XS, UK,
or by e-mail to s.kennedy@palgrave.com

General textbooks

Published

Desmond Dinan **Encyclopedia of the
European Union**
[Rights: Europe only]

Desmond Dinan **Europe Recast:
A History of European Union**
[Rights: Europe only]

Desmond Dinan **Ever Closer Union:
An Introduction to European Integration
(3rd edn)**
[Rights: Europe only]

Simon Hix **The Political System of the
European Union (2nd edn)**

Paul Magnette **What is the European
Union? Nature and Prospects**

John McCormick **Understanding the
European Union: A Concise
Introduction (3rd edn)**

Brent F. Nelsen and Alexander Stubb
**The European Union: Readings on the
Theory and Practice of European
Integration (3rd edn)**
[Rights: Europe only]

Neill Nugent (ed.) **European Union
Enlargement**

Neill Nugent **The Government and Politics
of the European Union (5th edn)**
[Rights: World excluding USA and
dependencies and Canada]

John Peterson and Elizabeth Bomberg
**Decision-making in the European
Union**

Ben Rosamond **Theories of European
Integration**

Forthcoming

Laurie Buonanno and Neill Nugent
**Policies and Policy Processes of the
European Union**

Mette Eilstrup Sangiovanni (ed.)
**Debates on European Integration:
A Reader**

Philippa Sherrington **Understanding
European Union Governance**

Also planned

**The Political Economy of the
European Union**

Series Standing Order (outside North America only)
ISBN 0–333–71695–7 hardcover
ISBN 0–333–69352–3 paperback
Full details from www.palgrave.com

Visit Palgrave Macmillan's
EU Resource area at
www.palgrave.com/politics/eu/

The major institutions and actors

Published

Renaud Dehousse **The European Court of Justice**

Justin Greenwood **Interest Representation in the European Union**

Fiona Hayes-Renshaw and Helen Wallace **The Council of Ministers**

Simon Hix and Christopher Lord **Political Parties in the European Union**

David Judge and David Earnshaw **The European Parliament**

Neill Nugent **The European Commission**

Anne Stevens with Handley Stevens **Brussels Bureaucrats? The Administration of the European Union**

Forthcoming

Simon Bulmer and Wolfgang Wessels **The European Council**

The main areas of policy

Published

Michelle Cini and Lee McGowan **Competition Policy in the European Union**

Wyn Grant **The Common Agricultural Policy**

Martin Holland **The European Union and the Third World**

Brigid Laffan **The Finances of the European Union**

Malcolm Levitt and Christopher Lord **The Political Economy of Monetary Union**

Janne Haaland Matláry **Energy Policy in the European Union**

John McCormick **Environmental Policy in the European Union**

John Peterson and Margaret Sharp **Technology Policy in the European Union**

Handley Stevens **Transport Policy in the European Union**

Forthcoming

Laura Cram **Social Policy in the European Union**

Bart Kerremans, David Allen and Geoffrey Edwards **The External Economic Relations of the European Union**

Stephen Keukeleire and Jennifer MacNaughton **The Foreign Policy of the European Union**

James Mitchell and Paul McAleavey **Regionalism and Regional Policy in the European Union**

Jörg Monar **Justice and Home Affairs in the European Union**

John Vogler, Richard Whitman and Charlotte Bretherton **The External Policies of the European Union**

Also planned

Defence Policy in the European Union

Political Union

The member states and the Union

Published

Carlos Closa and Paul Heywood **Spain and the European Union**

Alain Guyomarch, Howard Machin and Ella Ritchie **France in the European Union**

Forthcoming

Simon Bulmer and William E. Paterson **Germany and the European Union**

Phil Daniels and Ella Ritchie **Britain and the European Union**

Brigid Laffan **The European Union and its Member States**

Luisa Perrotti **Italy and the European Union**

Baldur Thorhallson **Small States in the European Union**

Issues

Published

Derek Beach **The Dynamics of European Integration: Why and When EU Institutions Matter**

Forthcoming

Thomas Christiansen and Christine Reh **Constitutionalizing the European Union**

Steven McGuire and Michael Smith **The USA and the European Union**

Also planned

Europeanization and National Politics

What is the European Union?

Nature and Prospects

Paul Magnette

First published in English in 2005 by
PALGRAVE MACMILLAN
Houndmills, Basingstoke, Hampshire RG21 6XS and
175 Fifth Avenue, New York, N.Y. 10010
Companies and representatives throughout the world.

This is a substantially revised and extended translation of the work first published by Presses de Science Po under the title *Le régime politique de l'Union européenne*.

PALGRAVE MACMILLAN is the global academic imprint of the Palgrave Macmillan division of St. Martin's Press, LLC and of Palgrave Macmillan Ltd. Macmillan® is a registered trademark in the United States, United Kingdom and other countries. Palgrave is a registered trademark in the European Union and other countries.

ISBN-13: 978–1–4039–4181–7 hardback
ISBN-10: 1–4039–4181–5   hardback
ISBN-13: 978–1–4039–4182–4 paperback
ISBN-10: 1–4039–4182–3   paperback

This book is printed on paper suitable for recycling and made from fully managed and sustained forest sources.

A catalogue record for this book is available from the British Library.

Library of Congress Cataloging-in-Publication Data

Magnette, Paul, 1971–
       What is the European Union? : nature and prospects / Paul Magnette.
       p. cm. — (The European Union series)
       ISBN 1–4039–4181–5 (cloth) — ISBN 1–4039–4182–3 (pbk.)
       1. European Union. I. Title. II. European Union series
     (Palgrave Macmillan (Firm))

JN30.M28133 2005
341.242′2—dc22   2005043891

10 9 8 7 6 5 4 3 2 1
14 13 12 11 10 09 08 07 06 05

Printed in China

Contents

Preface

The first version of this book was published in French in 2003, with the title *Le régime politique de l'Union européenne*. The idea to write it was not mine, and I would probably never have thought of it without Bertrand Badie's invitation. Then Editorial Director of the Presses de sciences-po, Professor Badie gave me a precise and demanding mandate: the book should be a concise and clear introduction to the EU, requiring no prior knowledge, complete though not exhaustive, jargon-free, and with a clear and if possible original analytical line.

This English version would never have seen the light without the initiative of a second person: Steven Kennedy, the publisher of the widely acclaimed European Union Series published by Palgrave Macmillan. A friend and colleague told me, before I met him: "You'll see. There are lots of editors, but there is only one Steven Kennedy." I now understand what he meant. Steven has been a constant and very generous supporter during the long revision of this book. Thanks to his comments and suggestions, and those of a very committed series editor, Neill Nugent, who also has written a very kind foreword, large parts of this book are new. Steven and Neill persuaded me to make the coverage of the book more comprehensive and helped me improve not only its structure but several insufficiently clear arguments. They also encouraged me to focus more on the central argument, which helped me clarify it in my own mind.

As I explain in the Introduction, the idea at the centre of this book is quite simple: most of our doubts about the nature and prospects of the EU would evaporate if we saw it as a sophisticated international organisation rather than a state-like polity. Contrary to what many euro-enthusiasts believe, interpreting it in these terms does not make the EU less but more valuable – and definitely more original. This view converges with those of many colleagues with whom I have recently had the chance to discuss the question posed in the title of this English language edition, notably Olivier Beaud, Richard Bellamy, Christian Lequesne, Anand Menon, Alan Milward, Andrew Moravcsik and Kalypso Nicolaïdis. Our discussions gradually convinced me that seeing the EU through this lens helps avoid optical illusions, highlight its originality and understand its proper value. The comments of my students in Brussels and at Sciences-po Paris also induced me to believe that such an approach may contribute to dissipating many of the misunderstandings generated by domestic analogies, both in analytical and in normative terms.

Most of the translation was done by Mrs Lesley Dalloz, and the full typescript was revised by Mrs Mary Long, and I am grateful to them for this.

Finally, the ideas developed in this book owe a great deal to discussions with dozens of colleagues. I can't cite them all, but I would like to acknowledge the pleasure I have in working with my colleagues in the Institute for European Studies at the Université libre de Bruxelles, as well as my brilliant colleagues and co-authors Olivier Costa, Renaud Dehousse, Justine Lacroix, Christopher Lord and Kalypso Nicolaïdis.

P. M.

Series Editor's Foreword

For many years there has been an ongoing debate amongst scholars of European integration as to the nature of the European Union. How is it to be characterized?

Initially, the dominant view was that it was essentially a rather special kind of international organization (IO). To be more specific, it was an international intergovernmental organization in which, to be sure, there was a broader range of policy responsibilities and activities than in other IOs and in which, too, there was a more developed and complex institutional system, but an IO nonetheless.

In more recent times, this view has come to be challenged by those who have suggested the EU is best viewed as a polity rather than as an IO. It may not be a completed polity – though some of those who see it as a quasi-federal system do not think it is so far off – but it is at least a fledgling polity. In this perspective, the EU exercises many of the same sorts of functions as state polities and has institutional arrangements and policy processes that can be compared usefully and meaningfully with those that exist in nation states.

Paul Magnette's book makes an important contribution to this debate about the nature of the EU's regime. Based very much in the IO camp, he argues not only that the EU today still very much bears the marks of its intergovernmental origins, but that it continues to function as 'a set of institutions and rules designed to strengthen the European states by encouraging them to cooperate' (p. 3). Rather than being an external force imposing unwanted policies and actions on member states, it is much more a framework in which governments cooperate on joint activities: 'In most cases it simply serves to coordinate or complete national policies' (p. 12).

In seeking to encapsulate the nature of the EU from an IO viewpoint, Magnette attaches great importance to the notion of 'cooperative sovereignty'. This term is employed to show how the EU is not, as is so commonly alleged, directed towards depriving states of their authority or sovereignty. Rather, it is about 'encouraging them to exercise their prerogatives in new and cooperative ways' (p. 3).

These new ways require us, Magnette argues, to move beyond conventional thinking in which only two forms of general union between states are possible: confederations (in which national sovereignty is retained and loose cooperation is the mode of operation) and federations (in which nation states join together to form a new common state). There is, he argues, something between these organizational forms, as the EU demonstrates.

Most of Paul Magnette's writings on the EU have hitherto been in French. It is, therefore, a great pleasure that his thought-provoking insights into the nature of the EU should now be available in English for the first time – in book-length form at least – via *The European Union Series*. I am confident that readers will find he provides a clear, incisive and distinctive analysis of the European Union. They will find, too, a book that is well organized, highly informed, and always lively.

Neill Nugent

Introduction

More than a decade after stormy debates over the ratification of the Maastricht Treaty, the nature of the European Union remains sharply contested. In the ten new member states which joined the Union in May 2004, the satisfaction of having been accepted into the club of rich and westernized nations has not put an end to the fears of seeing their (recently regained) sovereignty dying out in a Union often seen as a 'new Moscow'. This is also true for the older member states. The countries along the Union's Atlantic shoreline (the United Kingdom, Ireland, Denmark and Sweden), which had hesitated for a long time before joining the Union, constantly lament the loss of their sovereignty. Even in the Union's founding nations (France, Germany, Italy and the Benelux countries) and in countries that enthusiastically joined it after having rid themselves of authoritarian regimes in the 1970s (Greece, Spain and Portugal), a mistrust of Brussels – or disappointment with it – has been regularly gaining ground. After half a century of existence, the European Union is still perceived as a 'foreign' power, destabilizing political balances that had been patiently established since the postwar period.

The limits of the domestic analogy

Attempting to clarify the nature of the European Union, several scholars have argued in recent years that it is best understood as an ordinary 'political system', closer to national regimes than it might seem at first sight (Hix 1999; Lijphart 1999). Without denying the originality of its institutional organization, proponents of this approach underline its formal resemblance to federal systems, the similarity between national and EU policies, the increasing role played by political parties within it and the classic ideological cleavages which tend to 'normalize' European politics (Marks et al. 2003).

According to this viewpoint, the disconnection of the Union from its citizens is likely to be but a passing phenomenon: when European voters understand the stakes in terms familiar to them, they will consider the EU to be as legitimate as their own national democracies (Habermas 2001). Indeed, any new centre of power tends to prompt this type of hostile reaction in its early stages. For centuries, the political history of European nations has been marked by sharp criticism of the domination of the 'centre', just as Washington is still looked on with suspicion by American citizens. Seen in this way, Euroscepticism is just a European version of a universal phenomenon. The fact that the initial basis of European integration was the creation of a common market has fostered hostility and suspicion. By its very nature, the Union erodes boundaries and speeds up the circulation of people, goods, services and money. In this process, it is inevitably seen as an agent of the reform of labour markets and of the restructuring of public services and social protection mechanisms. And in endeavouring to regulate the single market it has created, it often upsets old traditions and patterns of life. Its strictures seem all the heavier and less legitimate as they come from remote and anonymous authorities: the Commission in Brussels, whose members' faces are familiar to few people; conclaves of ministers locked away behind heavy Council doors; the judgement of the Luxemburg-based court, cut off from the rest of the world on the Kirchberg plateau; or the decisions of the central bankers scrutinizing monetary Europe from atop their Frankfurt towers, not to mention an array of agencies and committees whose exact functions and numbers are a mystery even to EU insiders.

But while an approach that stresses what brings the Union closer to national political systems may help us understand some elements of its politics, it also tends to paint a picture of greater political coherence than really exists. It can be demonstrated statistically that the European political parties' manifestos are based on common cleavages; that European public opinion is, on the whole, shaped by a left–right opposition; and that this opinion is largely reflected in votes in the European Parliament. The fact remains, however, that this statistically verified coherence is not perceived by the citizens nor indeed by politicians.

This is the reason why other scholars argue that the Union should be seen as an international organization – albeit a sophisticated one – rather than as a 'political system'. In their view, European integration is primarily about coordinating national economic policies to adapt to an increasingly interdependent world market (Milward 1992). Citizens' and national opinion leaders' concerns with the 'democratic deficit' of the EU or its 'lack of legitimacy' are the result of misperceptions (Moravcsik 2002). If the Union was seen for what it is – a strongly developed international organization depending essentially on member states – citizens and political leaders would realize that it does not pose any serious challenge to politics as it has been practised in Europe for two centuries.

This book follows this latter view. It argues that the best way to understand the EU's structures and functioning is to see it primarily as an intergovernmental organization. Its institutional system, its decision-making procedures, the behaviour of the actors involved in European cooperation, all bear the marks of the EU's intergovernmental origins. The EU is not a federal state in the making, destined to absorb its member states. It is a set of institutions and rules designed to strengthen the European states by encouraging them to cooperate. This is what makes it so unusual: unlike classic international organizations, it is not confined to a specific function, but on the contrary induces the member states to coordinate almost all their policies; and unlike other international regimes, it is not based on strictly diplomatic and executive cooperation, but involves most of the states' organs and personnel (Slaughter 2004). On the other hand, in contrast to a federal state, the EU is very seldom based on constraint, authority and hierarchy. As one observer noted in the 1960s: 'It is in this fashion that the Community authority develops, rather as authority containing but a small element of constraint and a large element of consent' (Axline 1969:242). European institutions are not 'foreign' organs imposing their views on national authorities. They are 'frameworks' or 'networks' within which national actors seek to coordinate their interests and visions. The EU is not about depriving the states of their sovereignty. Rather it is about encouraging them to exercise their prerogatives in new and more cooperative ways.

Understanding cooperative sovereignty

It is precisely because cooperative sovereignty of this kind is so original that it arouses so much concern and so much misunderstanding. Some, stressing the 'constraints' cooperation entails, fear losing their national autonomy. Others, aspiring to more uniformity and more power on the international scene, regret the EU's lack of autonomy. Four centuries of state independence have accustomed us to think in absolute terms: either the state is fully independent or it is absorbed in a wider polity. We are still finding it hard to think simultaneously of sovereignty and of cooperation – with all the concessions the latter implies. But in a world where boundaries are agreed to be eroding, where the flow of people, material, cultural and financial goods between states is intensifying from year to year, the old concept of sovereignty is somewhat outdated. It evokes a political era which is coming to an end.

Yet, consciously or not, the language of the state and sovereignty continues to have a profound effect on our minds. Even if we are aware of the weakening influence of the state, and the increasing impact of globalization (for want of a better term), we continue to think in terms of sovereignty. Formed at the dawn of the modern age, this concept has profoundly shaped representations of politics – so much so that it is virtually taken for granted. In essence, it expresses the desire for a collective autonomy cherished by the classics of modern political theory, as epitomized by Rousseau's formulation of 1755: 'I should have wished, then, that no one inside the State could have declared himself to be above the law, and no one outside it could have imposed any law which the State was obliged to recognize' (Rousseau 1997a:115). The classic language of sovereignty encompassed two aims: within the state, subjecting any form of power to the rule of law; outside the state, accepting no form of domination.

This dichotomy has fundamentally shaped subsequent thinking on international relations, both among legal and political thinkers and in the everyday discourse of rulers and citizens. Since the seventeenth century, legal theorists have repeated that only two forms of union between states are possible: either the confederation, born of an international treaty concluded between sovereign states, where all decisions are unanimously adopted by state representatives; or the federal state, established by a constitution, where the law voted on by a bicameral parliament applies directly to the citizens. *Tertium non datur*. There is no third way. Either the state joins together with others to form a common state in which all are dissolved; or it preserves its sovereignty by establishing only loose forms of international cooperation.

Anything not falling into these two categories is merely an 'anomaly' and inevitably transient. A hybrid union will be dissolved, or it will be centralized, which, sooner or later, will give it the form of a state. This is what the political scientist Stanley Hoffman wrote, almost forty years ago:

> Between the cooperation of existing nations and the breaking in of a new one there is no middle ground. A federation that succeeds becomes a nation; one that fails leads to secession; half-way attempts like supranational functionalism must either snowball or roll back.   (Hoffman 1966:909–10)

In these, classic, political terms, the European Union is, strictly speaking, inconceivable.

This explains why it remains difficult to conceptualize the European Union. Admittedly, nothing in principle prevents us from overcoming the intellectual deadlock of this dichotomy by creating a new concept able to account for its hybrid character. Creating a third term would allow one to make the Union's originality (irreducible to historical precedents) understood. The concept of a 'Federation of States' (seemingly an oxymoron) has recently been unearthed to this end (Beaud 1993; 1995). Its great merit is to recall that federalism is not reducible to the formation of a federal state. Understood in a wider sense, federalism defines modes of relations between political entities based on peaceful cooperation and legal arbitration. For the eighteenth-century philosophers, Rousseau and Kant in particular, federalism constituted the logical extension of the formation of the state. In the language of that period, this amounted to the view that, just as individuals in the 'state of nature' had ensured their safety and liberty through a social contract to establish public control, states in turn should adopt a 'federal pact'. But this pact would be different from the one which gave birth to the state. It would not be a *pactum subiectionis*, erecting an authority with the power to impose its decisions on the states. It should rather be a *pactum societatis*, civilizing their relations without abolishing their sovereignty. It would mean using law and cooperation instead of force, and not dissolving the states into a European Leviathan. It would mean, in other words, establishing democratic values and habits not only within but also among nations (Bobbio 1995).

Federalism was, for the thinkers of the eighteenth century, the corollary of the making of the state. In *The Social Contract* of 1762, Rousseau resolved to show 'how the external power of a great People can be combined with the simple administration and the good order of a small State' (Rousseau 1997b:116) by establishing a federal link, while warning his readers that 'The subject is entirely new and its principles have yet to be established' (ibid.). Kant revived this idea a generation later, in his reflections on *Perpetual Peace*.

But it was outside Europe, on the other side of the Atlantic, that the theory of federalism was finally to be developed in a systematic way. Perhaps it is this historical circumstance that best explains the lasting misunderstanding of the federal doctrine in Europe. In the first half of the nineteenth century, Europeans observed the United States of America with a mixture of fascination and scepticism: the young federation claimed to have resolved the dilemma over sovereignty by 'dispersing' it, but it was undermined by divisions. De Tocqueville was one of the rare European voices to praise the virtues of this new form of separation of powers. After the American Civil War, when legal and political constraints were imposed on the States by the federal government, the Europeans considered their first impression to be confirmed: a federation can only be maintained by its setting itself up as a single state, in which the constituent states lose their autonomy. But far from having invalidated the standard dichotomy, the American experience had powerfully exemplified it. It showed that federalism is a form of state organization, rather than another way of creating political ties among sovereign states.

Historically, the European Union has followed a different route from that which led to a federal state in the United States,

Germany or Switzerland. Undeniably there are similarities between the four cases: in each the formation of a common market was the first stage, and many constitutional characteristics of these four regimes show an indisputable family likeness (Nicolaïdis and Howse 2001). It is, therefore, unsurprising that contemporary theoreticians often tend to refer to these historical precedents in examining the EU's experience (Lijphart 1999; Habermas 2001). But the contrasts are at least as outstanding as the similarities. Without even dwelling on the size differences and on the linguistic and cultural diversity of contemporary Europe, two major elements of the European experience can explain its peculiarity. First, the long interval between state formation and integration, and secondly, the presence or absence of an 'initial design'.

The EU was constructed a very long time after the European states were created. In the United States, only one decade separated the declaration of independence of the former colonies from the adoption of the Federal Constitution; in retrospect, the two events are best understood as two stages of a single revolution (Wood 2002). The two levels of power were born at practically the same time, whereas in Europe, the Union was formed by the reconciliation of pluri-secular states, which had developed a national awareness, a vast bureaucratic machinery and a large set of public policies in the course of the nineteenth and twentieth centuries. In these circumstances, the balance between the states and the Union in Europe cannot be comparable to one governing a federal state born in the eighteenth or nineteenth centuries.

No doubt this is where the 'fundamental fact' lies (to use the language of de Tocqueville). This difference is crucial in understanding the singular nature of the EU. No issue raised more debates in the postwar years and in the founding negotiations than that of preserving the states within the Union; and no issue had more impact during the succeeding enlargements. The British, like the Danes and Swedes, are still haunted by the idea that, by joining the Union, they have sacrificed a former independence. Today, in central and eastern European countries which have just joined the Union, fear of the Empire is resurgent.

Analysis of the successive treaties establishing powers and arrangements within the Union confirms that this is really the 'focal point'. One cannot but be struck by the extravagant precautions regarding the definition of the Union's competencies and the prerogatives of its institutions, and the care taken to balance the states' influence within them. All aspects of the Union's regime, and its daily functioning, are marked by this subtle balance.

The pace of European construction itself also differs from other forms of federal construction. The histories of the United States, Switzerland and the Federal Republic of Germany are punctuated by a succession of phases of centralization and, more rarely, of reflux (MacKay 2001). All three also have in common that each had a definite 'constitutional moment', which fixed the great institutional balances and contributed to bringing out a common political meaning. The EU, on the other hand, has experienced half a century of partial and continuous constitutional reforms. Its structure proceeds more from an experimental process and continuous adjustments (Laffan et al. 2000) than from a comprehensive plan devised through public deliberations. Again, these circumstances may explain some aspects of the Union's political regime. In the absence of an 'initial design', the construction of Europe has been characterized (much more than the other federal formations) by ambiguities and persistent misunderstandings, whose mark it still continues to bear. In the United States, the debate between 'federalists' and 'anti-federalists' remained lively up to the last decades of the nineteenth century, and has never completely disappeared. But the constitutional doctrine, nurtured by the inspiration of the Founding Fathers, channels this conflict (Ackerman 1991). There is no equivalent in Europe. Some, mainly seeing it as an international organization with an essentially commercial end, considered and still consider the Union from the point of view of international law; others, bearing in mind the project of a political union, conceived it and conceive it in federal terms. This initial ambivalence, and the fact that it has never been completely settled, explains why, in a way, the designers of Europe re-invented federalism – or at least invented a new variant of federalism, resolutely distinct from the American experience. What one calls the 'community method', is precisely this unlikely balancing point between supranationality and intergovernmental cooperation (Quermonne 2004).

Of course, federal states all experience conflicts between the states, cantons or *Länder* and the federal government; they all bear the mark of the fundamental ideological disputes between federalists and anti-federalists. But tensions between them never reach the same intensity as in the EU. The recent European Convention (2002–3), composed of ordinary politicians from 27 European states, was given the task of reflecting on the impact of European integration and its eventual destination or end state (its *'finalité'* to use the much more concise and evocative French expression) – and of re-conceiving its policies and institutions accordingly. But its debates have once again illustrated the weight of these ambiguities. After half a century of the Union's existence, European leaders continue to espouse radically contrasting interpretations of their common endeavour. As remote as their visions may seem from the reality of European integration, they remain widespread and influential.

Probably this stems from the fact that a debate has never fully taken place on the nature of this common endeavour. Historians of European construction have clearly established that the negotiations from which the first treaties ensued were driven by an openly utilitarian logic. Each government aimed above all at promoting its own economic and commercial interests, and integration always stopped where clashes of interest began (Milward 1992; Moravcsik 1998). Visions, ideas and principled reflections on Europe's future played only a limited role in these founding and re-founding moments. Europe might have a 'constitution', but it remains a 'constitution without constitutionalism' (Weiler 1999).

Without going back further over the historical and intellectual roots of this process (Magnette 2000), the rest of this book focuses on its consequences for the EU's institutional arrangements and decision-making, and for the perceptions of political actors and citizens. In other words, its central concern is with understanding the *regime* of the EU. The first three chapters focus on the nature of the 'Union of States' it comprises. A necessary first step in understanding the EU's political regime is an assessment of the dynamics of the process whereby national policies were progressively Europeanized, and what limits these dynamics came up against (Chapter 1). The coexistence of two major levels of power is one of the main features of any 'federal' entity, and one of the most outstanding dimensions of its political life. The way in which relations between the Union and its states are regulated on a daily basis and the mechanisms established to prevent or settle conflicts are part and parcel of its regime (Chapters 2 and 3).

The next section of the book is more directly concerned with analysing the Union's decision-making mechanisms. We will show how the rules governing the composition of the institutions and defining their prerogatives and relations all derive from this subtle balance established between the states and the Union. The famous 'Community method' conveys this peculiar form of synthesis between intergovernmental negotiation and supranational mediation (Chapters 4 to 6). Despite being the major decision-maker in the Union, the 'institutional triangle' formed by the Council, the Parliament and the Commission is not the end of the story. Upstream, the sphere of administrations facilitates joint decisions, while, downstream, jurisdictional control must allow for the management of conflicts or even for their prevention (Chapter 7).

Moving from internal decision-making mechanisms within the Union's machinery to the 'public space' surrounding it, the remaining chapters look at the way in which opinions and participating groups are affected by the formation of this new space of power. Representations and political attitudes cannot be formed *ex nihilo*; they are made up in relation to a given context. In the case of the EU, this process may be understood as the adaptation of pre-existing identities. We will see why the usual proponents of liberal democracy – political parties and trade unions – remain unstructured at the scale of the EU, and how the massive presence of pressure groups and thematic interests gives the European public sphere a very scattered morphology. We will look at how public opinion, formed at the national level, tends to become Europeanized in a still very relative way (Chapter 8). Analysing the different moves towards democratization that today are being debated in political and intellectual circles within the EU, Chapter 9 has adopted a more wide-ranging and resolutely more normative approach.

Chapter 1

Europeanization and its Limits

As all observers have emphasized, the 1992 Maastricht Treaty was a major turning-point in the history of European integration, not only because it extended Europe's field of action, but also, and perhaps above all, because the public debate which it gave rise to allowed citizens to become aware of the substance of the European project (Weiler 1999), in which, until then, most people only saw a colourless common market. Suddenly, the Europeans noticed that for forty years their states had been involved in a process affecting them more and more directly, and in a ceaselessly growing number of areas.

A quick look at the titles of treaties establishing the European Union may give the impression that no element of public action will be able to escape European control in future. From currency to foreign policy, to police and justice, agriculture, transport, industry, immigration policies and asylum, the environment, public health and consumer protection, research, culture, trade, development and humanitarian aid, the Union's competencies seem to cover everything, or almost. Occasional but highly publicized interventions by European institutions in national public life periodically illustrate the scale and weight of their influence: sentences passed by the Court in Luxemburg, reminding member states of their obligations; Commission decisions forbidding state aid to a sector in trouble, or a company merger, or reminding a government of its obligation to balance its budget so as to respect the Stability Pact; the silence of members of the European Central Bank in the face of political appeals for lower interest rates. These and many other similar examples mean that European citizens can hardly be unaware of the fact that member states' room for manoeuvre is limited by the commitments they have made within the Union.

This chapter will argue that this feeling of dispossession, encouraged by the attitude of many rulers who willingly resort to the 'European constraint' to justify their helplessness or carelessness, is largely exaggerated. On a closer look, the Union's sphere of activity remains limited, and strongly controlled by the governments of member states. When considering all the domains in which the Union can intervene, it must be pointed out that its working capacity comes up against two basic restrictions. First, as we will see in the following chapters, in bestowing these powers on the Union, governments more often than not have reserved a central role in the decision-making process and the implementation of these policies. The Union is not so much an 'external power' as a framework where governments come together to establish joint policies; it works more by a pooling of resources than by a delegation of power. Secondly, the strength of European action depends on the degree of convergence that member states have reached when new powers are bestowed on them: the areas where it acts as a substitute for state action are very limited. In most cases it simply serves to coordinate or complete national policies. This gradation of the intensity of European action reflects the strengths and the limitations of the dynamics of Europeanization started half a century ago – 'Europeanization' being understood here as a process of integration encapsulating both the formal process of institutional integration and the informal process of policy convergence.

The founding compromises

Like any political regime, the EU remains affected by the circumstances of its origin. In retrospect, the initial compromise can be perceived as a triple transaction.

Combining sovereignty and supranationality

Like other 'federal' experiments, the original pact first established *a balance between the sovereignty of states and the supranationality of some of the Union's institutions.* The advocates of a European federation were few in the wake of the Second World War. The profusion of European movements, and the euphoria of the 1948 Conference at the Hague, must not make us forget that most political leaders, and behind them citizens, remained attached to the sovereignty of their states. But, much more than the generation of 1930, they were also aware of the need to organize peace to make it lasting. The immediate postwar years were marked by a certain cooperative enthusiasm. The encouragement of the United States on the one hand, and the fear of the 'Soviet threat' on the other, combined to convince the Europeans that they must try to coordinate their reconstruction policies. In five years, more international organizations were created in western Europe than in the course of the preceding century. The European project was first of all an element, among many others, of the vast reorganization movement of the international order (Dinan 2004), which was also demonstrated through the creation of the United Nations, and the Bretton Woods and GATT agreements, and through the establishment of the IMF and the World Bank.

At first, the European leaders continued to adhere to a schema of standard international collaboration. Created in 1950, the Council of Europe symbolizes this first moment: envisioning large-scale cooperation covering areas such as the economy, culture, the development of democracy, it is based upon traditional institutions – a Committee of Ministers representing the governments and an Assembly made up of delegations of national members of parliament. From the beginning its activities were marked by the traditional opposition between the 'Carolingian' European countries (France and the nineteenth-century states of Germany, Italy and the Benelux countries), which have formed a deeply connected zone since the Renaissance and are inclined to cooperation, and the more reticent 'old nations' of the Atlantic front (the United Kingdom and the Nordic countries).

In contrast, the second phase of European construction was based upon the so-called method of 'functional integration'. The projects elaborated by Jean Monnet and his friends, for which the French government would act as a relay, are defined by a double rejection of the classic method. First, rather than seeking large-scale collaboration, it was deemed better to concentrate on strictly defined matters, with a limited number of partners. Secondly, in place of classic political institutions, new instruments were to be established. Such is the philosophy from which the European Steel and Coal Community (ECSC) proceeded in 1951: it concerned making solid and restricting commitments in defined matters, and establishing supranational institutions with real guarantees of independence and decision-making powers. The ECSC is the anti-Council of Europe: a more limited cooperation but with greater capacities.

This gradualist strategy had the virtue of making the different visions of the European project compatible. The skilfully maintained ambiguity on the 'ultimate finality' of integration allowed some to think that the joint management of coal and steel, as such, did not involve any other commitment; whereas others could hope that by dint of cooperation, the governments would compare their points of view and become aware of a community of interests. Ever since then, the European project has always been propelled towards this double temporal horizon: each new decision carefully negotiated by the governments is, in itself, only a modest element of cooperation; but each of these 'little steps' can also be interpreted (by those who keep hoping that a political union will be formed) as a contribution to the establishment of a more ambitious project. Functionalism reconciles the sovereignty of states and supranationality by playing on this temporal ambiguity.

Balancing politics and technocracy

The initial pact was built around a second transaction. The ECSC's institutional schema, which was to be the matrix of later arrangements, established *a balance between those in favour of political methods of integration and those defending 'technocracy'*. For the political leaders of that time, cooperation between states had to go through diplomacy, dialogue between governments, and inter-parliamentary deliberations, whereas for Jean Monnet's generation, the European project would be useless as long as these traditional forces were not counterbalanced by others, more independent of politics. The memory of the political crises of the interwar period persisted. Party divisions, the instability of the parliamentary regime, the importance of rhetoric, politicians' dependence on electoral cycles – in the 1920s, all this had given rise to a trend of thought marked by mistrust with regard to politics and an aspiration to increase experts' and civil servants' prerogatives (Meynaud 1964; Dubois and Dulong 1999; Radaelli 1999). In the days following the Second World War, Monnet was convinced more than ever of the need to correct the defects of the political game by using the virtues of technocracy. The necessary response to the instability of the electoral game was to rely on the continuity of public service; substitute long-term planning for the obsession with the short term; set the technical knowledge of economists and engineers against rhetoric; substitute the impartiality of jurists for private interests. In France this aspiration was represented by the 'Commissariat au Plan' (Planning Commission). The ECSC's functionalist plan extended it to the European level (Featherstone 1994). The High Authority which Monnet and his friends wanted to have established at the heart of the ECSC was meant to fashion the work of the politicians; the Commission placed at the centre of the European Economic Communities six years later corresponded to the same logic. The Six European rulers bowed to this same argument, but cautiously. The High Authority, then the Commission, had guarantees which established their supranational character and technical profile, but their prerogatives were strictly defined and they were counterbalanced by a Council of Ministers and an Assembly, ensuring the control of the politicians.

Positive and negative integration

The third arrangement entailed by the initial pact deals with the content of the commitments. Through the ECSC, and even more so, the EEC, the leaders of the Six established *a balance between the doctrines of the free market and public intervention*. The positive experience of the ECSC, and the aborted attempt to establish a European Community for defence in 1953–4, quickly convinced the governments of the Six to expand the scope of their cooperation to other economic sectors. Each of the states came to the negotiations that were to lead to the Treaty of Rome with its own priorities (Milward 1992). The Germans and the Benelux countries wished first to facilitate the circulation of goods and services by building a common market. They favoured a logic of negative integration, consisting in gradually dismantling the arsenal of national protectionist measures. The Italians supported this project, which they intended to extend to the free movement of workers, so as to encourage the migration of their nationals to northern countries. As for the French government, it remained attached to more planned economic policies and particularly wanted to extend the community logic to agricultural products. The agreement ratified by the Treaty of Rome was the first of a long series of package deals, in which each partner accepted the whole because it considered that its benefits outweighed the concessions it had to make. In its political trends, the initial pact would counterbalance the logic of negative integration of the common market with the sectorial policies of positive integration: national standards had to be abolished to allow for the circulation of production factors, while joint decisions had to be made to regulate this decompartmentalized market.

Although they were the cause of ongoing tensions, these three balances were never really questioned afterwards. The first decade of integration confirmed that this compromise was the only one possible at that time. All attempts at either accelerating the course of integration, or going back on commitments, ended in failure. By 1954, the plan to set up a European Defence Community (EDC), and to gather sectorial communities together to form a European Political Community (EPC), was hanging fire. Five of the six governments had ratified the new treaty, but strong opposition from the Gaullists and communists in France was to prevent it from coming into force. Four years later, the British project to establish a Free Trade Area which would include the Communities was rejected by the Six, showing their attachment to a Europe with sound institutions and market-regulation policies. Later, the refusal of the Fouchet Plan by the French partners in 1962 would show the determination of the other five to preserve community institutions, and their reluctance to embark on a process of political cooperation outside the Atlantic framework. Conversely, the institutional crisis of 1965 confirmed that Gaullist France remained suspicious of supranational institutions and majority voting. While the Commission suggested increasing its own powers and those of the Assembly, the French government had obstructed the Community's functioning by carrying out the policy of the 'empty chair' until its partners accepted a 'compromise' which bridled the autonomy of the European executive and strengthened the role of the governments.

A contrario, this agitated period confirmed the strength of the initial pact. In these first years, each time a political project was presented that aimed at increasing or reducing the degree of the Community's supranationality, at least one government vetoed it. The configuration of forces protected the status quo. In the long run, one effect was also to freeze the Community: if it was able to spread during the 1970s and 1980s, it was always by remaining within the framework defined by the initial pact. The Single European Act of 1986 was often to be presented as a sign of rebirth, but in substance it only extended the initial objectives. The measures envisaged mainly aimed at lifting administrative and regulatory obstacles, which continued to hinder the circulation of workers and capital, and the technical regulations restraining exchanges of goods and services. This meant the project of the common market was achieved.

However, the Single Act also marked a turning-point in the dynamics of integration, and started to break up one of the three initial balances: the one which concerned the basis of policies. Since then, negative integration has taken precedence over positive integration, which had slowly been taking shape since the mid-1970s (Scharpf 1998). Initially, to avoid the suppression of national standards leading to the formation of a market with no rules, a certain number of common regulations had been adopted in areas where they seemed necessary for the construction of the market, such as environmental concerns, public health and consumer protection, working conditions and sexual equality. Having neglected national regulation in these areas, which were new for the period, the governments were able to accept the proposals formulated by the Commission without too much difficulty (Dehousse 1994). Yet, the Commission's objective was not merely to promote the new regulations for what they were. Its attitude derived mainly from the fear of seeing governments introduce national regulations in these sensitive matters, which would have hindered the circulation of goods. The single market had to have a 'regulatory' side so as to avoid new barriers.

Besides, from the end of the 1980s, the European framework was used mainly to speed up the liberalization of vast economic sectors controlled until then by the individual states. At the time of its establishment, all governments wished to maintain the capacity to control certain key areas like transport, communications and energy, but the smallest member states feared that their enterprises would suffer from competition with public monopolies of larger countries. Therefore, it was decided that these areas would not completely escape competition, but that exceptions would be made in order to protect particular 'public services' and nationalized enterprises. For a long time, these arrangements were interpreted in a flexible way. Things began to change in the 1980s when the European Commission, to which the governments had entrusted the application of the principles of competition, became more incisive. Open to pressure from the industrial sector, and relying on the support of a majority of governments converted to the liberal creed, it was able to take advantage of the Court's audacious jurisprudence to control state aid more closely and to interpret exceptions protecting public monopolies more restrictively. Taking things one step further, it then proposed a gradual liberalization of the telecommunication sector, air transport and energy, which a majority of member states accepted.

This development profoundly altered the public's perception of the EU. Governments often claimed to be subjected to a 'European constraint', when they themselves had made these decisions – and when, in many cases, it is likely that they had made them in the absence of a European policy. Since then, in countries like France or Germany, where public power has long played an important role in the economic sphere, the EU has often been seen as a lever operated by the Commission to de-regulate public services. If it is true that the Commission has acted here as a 'political entrepreneur', inscribing the liberalization scheme, it was only able to attain its end because a majority of governments shared its vision. European integration is not driven by its own ideology; it reflects the governments' predominant preferences. In the 1950s, this led to the formation of a balanced market and to public regulation of some key sectors. Since the 1980s, the balance has shifted: the Union today extends the scope of the principle of free competition by regulating no more than the 'externalities' of the market.

The Maastricht moment

Without breaking the original matrix, the integration phase which opened at the end of the 1980s changed the meaning and scope of European enterprise. Some fifteen years later, it is still difficult to measure the impact of the fall of the Berlin Wall. European leaders very quickly understood that things would not be the same as before. What sense could the Union, initially conceived as one element of the rampart that the west wanted to build against the 'Soviet threat', still have after the collapse of the USSR and the disintegration of its camp? The implications of the upheaval of the global geopolitical order for European integration have remained uncertain for a long time. The Europeans reacted in stages, with no clear awareness of what they were doing.

Retrospectively, the Maastricht Treaty appears as a wavering response to this new external crisis. It started a double movement of enlargement and strengthening of the Union whose implications are still not clear. Today, no one can tell how Europe will function with 30 to 35 members; how the institutional framework conceived for six Carolingian European states, and gradually modified since, can adapt to the dimensions of an almost continental Europe, which stretches from the Baltic to the Mediterranean and from the Atlantic to the Black Sea. Those nostalgic for a little Europe predict an engulfment; from Aristotle to Kant, to Machiavelli, Montesquieu and Rousseau, all the theoreticians of politics have seen the spectre of Empire and despotism behind large confederations. But the American experience contradicts the Cassandras: the main institutional balances of the federation of thirteen small colonies, with a population of 4 million citizens, continue to operate in a union of fifty states and 300 million inhabitants. The foundations of a union often prove to be much more workable than it would seem, to begin with.

Beyond the single market

As far as public policies are concerned, the Maastricht Treaty includes two main changes which considerably extend the Union's sphere of activity and its meaning. First, the single currency: conceived at the beginning of the 1970s, then the subject of very long discussions, it formed a major advance in integration, materially and symbolically. Not only did the governments which have adopted it transfer their monetary power to the independent European Central Bank; they are committed to coordinating their economic policies and enforcing a strict budget discipline upon themselves. The constraint on the states, inscribed in the 'Stability and Growth Pact' adopted in 1997, has intensified. Yet, the governments remain influential: monetary decisions are made by a European system of central banks in which they are 'represented'; as to the coordination of economic policies, it is essentially a mechanism of multilateral surveillance between governments, where the Commission only plays a role of analysis, advice and control and where the Parliament is hardly consulted. Nevertheless, the constraint remains considerable, objectively and subjectively. When the German government urgently asks the French authorities to respect budget discipline – which compels them to reduce public expenditure or to postpone tax reductions – or when the Commission addresses a warning to four governments suspected of allowing their public deficit to increase, and blatantly threatens sanctions, interference in internal affairs is strongly felt – even if, hitherto, the governments have been unwilling to make concessions. On the other hand, the mechanisms of economic and social cohesion put in place to compensate for the cost of economic convergence in less advanced countries – as limited as they may be in budget terms and whatever might be their real economic impact – also contribute in pricking consciences. In the countries which are the main beneficiaries they are a reminder that solidarity between states is not totally absent from the European project.

The coordination of foreign policies and policies for internal security is the other great novelty of the Maastricht Treaty. The mechanism remains very intergovernmental: European institutions are largely cast aside and decisions are generally made unanimously. But again, the symbolic effect and the long-term range of this new commitment are far from negligible. Even if, to a large extent, they only institutionalize cooperation practices that have already been in existence for a long time, these two new pillars of the Union change the very meaning of European construction. This time the common market has been completed with more directly political points and brings into European negotiation regal powers (which have been at the heart of the definition of 'the State' since the dawn of modern times). By erasing the term 'economic' from the Community, by restoring the concept of the European Union formed in the 1930s, by setting up a Union citizenship, and by bestowing a power of legislative co-decision on the European Parliament which it had been claiming for decades, the initiators of the treaty intended to emphasize the rupture which accompanied the end of the Cold War, and which offered the prospect of the continent's unification.

The enlargement process, and the acceleration towards a market economy, the rule of law and liberal democracy that was imposed on the applicant countries, are supposed to prolong the virtuous effects of the initial project: the new member states would have to establish peaceful relations, consolidate their democratic basis and see their standard of living meet that of the west. In other words, they should, in their turn, reap the benefit from integration enjoyed by the six founder members and, thirty years later, by the southern European countries. These high ambitions remain uncertain. At least a generation will have to elapse before the results can be evaluated. It must be acknowledged today that it is not known how far the 'revolution in number' will affect the functioning of institutions, and how joint policies will adapt to the growing heterogeneity of the Union.

Beyond Maastricht?

It seems that the 're-founding compromise' of Maastricht is, like the Treaty of Rome in its time, the only one welcomed by all governments, and European integration has no doubt reached a level which, unless there is a major unforeseeable crisis, should not be surpassed. Since then, the Treaty of Amsterdam has spread the logic of coordination to certain social and employment policies, but without tampering with the heart of the national welfare states. Furthermore, the Union's budget has not been increased, while the needs of the new member states are considerable. Competition policy and economic and social cohesion have been partly decentralized, and the re-nationalization of some European policies – such as the expensive agricultural policy – is the subject of constant debate. Broad discussions conducted within the Convention on the Union's future in 2002–3 showed that, on the whole, state representatives have aspired to rationalize acquired attainments, rather than to bestow new powers on the Union. On the one hand, the conventioneers suggested that a qualified majority should be used more often within the Council, and that the Commission and the Parliament should participate fully in all of the 'shared powers', whose effect could be to intensify European action. But on the other hand, the conventioneers 'froze' the Union's margins of action by a clearer delineation of its powers, and by emphasizing the Union's need to respect state and regional prerogatives.

With hindsight, we see that the spill-over effect which the Founding Fathers and certain academics banked on was to be only partially deployed. The most optimistic scenarios of the 1950s saw European integration as a dynamic which was broadly similar to that of the formation of a state. Sectorial cooperation was to expand 'step by step' until it covered most national public policies; it would quickly seem necessary to increase the Union's budget, and to levy European taxes; the elites would become aware (in the business sector, trade unions and political parties) that the real places of power had been shifted to Brussels, and would be reorganized on that scale; opinions would follow, becoming Europeanized in their turn under the influence of the circulation of goods, people and ideas and the homogenization of lifestyles. Something like a European state, even if it were federal, would emerge.

This prophecy was not fulfilled. Admittedly, there were some consequential effects here and there. But the conditions required for governments to accept the transfer of some of their powers to the Union, or the coordination of their policies, were only met in rare circumstances.

The uneven vectors of Europeanization

This has been for a long time, and partly remains today, one of the fundamental issues of studies devoted to European integration: how does one explain that sovereign states are involved in a joint enterprise and must be prepared to suffer its consequences? What is the motive of this 'dynamics of integration'?

Almost like caricatures, researchers were first divided into two groups. On the side of the 'functionalists', stress was laid on integration vectors. Supranational institutions are perceived as 'political entrepreneurs' driven by their own interests, which they manage to promote by using and by amplifying powers bestowed upon them by governments in successive treaties, and by relying on extra-governmental interest groups whose causes they promote. A tacit alliance between the supranationalized elite and interested parties favourable to the erosion of commercial boundaries is supposed to take hold of governments, and narrow their room for manoeuvre. The Commission uses its right to initiate legislation to organize the Council's agenda, and relies on the numerous private interests it consults to establish coalitions supporting it; the European Court, when cases are submitted by firms, uses its power to impose a very integrationist reading of the treaties; the Parliament, open to lobbying pressures, uses its capacity to advise and amend to reorganize the agenda and decisions and to extend its own prerogatives (Stone Sweet et al. 2001).

By contrast, for the 'intergovernmentalists', emphasis is laid on the governments' resistance against integration (Milward 1992; Moravcsik 1998). The successive stages of Europeanization are analysed in terms of simple bargaining by governments exclusively out to defend their own commercial interests. In the long run, European construction is perceived as a method of adapting national policies in a global economic and commercial context, and corresponds to a simple fixed rule: 'integration was chosen only when interdependency was regarded as an inadequate framework to promote important objectives of national policies' (Milward and Sørensen 1993:3). According to this approach, European institutions and private actors have played only a marginal role in these crucial negotiations. The governments themselves drew up the terms of the compromise.

After paradigmatic contrasts, comes the time for syntheses – according to the law of the history of sciences established by Thomas Kuhn. Most researchers today acknowledge that it is impossible to devise a 'general theory of integration' based upon simple causes and mechanisms. Some first recall that, as in any political entity, the decision-making process largely depends on the nature of the stakes. John Peterson and Elizabeth Bomberg thus distinguish 'historical' decisions (which, in their view, mainly pertain to state bargaining) from the creation of new public policies, or new orientations within them, where European institutions and private actors counterbalance any influence from the states (Peterson and Bomberg 1999). Functionalists and intergovernmentalists would therefore each hold part of the truth; the clash of interpretations would only be due to a difference in viewpoint. Other attempts to synthesize intergovernmental and functionalist approaches have been outlined. Accepting the hypothesis according to which governments are at the centre of integration dynamics, Paul Pierson intends to show how they are nevertheless, in certain circumstances, compelled by the action of community institutions (Pierson 1996). He underlines more particularly that governments are sometimes incapable of predicting the long-term consequences of new policies, and that *a posteriori*, the rule of unanimity governing the revision of treaties prevents them from going back on their commitments, or reducing the powers of community institutions. While we cannot talk of a chain effect, what is at play here is at least a 'ratchet effect'.

In any event, Europeanization first presupposes that the governments' viewpoints will converge. The treaties can only be modified unanimously, and even in areas where a qualified majority is possible, it requires the agreement of at least two-thirds of governments. What therefore needs to be explained, in order to understand the phenomenon of Europeanization in the long run, is the way in which national stances are converging.

The abundant literature that this issue has given rise to enables us to identify three variables.

External pressures

From the outset, and throughout integration, it has been because they perceived a 'common challenge' that governments have been prepared to cooperate. The genesis of the Treaties of Paris and Rome cannot be explained without bearing in mind the growing economic interdependency in the postwar period, along with American pressure and the recognition of a 'Soviet threat'. For a historian like Eric Hobsbawm (who dedicated two out of eight hundred pages to European construction in his history of the twentieth century), the formation of the EU is reduced to a 'Cold War effect' (Hobsbawm 1994). The Maastricht agreement would have been impossible also without the psychological shock caused by the fall of the Berlin Wall, and the fear of 'migratory pressure' and 'new threats' that it created. The decision to establish a single currency would not have succeeded if most of the governments had not become aware of their weakness on the freer and more and more speculative financial markets. More recently still, the events of 11 September accelerated the adoption of directives concerning the fight against crime, which had for long been under discussion and seemed to be stalled. Like classic federal systems (MacRae 1997), the EU owes its first foundations to external constraints.

External pressure alone does not suffice. In many cases, faced with common challenges, governments have responded very differently. Monetary fluctuations in the 1970s did not convince them to adopt a single currency, although the idea had been put forward. Far from favouring the coordination of economic policies, oil shocks of the same period saw them increasing competition rather than seeking a common response. Fifteen years later, the 'Yugoslavian crisis' emphasized differences in strategy rather than contributing to some convergence. As for the 2003 'Iraq crisis', it was to exacerbate the differences in vision and strategy. External pressure only favours the quest for a common solution when governments perceive it at close quarters. In other words, Europeanization requires a convergence of representations. A fellowship of interests is not enough to persuade governments to coordinate their actions. At the least, they would have to be aware of this fellowship.

Convergence of ideas

In the long run, European integration reflects the successive patterns of public policy. The Treaties of Paris and Rome, as has been said, institutionalized the doctrine of the 'social market economy' predominant in the 1950s. The wave of liberalization in the 1980s in turn elucidated the progressive conversion of leaders to 'neo-liberalism' (Hall 1998; Schmidt 2002), in the same way that the process of convergence to a single currency was inspired by the new monetarist wave. The EU framework can amplify and institutionalize these ideas, but it is not in a position to impose them by itself.

Moreover, the convergence of representations is slower and more partial when it is a question of designing the Union's institutions. Ideas do not converge in the same way in creating policies as they do in the reform of polity. When governments debate *policies*, they waver between their national traditions and trends in transnational opinion. Many studies have convincingly shown that socio-economic paradigms are widely spread beyond borders, and that the progressive convergence of the leaders' doctrines are paving the way for new European commitments (Muller et al. 1996). The logic is different when it is about revising the rules of the game and the structures of the *polity* itself. When national leaders debate institutions, their reasoning is essentially guided by the calculation of their own interests, but it is also orientated by their national civic culture. Moreover, legal formalism counterbalances the weight of these contrasting visions (Weiler 1999; Kohler-Koch 2000). If the governments have constantly reinforced the European Parliament, when the latter was rarely in a position to enforce its decisions; if the co-decision procedure was broadly extended after the Maastricht Treaty; if the European Convention debated at great length the 'simplification' of decision-making procedures, it is because the political actors, consciously or not, tend to think of institutions through conceptions familiar to them. The process is somewhat dialectic: concerned about protecting their interests, the governments adopt compromises that have not been fully thought through and give rise to complex and unstable institutional arrangements; the latter, in turn, lead to a continual reflection on the need to 'rationalize' the system (Olsen 2002a); this rationalizing ambition finally induces reforms prompted by formalizing motives.

From the mid-1970s, two *leitmotivs* were established in leading European circles which largely influenced later institutional reforms. First, the theme of 'complexity': the Union, created by the addition of partial treaties and constantly being reformed, was deemed too complicated and incoherent. According to a very widespread discourse, it required simplification as much in the definition of its powers as in its decision-making procedures. The theme of a 'democratic deficit' completed this discourse. Based essentially on negotiation between governments and European administrations, the Union was accused of privileging the executive sphere at the expense of parliaments. Here too, the response seemed to be self-evident: the governments and administrations were to be more answerable to the parliaments. Educated in parliamentary democracies, often with legal training, political actors responsible for big European decisions almost naturally tend to reason in classic constitutional terms whenever it is a question of revising the rules of the game.

The convergence of representations is a phenomenon whose mechanics cannot easily be established. It partly rests on the preliminary presence of a common foundation of convictions, such as an attachment to the 'parliamentary model' or to the 'social market economy'. It is also explained by mutual training: governments sometimes draw the same lessons from the same failures and, by watching each other, take inspiration from their neighbours. Community institutions can, in some circumstances, also contribute to reconciling the diagnoses and preferences of governments.

The mediation of institutions

The circumstances in which community institutions are able to impose their will are rare. As we shall see, the Commission, backed by the Court, has sometimes been able to use the powers with which the governments vested it in order to promote policies whose development they had not anticipated. For its part, the European Parliament has exerted continuous pressure on the governments. But they generally had a limited capacity of constraint: the decision always relying eventually on the governments' agreement, European institutions are reduced to playing on their influence (Pollack 2002).

Influence can be exerted in three ways. When EU institutions manage to unite around them actors that governments cannot ignore – as was the case with the main industries in the 1980s – they invest themselves with power to exert *pressure* on member states. Where industries based on their home-ground support the Commission, the governments are subjected to pressure from below, and encouraged from the top. The single market programme of 1987 is generally perceived in these terms, and even supporters of the strictest intergovernmental interpretations acknowledge that, in this case, community institutions were able to play a certain role (Moravcsik 1998).

In other circumstances the Commission or the Court were, moreover, able to make compromises which facilitated negotiations, because they took the interests of all the governments into consideration; here they were playing a classic role of *mediation*. The frequently quoted examples to illustrate this mechanism are the Court's jurisprudence on 'mutual recognition' at the end of the 1970s, which facilitated the implementation of new policies on the free circulation of goods and services, and 'budget packages' conceived by the Commission at the end of the 1980s, which simplified subsequent intergovernmental negotiations.

Finally, in so far as they develop a 'vision' of policies and institutions of the Union that they steadfastly defend, the use of *persuasion*, can contribute to securing it in the representations of national governments; the Commission's continuous defence of the 'Community model', and the European Parliament's permanent criticism of the 'democratic deficit', partly explain the weight of these institutional models. But, here again, it is only a question of influence.

It is rare for these modes of action to be combined. Analysts agree for example to acknowledge that the 'liberal turning-point' of the 1980s, prefiguring the liberalization of the telecommunications sectors, air transport and energy, was facilitated by the court's jurisprudence and the Commission's proposals. But they concede that, as a last resort, it was the governments' agreement which was the determining factor (Scharpf 1998). As to the intergovernmental conferences that fashioned the legal framework in which the Union acts, it appears impossible to show empirically that they were re-orientated by the action of the Commission or the European Parliament (Pollack 1997).

The Europeanization phenomenon cannot therefore be perceived as regular and uniform. The need for adaptation when faced with external pressure, the convergence of representations and the mediations of supranational institutions act at varying levels according to the times and areas of integration, which in turn explains how, far from following a single model of joint management, governments have established different forms of action according to the level of convergence reached.

Taken together these fields of action give the EU substantial power. Nevertheless, relations between the states and the Union cannot be conceived as a zero sum game. The areas where the Union is substituted for the states, depriving them of their decision-making ability, are in fact limited to the customs union, and competition, monetary and commercial policies. In all other sectors, the Union's action completes and coordinates that of the state, much more than it substitutes for it. Europeanization is not related to a 'centralization of power', comparable to the process of the state's historical formation; and vast areas of national policy escape its hold.

Chapter 2

Policy-making in a Union of States

Contrary to widespread opinion, the European Union is not a sprawling political system which is gradually substituting for the member states and depriving them of their substance. In the first chapter, we have seen that even if the preamble to the treaty evokes an 'ever closer union among the peoples of Europe', the dynamics of Europeanization remain uncertain. States are only prepared to increase cooperation after having scrupulously weighed what they can gain from it. Moreover, as we will see in the next chapter, in the last ten years the governments have also stepped up their control over the Union's actions. Concerned with preserving their identity and conserving their room for manoeuvre, they have continually reinforced the principle of subsidiarity and scrutinize European policies with ever more sustained attention.

The governments' vigilance is also shown in the way the Union's policies are made. In this chapter we will see that the states only really accept constraints on their sovereignty in matters tied to market regulation. Elsewhere, in whatever affects the heart of public action, they embark more cautiously on ways of coordinating national policies. If the governments have continued to extend the areas in which they pool their sovereignty, they have maintained the transfer of competence to supranational institutions within narrow limits. Whenever it seems possible, national leaders prefer to opt for flexible forms of Europeanization which do not involve the recognition of new European competence. And when they nevertheless agree to collaborate within the framework of treaties, they only accept supranational constraints with caution.

In which spheres does the EU matter?

Citizens understand that most national policies are now included within a framework of European cooperation, but they struggle to assess the weight of this constraint accurately. At the same time, they can both denounce Brussels' interference in their domestic affairs and regret Europe's weakness at the social level or on the international scene. The European Convention tried hard to correct this failing by proposing a new typology of competencies but, since the greater part of European policies come under the category of 'competencies shared' between the Union and the member states, it is likely that confusion will continue to reign.

Rather than making an inventory of European 'competencies', it may be useful – in order to measure the impact of the Europeanization process – to reason *a contrario*, that is to say, to recall that these competencies only concern the more recent public policies, and leave the states with control over their traditional sphere of activity. According to the Norwegian political scientist Stein Rokkan (1999), our contemporary states were formed in four stages. We will see in this section that only the last stage, which concerns market regulation, is truly Europeanized. The others – those covering a state's historical essence (territorial protection, the making and upholding of the nation, the establishment and reforms of democratic life) – for the most part remain national. The governments sometimes take their neighbours as a model, they sometimes coordinate their policies within the Union, but they are careful not to transfer their powers to European institutions. European construction, having started when the states were already established within these four dimensions, will, in the end, only have a profound effect on what pertains to the state's relations to the market, that is to say the 'Fourth Age' of the state.

Security policies

Contemporary European states continue to attach cardinal importance to the sovereign competencies which were their cornerstone. Modern states asserted their authority by marking out their boundaries, by ensuring their control and by assigning to their subjects a legal status as 'nationals'. These essential missions called for the deployment of a police force and legal institutions to establish peace within the territory. They also presupposed the development of an army and diplomats to take charge of defence against the outside world. In turn, these first elements of the state engendered the installation of a huge administrative system as well as tax levying and fiscal redistribution mechanisms.

Today, this key area of public power is only partially affected by European integration. It is true that the creation of a single market leads to the abolition of physical controls at domestic frontiers, but the states remain in control of granting nationality: 'EU citizenship' is added to that of the states, without taking away any of their power to determine who comes under their authority. Moreover, the resources on which security policies depend continue to pertain solely to the individual states. The Union does not levy taxes and its budget remains thirty times lower than that of most member states. If an embryo of a European army corps exists, as well as the beginnings of a public prosecutor's department and a common police force, these coercive forces are only a combination of national divisions. The Union does not have its own army, nor customs officers, police forces, enforcement administration, higher and lower courts. Moreover, in these areas, the states undertake to coordinate their national policies only by resorting to flexible methods that merely impose weak constraints upon them. They establish certain common principles, facilitate the exchange of information between their administrations, mutually acknowledge their decisions, and can carry out joint action. Along with control over the coercive apparatus, security policies remain almost exclusively state-owned property.

However, this does not prevent a more indirect form of Europeanization from spreading. Over recent decades, almost all European states have modified the rights of citizens to nationality, and differences between national traditions have become less marked. States more attached to 'blood rights' are slowly opening up their citizenship to foreign residents (Weil and Hansen 2001). In the same way, the evolution of criminal law appears to be converging (Weyembergh 2004): the legalization of abortion, the control of firearms and the abolition of the death sentence (once topics of the sharpest controversy) today are asserted with more coherence in the EU than in the United States. But we must not lose sight of the fact that this is a 'spontaneous' form of Europeanization. European societies experience similar evolutions and carry out similar experiments: the convergence of the law simply reflects these reconciliations of facts and values. While it is clear that membership of a union will lead to comparisons and the exchange of practices, this is difficult to quantify and will, in any case, be subjective. Yet it is true that constraints are heavier for countries that have applied for EU membership. Thus, Turkey abolished the death sentence during the summer of 2002 as a signal of its intention to draw closer to the 'European model', and the Turkish government has undertaken to revise its policy with regard to national minorities. States wanting to join the EU are compelled to join the European mainstream, but beyond these general principles, they remain in control of the greater part of their domestic security policies.

Identity policies

Nor does the EU act as a substitute for the states when it comes to policies contributing to shaping the identity of nations. We know how much the setting up of free and compulsory education systems, cultural and sports policies and the spreading of 'state propaganda' have contributed to forming national identities (Gellner 1997; Hobsbawm and Ranger 1983). Here too, most decisions continue to come under the state – or federated entities. The EU does not finance schools and universities, it does not establish school programmes or train teachers. In these matters, its intervention is limited to encouraging the movement of students between member countries. Each time community institutions have suggested the harmonization of school programmes, or the creation of European curricula for civic education, they have come up against a polite refusal from the governments. Attempts to write 'European texbooks' have aroused the hostility of the vast majority of academics, who are opposed to harmonization and wary of an inclination to instrumentalize history.

In the same way, proposals (formulated in the 1980s) for the creation of sports teams, lotteries and European academies have fizzled out. The Union has been content with an anthem and a flag, whose impact on national identities remains to be analysed (Forêt 2003). The Union does not finance television or radio channels, and the support it gives to the audiovisual field is marginal. So far, its public information services have remained protected from competition rules. Interference from the court of Luxemburg in sports matters has given rise to such strong political reactions that it will certainly be difficult to intervene further in these areas. Many other national policies which contribute towards shaping social life, like civil rights or urban and regional development, almost completely escape the Union's powers.

Again, this does not prevent spontaneous forms of European convergence from taking shape. For example, the reorganization of higher education in Europe is leading to the standardization of degree courses – moreover, from a widely American-inspired model. But this depends on unrestricted cooperation between governments, conducted outside the Union framework and with an essentially economic end. Judging by the opinion polls, European citizens would like cultural and educational policies to remain within the competence of individual states.

Institutional policies

Are the forms taken by European liberal democracies determined by their EU membership? This issue, which has given rise to extensive literature (Olsen 2002b), calls for a balanced response. First, it must be emphasized that a respect for the principles of the rule of law and of democracy is a basic condition for Union membership. Until 1997 the treaties did not specify anything in this respect, but authoritarian states (such as Spain and Portugal until the mid-1970s and Greece during the dictatorship of the Colonels) remained on the Union's sidelines, although they were members of other European organizations like the OECD (Organization for Economic Cooperation and Development) or EFTA (European Free Trade Association). Portugal had been a member of NATO since 1949, of EFTA since 1959 and of the OECD since 1961. It was only admitted to the Council of Europe after the fall of the dictatorship in 1976, and to the Union in 1986. Spain was also a member of the OECD from 1961, like Greece and Turkey. The 1997 Treaty of Amsterdam made this condition explicit, and matched it with a control mechanism. Member states can now decide to suspend the rights of any state unanimously found guilty of a 'serious and persistent breach' of democratic principles. A *fortiori*, they reserve the right to refuse membership to a state which – according to their assessment – would not respect the criteria of democracy and the rule of law. These mechanisms seem to be symbolic and are intended to prevent wavering rather than to impose sanctions. So far it has not been possible to measure their effect.

Beyond this fundamental requirement, EU membership does not carry with it any precise constitutional obligations. Most of the members are unitary states but three of them are federal and many of them are familiar with forms of decentralization. The parliamentary model is the most widespread, but in some cases it has a presidential corrective. Constitutional monarchies are as numerous as republics. Referenda are forbidden in some countries, whilst they are frequently used in others. The current voting methods include almost all the possible variants, from the majority system to the purest proportional representation, as well as mixed methods. Some give a key role to a constitutional court, whereas others are wary of it. The bicameral system survives in most states, but the upper legislative chamber has been done away with in some of them. In short, unlike the United States, where the constitutions of individual states all draw on the same sources and reflect the Federal state's balances, Europe is still characterized by a vivid constitutional diversity. The only precise constraints that EU membership entails are the marginal aspects of political regimes. Member countries of the Euro zone were made to reform the status of their central banks to make them more autonomous. In certain states, as in the United Kingdom and Sweden, the Court's jurisprudence on the 'right to a judge' made it necessary to set up new types of judicial recourse, open to private individuals, in the Union's spheres of activity. Though far from insignificant – and sometimes having a considerable symbolic impact – these constraints do not substantially affect the regime.

Constitutional convergence is very relative (Grewe and Ruiz-Fabri 1995). Achieved in the last half-century, it stems, here too, more from copying each other and mutual experience than from a formal dynamic of Europeanization. If we have seen rulers establishing constitutional jurisdictions almost everywhere, this is explained more by the lessons drawn from the abuses of the interwar period than by the pressure of a 'European model'. If most of the unitary states have delegated some of their tasks to local or regional entities, this is mainly due to the continuous development of public authorities and to the resurgence of infra-national identities – without it having been convincingly shown that EU membership was (be it only partially) responsible (Le Galès and Lequesne 1998; Keating 1998). As for the rest, convergence, which again is not confined within the EU's borders, can only be observed in the detailed structures of European regimes. Mimesis (relative insofar as each adapts methods common to the national context) is especially shown in administrative reforms and in the creation of independent executive agencies (Lippert et al. 2001; Grabbe 2001; Malova and Haughton 2002). It does not affect civil rights, the parliamentary sphere and national political life.

Market formation and regulation

Finally, only the states' monetary and economic policies are profoundly affected by European integration. Still it should be specified that the intensity of European regulation varies widely from one area to the next. In the vast entity formed by the generality of economic policies, we find very different methods of action, as we will see in the second section of this chapter. Moreover, one should not lose sight of the fact that the Union's extremely limited budget (1.27% of the combined GDP of its member states) in fact prevents the conduct of extensive policies on a European scale for the construction of infrastructures, the running of public services, and social security. Only the common agricultural policy (CAP), economic and social cohesion and research have a redistributive impact, which does not exceed 3 per cent of their GDP for countries which benefit the most from the community budget. If CAP (which largely depends on price maintenance and subsidies for producers) could be labelled an 'agricultural welfare state', all the other social policies continue to come under individual governments and national systems for social protection. In these areas, governments are only prepared to compare their respective policies and to give themselves very general guidelines in a so-called logic of 'open coordination'. Over recent years, much attention has been focused on another form of Europeanization: judgements by the Court, which appears to want to apply the principles of competition and/or the free circulation of goods and services to areas falling within social protection, has seemed to threaten the specificity of these 'non-market' sectors. In its decisions, the Court has nevertheless shown a wish not to jeopardize the financial balance of social security systems (Maduro 2001; Leibfried and Pierson 2000) and so far the direct consequences of its decisions seem marginal. Moreover, reactions from numerous governments could lead towards legally guaranteeing the particularities of these sectors.

'European constraints', which are so often denounced, mainly pertain to political rhetoric. If it is unquestionable that EU membership obliges the member states to adhere to certain general principles limiting their room for manoeuvre, and that in many areas connected with market regulation it forces them to negotiate with their partners, they nevertheless retain control over the main part of their policies. Decision-making methods, adapted to specific areas of public action, convey the states' reservations concerning the 'community method' beyond policies linked to the single market.

How are the Union's policies made?

In the EU as in any political entity, the decision-making logic varies widely from one area to the next. The procedures, configurations of actors, tensions and strategies obviously differ, be they concerned with adopting or implementing agricultural measures, coordinating economic policies or outlining joint action to do with foreign relations. The EU pushes this differentiation much further than do the states, even the federal ones. This is largely due to the way in which its treaties have been negotiated. In drawing up new policies, the governments have adapted decision-making methods to suit the circumstances. When they agreed on large, clear priorities, as was the case for the single market project in the 1980s, they were to establish decision-making methods where a majority vote is usual and where community institutions play an important role. By contrast, when (as in the domain of foreign policy) the consensus on which their commitment was made remained minimal, they made sure they safeguarded their independence by preserving a right of veto, and only gave the Union's institutions a secondary role. Successive intergovernmental negotiations have constantly accentuated this specialization. At each stage, governments scrupulously weighed cooperations that they were prepared to accept and the guarantees that they intended to obtain in order to protect their national interests. The exchange of concessions led them to adjust decision-making processes from one area to the next.

If we look at them in detail, the result is that almost every policy is governed by a specific mechanism. Even without taking into account areas falling within intergovernmental cooperation, twenty-two different legislative procedures and more than thirty legal instruments were listed. The European Convention agreed to simplify these historical acquisitions. Many *ad hoc* norms and procedures could be done away with, to make way for 'European laws' or 'European framework laws', adopted according to a single legislative procedure. For all that, the way the Union works cannot be reduced to a single decision-making procedure. Many matters pertain to the cooperation or coordination of policies between governments, without inevitably producing European laws. They call for particular mechanisms, and these, according to the Convention, should be maintained.

Consequently, it remains difficult to reduce European decision-making to a single outline (Peterson and Bomberg 1999). The very extensive empirical research concerned with individual European policies highlights the particularities of each one of them. Concerned with not marring this diversity, political scientists are struggling to bring out a comprehensive analytical description. The 'multi-level governance' notion, which attempts to account for the complexity of policy-making in the Union, has enjoyed a certain success over recent years (Marks et al. 1996). Overall, it shows that, unlike a state, the Union is not a centralized system in the form of a pyramid, but a flexible organization of different levels of power. It underlines that decision-making is not limited to the 'government', because many others, both private and public, play a part in 'governance'. It highlights the fact that the Union's methods vary from one area to the next and it stresses the interdependence of the internal and external dimensions of contemporary politics. Such an approach has the virtue of widening the Union's perceptions, and of casting doubt on interpretations which reduce it to a banal international organization or set it up as a federal state. It allows one to account for the multiplicity of integration methods and the profound interpenetration of public and private, national, infra- and supranational spheres which our analytical distinctions tend to bring out. What constitutes the weakness of this notion is also where its great strength lies. Overstressing the flexible, malleable and variable nature of governance can lead to two types of analytical deadlock. The first would consist in highlighting the Union's originality in caricaturing the state: setting a complex European governance against a simple national government would mean forgetting that our states are also, increasingly, forms of 'multi-level governance'. Decentralization, contacts with organized interested parties and the emergence of 'policy networks', cooperation between different levels of power, variation in methods of negotiation and decision-making, all characterize the contemporary state. On the other hand, by showing that the same tendencies are at work in the Union and in the states, one runs the risk of setting 'multi-level governance' up as a hegemonic analytical category so that it loses its distinctiveness.

One must therefore aim at a more modest evaluation which (without reducing European decision-making to a juxtaposition of particular configurations) emphasizes the persistence of distinct decision-making schemas. Three simple, formal criteria allow a little order to be put into this tangle of procedures. First, the degree of involvement of community institutions: in order to give shape to their cooperation, governments can either involve the Commission and the Parliament in policy-making, or choose to keep them in the background. Secondly, the decision-making criteria: giving up unanimity in favour of a qualified majority also shows a desire to step up joint commitments. Finally, there is the legal nature of the motions adopted, which underlines the degree of constraint the governments are willing to accept. Although they have not always tallied, these criteria tend to be taken up with the passing of time. The typical 'Community method' associates the three points of the institutional triangle, has recourse to majority voting and produces binding law. The other ways in which it works are limited by its ability to move away from this 'model' (Scharpf 2000).

Taken as a whole, these criteria allow one to distinguish three predominant decision-making frameworks in the EU: the 'Community method', cooperation between governments, and 'open coordination'. The first two have for a long time provided a choice in the development of integration: either the governments decided to establish a real common policy by having recourse to Community institutions and instruments, or they only undertook to coordinate their national policies within a classic intergovernmental arrangement. The third, more recently established, method attempts to put forward a compromise between these two options, by combining the approaches. A framework of 'centralized regulation' must be added to this trilogy: in some strictly defined areas, governments have chosen to delegate their power to an independent third-party organ rather than making joint decisions.

The Community method

The essence of the 'Community model', which is the usual pattern for ordinary decision-making in the Union, involves collaboration between governments and European institutions. In its present version, the governments accept two constraints limiting their autonomy. On the one hand, decisions are most often made by a qualified majority within the Council, thus depriving governments of their right of veto. On the other hand, they come to a decision on the basis of a proposal from the Commission and in agreement with the European Parliament. Legally speaking, the directive (or European framework law, according to the vocabulary proposed by the Convention) is, and should be, the instrument of choice in this case. Binding as to the result to be achieved, it must be interpreted by the authorities of each member state, which gives them the power to adapt it to their specific context. This decision-making method mainly governs the regulation of the single market (including most policies for the protection of public health, the rights of consumers, and the environment), some policy areas like research or transport, development and humanitarian aid, and some precise social measures (concerning vocational training and work safety or the fight against discrimination). If the constitutional treaty comes into force, it will also cover certain aspects of asylum and immigration policies.

This hybrid form of cooperation, which we will come back to in the following chapters, conveys the delicate balance of a federation of states: it leaves the states with the essential decision-making power, but it gives to the Commission the power to bring about an entente between the governments, and to the European Parliament the possibility of influencing parliamentary bills. Although the Parliament and the Commission have constantly spoken in favour of expanding this arrangement to cover all or most of the Union's activities, the governments have nevertheless preferred to establish either more flexible or stricter methods in some of these spheres.

Intergovernmental cooperation

When they undertook to widen their cooperation beyond matters tied to market regulation, getting into areas they regarded as being at the heart of their sovereignty (foreign policy, security and defence, judicial and police cooperation), most governments thought that they could not accept the constraints of the classic Community method. It seemed premature to give the Commission a monopoly of the right to initiate legislation in these matters, to run the risk of being defeated in a majority vote and to give the European Parliament a power of amendment. In Maastricht, the governments therefore established 'intergovernmental pillars', governed by decision-making methods which were much less restrictive. They decide unanimously that in intergovernmental matters, the Commission should have only a very limited right of initiative, which should be shared with the governments, and at best, the Parliament should only be consulted on certain aspects. In these areas, the decisions made are *ad hoc* legal instruments, are not of a legislative nature and escape jurisdictional control. As for the coordination of asylum and immigration policies, as well as for cooperation in police and criminal matters, the laws produced are subject to the Court's control solely under limited conditions. This situation is therefore formally close to what is the usual practice in classic international organizations.

The intergovernmental method is the subject of varied interpretations. Certain governments, supported by the Commission and a majority of MEPs, claim to be hostile to it and frequently call for the 'Europeanization' of these spheres of activity; others do not intend to go beyond this slightly restricted form of cooperation. Many observers regularly denounce the impediments inherent in the rule of unanimity and the weakness of negotiations that depend on bargaining rather than on a willingness to find common solutions (Scharpf 1988). Others underline that these minimum commitments amount to useful forms of learning because they enable one to go beyond non-cooperation and progressively socialize those involved in implementing national policy, without causing the most reticent governments to fear being committed against their will. The routine which has been established over the years, reducing clashes and the most blatant forms of competition, has contributed to this movement towards flexible convergence.

The Convention's debates and compromises on the Union's future have shown that European leaders are still attached to this somewhat restrictive method. In spite of strong appeals from the Commission and Parliament, backed up by the governments of the Benelux countries and some others, and despite the threat of complete paralysis in an enlarged Europe where each of the twenty-five governments enjoys a right of veto, the European Convention has not suggested abandoning intergovernmental cooperation. Formally, the constitutional treaty will abolish the 'pillars' established in Maastricht. But this does not mean that all spheres of activity will be subject to the classic Community method. As regards foreign and defence policy, as well as the tax system and sensitive social policies, unanimity will still be necessary.

The Commission and Parliament's role will also remain limited: as regards foreign policy, the constitutional treaty states that the right to initiate action will be shared between a minister of foreign affairs, designated by the governments, and the Council (made up of the governments' representatives). Some have considered that a more integrated method (inspired by the one governing the Union's commercial policy) could be extended to the whole of the Union's external affairs. The Commission would have obtained the power to submit proposals to the governments, which would have come to a decision by a qualified majority and would have entrusted the Commission with their execution. But a wide majority have reckoned that this method (which has shown its efficiency in the area of trade, where governments are represented by the Commission in international organizations) would be impossible in areas where urgent decisions have to be made. The commercial policy only works because governments have the time to examine the Commission's proposals in detail, to modify them and to control the Commission's actions throughout multilateral negotiations. In the event of an international crisis, this process would deprive the Union and its states of their capacity to react rapidly.

We would be wrong, however, to attach too much importance to procedures governing decision-making. Everyone knows that in circumstances like those of the war in Iraq in the spring of 2003, voting by a qualified majority would, on its own, have been unable to reduce opposition. This is why the most ardent advocates of the Community method acknowledge that in these sensitive matters, it would be more efficient to encourage dialogue, which could, in the long run (if viewpoints are drawn closer together on a lasting basis), make recourse to a majority vote possible. These reforms of the Union's external affairs (stepping up the role of dialogue between governments, entrusting the Union minister for foreign affairs with the power to bring together the governments' decisions and to represent them on the international scene, improving the use of common resources) aim at improving the intergovernmental method, but do not call its foundations into question.

'Open coordination'

A third mode of action, seeking a median channel between inter-governmental cooperation and the Community method, was outlined more recently. Starting from the Maastricht Treaty, governments have established an original form of flexible coordination in the area of the Economic and Monetary Union. By adopting a single currency, which is entrusted to the care of the European Central Bank, they in fact undertook to coordinate their economic and budget policies. Some years later, at the time of the adoption of the Treaty of Amsterdam, they extended this logic to certain elements of their social and employment policies, and then, in Spring 2000, to a group of new areas linked to social security and vocational training. While at the same time undertaking to reduce clashes between their national policies, governments preferred not to entrust the Commission and the European Parliament with too wide an influence in this area, on which most of their national policies depend. Consequently, strictly speaking, they do not make common policies in these areas, but establish criteria through which to channel their national policies. The logic of this form of flexible coordination, which has experienced some variants depending on circumstances, is substantially as follows: the governments first adopt general attitudes and guidelines that they undertake to follow when conceiving their national policies. These norms, pertaining to a form of 'soft law', are not directly applicable, nor even translated into domestic law. They make up 'criteria' which national authorities agree to take into account when making their own policies.

In the decision-making phase, strictly speaking, the Commission only plays a limited role. The power to initiate legislation (for which it has the monopoly in matters pertaining to the community method) is weakened here. The Commission elaborates recommendations or proposals, but does this on the basis of reports and conclusions established by the governments themselves (within the framework of the European Council or the Council of Ministers).

The Commission's power of control is also diluted. To ensure that these objectives are effectively pursued, a mechanism of 'multilateral surveillance' is established. The governments themselves can decide to address recommendations or reprimands to states that have failed to adhere to jointly agreed criteria. Here, the role of the Commission is confined to analysing national situations on the basis of reports established by the governments, and proposing the adoption of recommendations to the Council. Until now, moreover, the governments have been hesitant to point a finger at one of their own: although the Commission has proposed recommendations with regard to the least efficient governments, this was only after many warnings and reconciliation attempts.

Sometimes described as an 'open method of coordination', this new mode of action was conceived because the governments were aware that in the absence of cooperation they would be forced to compromise, but they nevertheless refused to adopt truly 'common' policies in these matters. In order to avoid unfair competition due to 'social and fiscal dumping', and while at the same time shirking the constraints of the classic community method, the governments brought policy 'coordination' in line with current tastes and methods based on emulation more than compulsion. Nurtured by concepts of public management, this method is intended to favour a gradual convergence of national policies without imposing heavy constraints. By establishing criteria backed up by figures so that results can be compared (benchmarking), by accepting that the benefits be assessed by their peers (peer review) and by the Commission (monitoring), by informing their partners of successful initiatives (best practices), they are aiming at mutual learning (policy learning).

Centralized regulation

Centralized regulation makes up a fourth mode of action in the Union. In some very limited areas, governments have considered that 'good decisions' could only be made if they were entrusted to a supranational and independent institution. Starting with the Treaty of Paris, member states established a Court of Justice and a High Authority enjoying strong guarantees of independence in order to ensure that European law was respected by everyone. Aware that it was in their interest to see their decisions being correctly applied by their partners, and that clashes could spring up between them that they themselves would not be able to resolve, they established these third-party institutions to act as arbitrators and guardians. Later, when the Commission was entrusted, by stages, with applying the principles of competition, this answered to the same logic. It was in the interest of each state to see to it that its partners respected these principles, and they presumed that they would be scoffed at if the governments themselves were in charge of their application. The setting up of an independent European Central Bank, responsible for decisions concerned with currency, falls within the same reasoning.

Political scientists have undertaken to explain (and at times to justify) this phenomenon of delegating powers to third-party organs. Some have highlighted the different nature of so-called 'redistributive' public policies – which presuppose government arbitration because they affect the distribution of resources – and of 'regulating' policies which, in their opinion, are better conducted by independent experts (Majone 1996). Even if it exerts a certain appeal for the leaders themselves, this distinction remains weak: 'regulatory' measures, like those adopted by the European Central Bank or by the Commission as far as competition is concerned, can, in practice, have a strong redistributive effect and often imply a choice between values rather than a simple technical decision on the means of distribution. As has been emphasized by a political scientist, 'severing ties to democratic representatives and relying on technocratic expertise does not apoliticise monetary policy. Rather, delegation to independent central banks produces partisanal policies, with significant distributional effects that raise important questions of democratic accountability' (McNamara 2002).

Other political scientists, inspired by analytical outlines constructed in the United States, stress the interests governments can have in relieving themselves of the burden of some of their duties (Pollack 1997; Tallberg 2002). In matters exposed to market reactions, as in monetary policy or control over competition, they may consider that the commitments they make will be more credible if they are entrusted to the care of an 'agent', that is to say, a third party. The second motive that political authorities can have in entrusting an agreed mission to an agency is, more simply, to gather information and expertise at a lower cost than if they were to do it themselves. Thus, many agencies composed of experts were established in order to help political decision-makers in highly technical domains. Sometimes, the governments may go so far as to entrust agents chosen for their competence with the decision-making itself in a fixed area, intending to improve the quality of public policies. Finally, a fourth motivation frequently put forward lies in the politicans' willingness to 'shift the blame', by leaving unpopular decisions to external organs. In actual fact, these motives more often than not become confused in practice. The creation of an independent central bank proceeds from a willingness both to entrust a competent and impartial organ with decision-making, and to make it bear the responsibility.

There remains, however, an important difference between the agencies with both decision-making power and solid guarantees of autonomy, and those that simply provide information and consultancy, and are subject to political control (Majone 2001a). Even if the responsibility for errors committed in certain sensitive matters like public health protection has sometimes been attributed to the role played by experts in decision-making, it is, above all, the first type of agency which has been the subject of debate. Entrusting crucial decisions to organs protected from political influence might seem to go against the spirit of parliamentary democracy. Criticism directed at 'stateless Areopaguses' is nevertheless tending to be toned down. Within the European Convention, virtually nobody has seriously called into question the role and status of the European Central Bank – even if those furthest from the political hub continue to regret that the members of its board of directors cannot be made more fully and openly accountable for their decisions. It may be observed, however, that the governments are extremely reticent about creating other agencies on the central bank model: most independent organs created over recent years mainly carry out the duties of informing and awareness-raising, and remain under the governments' attentive control. There is every indication that, in the years to come, governments will continue to favour more flexible and less restrictive forms of coordination, only sparingly making use of delegation to a third party or sharing decision-making with Community institutions.

Chapter 3

Cooperation and Conflict: the Union and its States

Tensions between different levels of power are part and parcel of any political system. Even unitary states, or those only experiencing flexible forms of decentralization, must periodically face the opposition of local or regional authorities. This chapter will show that this phenomenon is particularly pronounced in regimes which, like that of the European Union, have installed complex forms of task distribution among the different hierarchies. As political actors naturally tend to be defensive of public entities on which they depend, conflicts are inevitable, especially as European public policies, blurring the boundaries between the private and the public sphere, and based on subtle partnership and collaboration mechanisms, increase the risks of imposition or competition.

In the European Union, as in any federal entity, two sets of mechanisms are supposed to prevent or resolve 'vertical' conflicts. First, in participating in European decision-making, states need a guarantee that each one can make itself heard to avoid disagreements as much as possible. As will be seen later in this book, the composition of European institutions ensures that their rules for internal decisions and inter-institutional decision-making procedures allow state authorities to intervene at all stages in order to defend their interests. The EU not only intensifies this classic federal mechanism, it also completes it with a demanding doctrine of 'subsidiarity', offering state authorities the opportunity to control the initiatives of EU institutions *ex ante*.

With no preventive mechanism able to avoid competition entirely, the EU has also developed a subtle technique for resolving conflicts that arise after decision-making. While states intend to control the action of the Union's institutions in order to prevent them encroaching upon their powers, they are also aware of the need to control themselves. With European law being essentially implemented by state authorities, it is in their interest that their partners respect joint commitments. This explains why they granted the Commission and the Court of justice the power to force states to keep to their obligations.

How the states control the Union

At the outset, the principle was simple. The EU only had powers of attribution. The treaties, adopted with the agreement of each of the member states, defined a certain number of areas for joint action, and specified the European institutions' role in their design and implementation. Everything not formally pertaining to the Union's activities continued, in principle, to be the prerogative of the member states. Defining the respective capacities of the Union and the states seemed to show a clear logic of separation. Moreover, legal mechanisms allowed the states to have European decisions annulled when they infringed on their prerogatives.

Things rapidly proved less simple than they had appeared at first glance. To begin with, rather than establishing a strict list of powers, the treaties resorted to different ways of defining the Union's functions. The preambles and principles set out the objectives that European action must follow. Broad and imprecise, the latter cover

> a harmonious, balanced and sustainable development of economic activities, a high level of employment and of social protection, equality between men and women, sustainable and non-inflationary growth, a high degree of competitiveness and convergence of economic performance, a high level of protection and improvement of the quality of the environment, the raising of the standard of living and quality of life, and economic and social cohesion and solidarity among Member States.   (EC Treaty, article 2)

As far as its external role is concerned, the EU is also supposed to

> safeguard the common values, fundamental interests, independence and integrity of the Union in conformity with the

principles of the United Nations Charter, to strengthen the security of the Union in all ways, to preserve peace and strengthen international security ..., to promote international cooperation, to develop and consolidate democracy and the rule of law, and respect for human rights and fundamental freedoms.   (EU Treaty, article 11)

If state objectives were to be defined, no doubt the wording would not be very different. These principles and objectives do not initiate a capacity of action for the Union, but they are not strictly declaratory for all that: put forward by the Commission, they can be used to justify a new proposal for action. For its part, the Court of Justice may refer to them in order to specify the impact of the Union's powers in particular cases.

Beyond the assertion of these principles and objectives, the treaty sets out more precisely the 'policies' required to bring them into existence, and establishes for each of them a specific field and mode of action. Being the fruit of long and meticulous negotiations, the measures defining the impact and means of these policies are generally precise and detailed. When, for example, the Maastricht Treaty introduced new chapters or paragraphs relating to culture, the environment, public health, and so on, in each case it specified the limits of these policies, conceived for the most part to complement national activities. Moreover, these measures aimed as much at restricting the Union's margin of activities (by setting clear limits to it) as at opening new fields for it.

But such measures cannot suffice to eliminate the risks of conflicting interpretations: it frequently happens that a measure deemed necessary by the Commission to pursue the Union's objectives will be regarded by a member state as encroaching on its prerogatives; or that an action which, according to some members, pertains to the European policy on competition, will be seen by others as an attack on national social policies. These divergences are all the more frequent as in most of its spheres of activity the Union shares its powers with the member states. Rather than attributing prerogatives exclusive to the Union in specific areas, as was originally the case in the federations established in the eighteenth and nineteenth centuries, the governments, more often than not, have established mechanisms of cooperation and coordination or bestowed the Union with so-called shared or complementary powers. The near-totality of national public policies thus ended up 'framed' or 'completed' by European measures, which has increased the risks of competition or contradiction.

The problem is still worse because, far from having been definitively set, the Union's sphere of activity has been regularly revised since the time of its establishment. Aware that they might be required to envisage new cooperations, the initiators of the original treaties resolved to preserve the open definition of the Union's powers. They thus anticipated the possibility of modifying the treaty itself to establish new spheres of activity, and this track has frequently been followed since the mid-1980s. They also gave the Council (made up of government representatives) the power unanimously to adopt actions not anticipated in the treaty, and this power was also often used in the 1970s and the 1980s. These slow and partial increases in the Union's powers did not arouse any tensions, at least up until recently. Subject to the rule of unanimous decision-making, the new policies were accepted by each of the member states.

It is true that in some cases, progress on integration has escaped their control. The Court of Justice soon formulated a doctrine of 'implicit powers' and 'pre-emption' which allowed the Union's powers to develop beyond what the governments themselves had envisaged. Without exploiting its ability to interpret the treaty too openly, contrary to the wishes of the governments, it nevertheless favoured an increase in the Union's powers. Thus, in particular, in the 1970s it established that where it enjoyed an internal competence, the Community should have the capacity to exercise it as far as the outside world was concerned, even if this had not been anticipated in the treaty. This amounted to depriving the states of their right to enter into international engagements in matters where they acted together within the Community.

Until the end of the 1980s, this flexible system for the division of powers functioned unhampered. Of course, some governments have sometimes found the Commission's proposals excessive, and tried to block them or get the decisions annulled by the Court. But none of them considered it pressing to revise the principles governing the attribution of powers to the Union. The rules guaranteed that no extension would be possible without the unanimous agreement of the member states, and procedures of appeal were open to them.

On the eve of the Maastricht Treaty, the concerns of those fearing a gradual centralization of power in Brussels grew stronger and more widespread. Throughout the 1980s, the governments had invested the Union with new powers. No doubt these decisions had been made unanimously, but this formal guarantee seemed to be less and less sufficient. Some governments which had recently come into power, and been compelled to accept concessions made by their predecessors, intended to control more strictly the transfer of national powers to European institutions in the future. Moreover, the gradual increase in votes passed by a qualified majority caused them to fear that they might be relegated to the minority for the long term with regard to the implementation of these policies. At the same time, European standards tended to become more and more precise. On the pretext of ensuring the functioning of the internal market, the Commission proposed strict measures for the regulation of goods and services; concerned with preserving their own interests, governments negotiated these texts to the smallest details, making European legislation still more complex and more restrictive. In spite of a broad consensus about the goal of completing the single market by 1993, this intense regulatory activity generated the fear (in European leaders and in public opinion) of seeing the development of ever more pernickety European legislation, which would gradually escape from the governments' control. More and more often, farmers, hunters, craftsmen and consumers have denounced the 'regulatory fury' of the Commission, suspected of wanting to dictate everything from Brussels, from labelling shoe boxes to grading strawberries, to the conditions of livestock in transit, the length of leek stems or the living conditions of animals in zoological gardens. Related by a press greedy for striking facts, these criticisms became commonplace.

Theory and practice of subsidiarity

In this climate of distrust and tensions, negotiations which were to give rise to the Maastricht Treaty saw the emergence of the 'subsidiarity' theme. The German *Länder*, concerned about seeing the government of the Federal Republic entrust the Union with missions pertaining to their own areas of competence, wished to see the principle of power attribution more clearly reasserted. This wish fell in with the preoccupations of the majority of governments, concerned about reassuring their worried populations about the interference of 'Brussels' in their daily life. Thus the governments agreed to insert an article in the treaty setting out the famous principle of subsidiarity. This concept, stemming from the social doctrine of the Church, had initially been designed to govern relations between hierarchies within the Catholic Church, and to alleviate Roman centralism. It was then applied to temporal power, with the intention of containing public intervention by making the case for the autonomy of families, corporations and charity institutions (Millon-Delsol 1992). So, at the outset, this concept was foreign to constitutional terminology, which made it particularly adaptable and allowed difficult debates on establishing a list of powers to be avoided. On its own, it brought no clear response to preoccupations linked to the division of powers: by asserting that the Community could only intervene 'if and in so far as the objectives of the intended action cannot be sufficiently achieved by the Member States ... but can rather, by reason of the scale or effects of the proposed action, be better achieved at the Union level' (EC Treaty, article 3B), the treaty merely begged the question. Moreover, this new article was interpreted by most commentators as a political signal much more than a real mechanism for regulating conflicts. It was about showing members of the public that their concerns had been heard, and that the European political players would thereafter be more attentive to the states' prerogatives, while at the same time leaving at the more federalist margins of public opinion the hope that new commitments could be made on this basis. The rejection of the Maastricht Treaty by Danish voters, and its acceptance by a narrow margin in France, confirmed that, although necessary, this precision was insufficient.

As it figured in the treaty, the principle could be perceived in two ways. On the one hand, it was a kind of political warning addressed to the Commission by the governments: being the mainspring of European construction, and the initiator of text proposals adopted by the governments, it was encouraged to justify more rigorously the need for the actions it promoted. The Commission itself, aware of its worsening image, had supported this proposal. On the other hand, this principle was also justiciable: the governments could refer to it before the Court when trying to oppose measures which they thought went beyond the Union's functions (Dehousse 1994). Since then, these two meanings of the concept have been confirmed, the first more clearly than the second.

The governments were actually very reticent to entrust the Court of Justice with resolving their conflicts – they no doubt thought that the Court would rather be inclined to defend the EU institutions' viewpoint. The Court itself only entered into this delicate matter with extreme caution. In many cases submitted to it, it pretended not to see that the issue of subsidiarity was being referred to by the governments, and responded to those making the appeal on more traditional grounds. In only two cases was the Court brought to give an explicit opinion in respect of the principle of subsidiarity. In 1994, the United Kingdom tried to oppose the adoption of a directive harmonizing weekly working hours. The Commission had presented this proposal as a contribution to the improvement of working conditions, which implied that it pertained to a sphere of European activity where decisions are adopted by a qualified majority; the United Kingdom, however, brandishing the notion of subsidiarity, considered that such a measure was unnecessary within the framework of this policy, and that it could therefore only be adopted unanimously. That same year, for the same reasons, the German government opposed the adoption of a directive relating to bank deposit guarantees. In both cases, the Court decided against the state which tried to oppose the adoption of a European standard, considering that the fact alone that the Council chose to act in this regard showed the need for a European decision, without demanding a more detailed justification in reference to the principle of subsidiarity (de Bùrca 1998).

In the months following the adoption of the Maastricht Treaty, the governments again took the political initiative, and sought to specify the impact of this principle. A protocol appended to the 1997 Treaty of Amsterdam and taking up the terms of previous agreements, tried to make this principle operational. It first states that the subsidiarity notion cannot be separated from one of the Union's major principles: proportionality. The Court had already asserted the importance and specified the impact of this principle. In many cases, in fact, it is not about whether the Union must act or not, but *to what extent* its intervention is necessary. The criticisms expressed by national politicians, and echoed by public opinion, do not denounce Community policies in themselves as much as the propensity to govern areas that are tackled in the minutest details, when it could content itself with setting the main lines and leaving the states to deal with the practicalities.

The political assertion of the importance of proportionality is shown through an invitation addressed to the Commission, asking it to give preference to forms of cooperation and flexible coordination in such a way as only to propose European legislation where coordination does not suffice, and to opt as far as possible for framework legislation rather than for precise regulations when legislation seems necessary. In other words, it is about returning to the spirit of the Community's origins: the Treaty of Rome reserved legislative harmonization for defined areas and saw the directive as a more general instrument of flexible convergence, leaving the choice of methods to the member states. In addition, the governments specified that subsidiarity had to be understood in a double sense. If they intended to preserve what had been acquired, in particular the exclusive powers linked to the single market, they also emphasized that the principle of subsidiarity is not only a means of conceiving new policies, but must sometimes allow for the limitation or even the abrogation of European action when the latter is no longer deemed necessary. So the political message is clear: if hereafter the Union acts within a wider field of competencies, the governments intend to keep a strict eye on the growth of European policies.

In practice, this can be interpreted in two ways. Before decision-making, the respect for the principles of subsidiarity and proportionality must be guaranteed by more intense consultation and justification mechanisms. In other words, before putting forward a new proposal, the Commission must carry out broad consultations in order to verify the relevance of the measures suggested, and strictly justify their necessity. It must also anticipate and explain the financial impact of these actions and make sure that that impact is as little as possible. Without defining a specific procedure, governments have indicated the criteria that it is the Commission's duty to take into account in this exercise. It means showing that the issue tackled involves transnational aspects such that it could not be treated in a satisfactory way by states acting separately, and that a joint action would provide obvious advantages because of its size or its effects. Of course, the interpretation of such criteria remains wide open: rare are the cases where governments unanimously consider that an issue is transnational by nature or that a joint policy objective offers an 'added value' in comparison with the Union's objectives.

The principles of subsidiarity and proportionality do not resolve power conflicts. They simply offer a way of itemizing political debates. Furthermore, they are conceived as part and parcel of a political dynamic: if the Commission must justify its proposals before making a decision, reporting on the application of these principles is incumbent upon it afterwards. By making an annual assessment of the way in which they reorientate the Union's actions, the Commission justifies its proposals *ex post*, and shows how it intends to interpret them in the future.

It is difficult to give a precise estimate of the impact that this new scale of argumentation between the states and European institutions has on the Union's practice. There are many indications that the Commission, the Parliament and the governments acting within the Council take these principles seriously. Even if it only offers a rough image of European action, the decreasing number of proposals for standards presented by the Commission each year shows a desire to reduce the amount of European legislation imposing legal constraints on the states.

Further, the Commission regularly emphasizes its willingness to promote flexible methods of coordination (when this does not jeopardize the Union's objectives), rather than restricting harmonization techniques (European Commission 2001). In this way, for instance, it encourages agreements concluded directly with industries in the sphere of environmental protection. Elsewhere, it favours self-regulation within the enterprises, or social dialogue between employers and trade unions. More generally, it often advocates coordinated approaches, or agreements of mutual recognition, rather than seeking to harmonize national rules, and it puts forward more recommendations than proposals for legislative acts. All these initiatives move in the same direction: the Union must better distinguish the priority spheres of activity, where common standards are necessary, from policies in which it only intervenes subordinately and where flexible techniques of coordination will be privileged. In the long run, this should clarify the public's perception of the Union's role, and reduce the strength of its legislative action. Even if hasty conclusions should be avoided, we cannot help but notice that this corresponds to the expectations of the employers' organizations, who want single market regulation to engender only a minimum of legal restrictions.

In a white paper devoted to 'European governance' (published during the summer of 2001), the Commission presented this perspective as the fate of a Europe enlarged to encompass the whole of the continent. Defending the 'Community model', it expressed the wish that the Union should thereafter concentrate on a few key themes, and act in a more flexible and more decentralized way in all other spheres. Sharing this concern, the members of the European Convention, who considered global remodelling of the Union's 'constitution' in the course of 2002 and 2003, deemed it necessary to deal further with this principle of subsidiarity. Debates in this field have shown that national political leaders remain very concerned about the issue of the definition of powers, and that the practice of subsidiarity did not meet their concerns. That is why, at the request of members of national parliaments, anxious to control more strictly the shifting of powers to the Union, the Convention suggested instituting an 'early warning' system, which would allow national members of parliament to draw the attention of European institutions when they consider that a proposal of European norms might encroach upon their powers. If such 'reasoned opinions' are expressed by a third of the parliaments, the Commission will be obliged to re-examine its proposal, and decide whether to maintain it or to withdraw it, but should in any case again justify its choice. Such a mechanism remains essentially preventive: the state parliaments will not be able to block the Commission's initiatives, but their warnings will oblige it to be more cautious. In addition, the states retain the right to bring cases to the Court when they consider that a legislative act violates the subsidiarity principle.

The states under the Union's control

The balance between power levels is not only shown in the way member states supervise the Union's action. It is also conveyed through the control exerted by the European institutions on the authorities of member states. Giving rise to fewer debates, this other dimension of 'vertical relations' is of no less importance. With rare exceptions, the Union's policies are implemented by the national authorities. European laws must be transposed into national laws by the legislators; implementing norms are more often than not adopted by state executives, and it is their courts which ensure the daily application of European law. In other words, the formation of the Union did not give rise to a broad federal administration. There are about 30,000 European civil servants, two-thirds of whom work within the Commission (Stevens and Stevens 2001), which hardly exceeds the number of civic employees in an average town, and represents less than one-hundredth of the American Federal administration, or one-tenth that of the Federal Republic of Germany. The Union has neither firemen, nor policemen, nor health personnel, nor teachers, nor customs officers, nor servicemen. Its civil servants mainly deal with drawing up policies and only take part in their management and execution in limited areas – as in the control of competition, or social cohesion policies. This is how the initiators of European administration would have wanted it. In this connection, Monnet writes in his memoirs: 'Some hundreds of European civil servants would suffice to set thousands of national experts to work and have the powerful machinery of enterprises and governments used for the treaty's missions' (Monnet 1976:436). Even if the size of the European civil service has increased since then, this logic has not been fundamentally questioned.

In such a system of task division, it seems inevitable that the way national authorities implement joint decisions will be the subject of control by European institutions. Besides, from the time of the Treaty of Paris, it is the governments themselves who have wanted it that way. Not one of the founding members intended to substitute a centralized European administration for its own national civil service. But each was aware that, in such a decentralized system, some states were likely to try to escape from their obligations. Indeed, the treaty obliges the states 'to take appropriate measures, whether general or particular, to ensure fulfilment of the obligations' arising from their membership of the Union; to 'facilitate the achievement of the Community's tasks' and to 'abstain from any measure which would jeopardize the attainment of the objectives' of the treaties. But such a statement has never sufficed to guarantee loyalty. Very early, negotiators of the treaties of Paris and Rome understood that the mission of 'guarding the treaty' had to be entrusted to supranational institutions (Pescatore 1981). Any system of multilateral surveillance might have stirred up tensions between governments.

It was to respond to this need that the remedy for breach of EU law was conceived. Mixing amicable resolution and legal recourse, it established the Commission and the Court as 'guardians of the treaties'. In substance, the process is as follows. The executive authorities of the member states are under an obligation to inform the Commission of the way in which they have interpreted European standards, and more generally of the measures they have adopted to fulfil their obligations. Moreover, the Commission also receives complaints from private individuals (which in fact come, more often than not, from enterprises and interest groups), accusing national authorities of violating Community law, and can lead its own investigations. The number of cases brought before the Commission is relatively stable, and most of them are brought to its attention by private individuals. Statistics established by the Commission show that matters linked to environmental protection (38.75%) and the domestic market (22.71%) represent the main part of the issues it examines. Next come health and consumer protection (7.41%), the tax system and the customs union (6.46%), employment and social affairs (5.30%) enterprises (4.08%) and energy and transport (3.81%) (European Commission 2001).

The handling of these affairs responds to a political logic conceived to favour amicable arrangements between the Commission and national administrations, and to delay legal solutions as far as possible. To begin with, the Commission's departments gather information in order to check that the complaints are justified; they then inform the national authorities. A considerable number of cases are discreetly resolved through informal exchanges. The departments of the Commission sometimes take the initiative of organizing a meeting with their national counterparts to tackle broad contentious issues or seek a compromise on a 'pack' of violations. If these processes do not suffice, the Commission can initiate the formal procedure. The latter also includes pre-contention phases intended to iron out differences: first, the Commission enjoins the state in question to make its standards and practices conform to Community law; then, if this does not prove sufficient, it issues a 'reasoned opinion' on the matter. Of the two thousand files processed each year, almost half reach a solution at this stage. Then comes the so-called contention phase. The Commission has the power to bring the matter before the Court. In practice, it only uses this power sparingly: only a third of cases that have given rise to a 'reasoned opinion' are prolonged by being brought before the Court. The Commission in fact enjoys a discretionary power in this respect. Sometimes, it will consider that a case is too confused or too insignificant to justify legal proceedings. Sometimes, however, it deems it opportune to go into open conflict with a member state, because the case is important or may serve as a warning. On this basis, each year the Court pronounces about fifty judgements condemning a state – which represents only 4 per cent of the violations detected, and 15 per cent of the cases referred to it within this framework.

The treaty also provides for a variant of this procedure, in which the Court is directly approached by a state. In practice, this way of resolving conflicts is extremely rare: first, because state governments balk at directly attacking their partners before the Union's jurisdiction, and prefer to leave this thankless role to the Commission; and sometimes because, hoping to avoid sharpening tensions, the initiators of the treaty have anticipated that the Commission must first seek an amicable solution: after having heard the arguments of the parties, it addresses a 'reasoned opinion' to them indicating how the case might be resolved. It is only at the end of this conciliation phase that one state can bring another before the Court of Luxemburg. This explains why only four judgements have been pronounced on this basis since the implementation of the initial treaties. More often than not, the states have found a solution to their disagreements through bilateral negotiations, or have put the Commission in charge of prosecuting recalcitrant national authorities. The Court was therefore able to avoid (we will revert back to this in Chapter 6) appearing to be an 'international court' needing to be acquainted with conflicts between states, and to present itself as a 'constitutional court' ensuring the uniform interpretation and application of the law.

Although they sometimes end up paying for it, the governments have always supported this control mechanism. During negotiations on the Maastricht Treaty, they even increased the sanctioning powers granted to the Commission and the Court. Until then, no sanctions could be imposed on a state guilty of not respecting a court judgement. Aware of the risks that this represented for the application of the law and the credibility of the authorities in charge of 'guaranteeing' the treaties, the governments then established a new mechanism that allowed for the imposition of financial sanctions on states at fault. After again having addressed a 'reasoned opinion' to the state in question, giving it a last chance to conform, the Commission can hereafter take over the Court and propose that the state concerned be condemned to pay a lump sum or penalty. The amount of the fine proposed by the Commission takes into account the duration of the violation, its implications and the financial capacity of the state in question.

The fines proposed since 1997 have ranged from 6,000 euros (against Luxemburg, regarding medical assistance on board ships) to 185,850 euros a day (against Italy, regarding the processing of waste-water). Here too, the Commission will only exercise this power with caution. Although the treaty came into force in 1993, the Commission did not resort to this mechanism before 1997. That year, nine appeals were initiated, levelled at four member states (five of which concerned matters linked to environmental protection). Subsequently, the Commission has acted in an even more selective way, opening such a procedure in only three or four cases each year. To date, only one of these cases has led the Court to fix daily fines against a state (in the case of Greece, which paid 5,400,000 euros for an infraction relating to a discharge of toxic products which had lasted eight months), the others having changed their legal and administrative practices before the Court reached its decision.

The public rarely becomes aware of it, but the continuous control of the member states by European institutions makes up one of the main elements of political relations in the Union. The issue of incomplete or imperfect implementation of Community law, at one stage, gave rise to some debate among academics and in political spheres: faced with the increase in European regulations, some states were suspected of trying to escape their obligations by 'forgetting' the law. Since many violated standards had been adopted by the qualified majority, the EU might have been weakened, in the medium term, by this more or less deliberate form of carelessness. Since the end of the 1990s, this concern seems to have been taken seriously. On the one hand, the *leitmotiv* of subsidiarity led to a decline in European legislation: fewer and more flexible rules are more easily implemented than pernickety regulations. On the other hand, the Commission demonstrated the efficiency of the control mechanisms and, by using them more often than not as a warning, could persuade the governments to see that European decisions were interpreted and implemented more scrupulously.

Controlling law enforcement by the national authorities nevertheless remains a major concern of EU politics, confronted today by a double challenge. The Union's enlargement has doubled the number of states, and complicated the Commission's task of surveillance even more, which may necessitate resorting to the services of private experts to examine whether national practices conform to European commitments. On the other hand, the relaxation of methods of European integration calls into question the role of the Commission and the Court as 'guardians of the treaties'. When governments resort to cooperation or to 'open coordination', rather than producing common legislation, the margin for control narrows. No doubt, in years to come, the issue of 'vertical' political relations in the Union will once again be at the heart of the political agenda.

Chapter 4

Competing for Leadership: Commission vs. Council

The intricate rules for the distribution of competencies between the states and the Union, and the mechanisms for preventing and resolving conflicts accompanying them, constitute one of the major elements of the European Union's regime. This, in substance, is the argument of the first three chapters of this book. The following four chapters will show that the balance between the states and the Union is also expressed in the way its institutions are conceived, and in its decision-making procedures. We will see how, by designing a 'Community model' which was deliberately different from federal arrangements, the Union's founders and reformers attended both to protecting the states' identity and also to making their cooperation possible.

This chapter will begin with the core of the Community model: the institutionalized form of negotiation between governments taking place within the Council sphere, with the support of the Commission. The balance between intergovernmentalism and supranationality is indeed the cornerstone of the 'Community way'. It distinguishes the EU both from classic international regimes and from federal polities.

What is the Community model?

When analysing the Union, there is a great temptation to project onto it constitutional principles familiar to us. On paper, today's European institutions seem unoriginal. Like contemporary federations, the Union is composed of a central executive (the Commission), counterbalanced by authorities representing the states on the one hand (the Council) and the Union as a whole on the other (the European Parliament); the European

Council, which exercises the functions of a 'head of state', and the Court, which arbitrates conflicts, complete the system. The formal resemblance to classic federal arrangements, in particular those of the Federal Republic of Germany, is striking. A political analyst as influential as Arendt Lijphart sees an altogether banal form of the federal state in the Union (Lijphart 1999). And the German social scientist Jürgen Habermas echoes a widespread view when he regrets that the Union does not conform more to the German federal model (Habermas 2001). Not only is this analogy simplistic (Costa and Magnette 2003), but one must not lose sight of the fact that, in practice, the Union's regime is very different from that of the federal states. First of all, the federal analogy conceals the fact that the Union's international nature continues to have a marked influence on the composition and functioning of these institutions (Menon 2003). As we will see in this and the next few chapters, the three major EU institutions are best understood as mechanisms designed to manage national oppositions. Secondly, this analogy hides a major feature of the 'Community model': the fact that, contrary to what happens in federal systems, in the EU none of the three key decision-making organs (Council, Commission, European Parliament) has ever managed to dominate the political game on a long-term basis. The Commission is not and cannot become the Union's government. The Union remains a 'headless' regime, based on continual negotiation between three poles, none of which manages to monopolize the leadership functions. Far from revealing a growth crisis, or being an anomaly, competing for leadership is normal in such a regime. From the outset, continuous competition between the supranational Commission and organs representing the governments, has been a distinctive feature of the 'Community model'.

The principles of the Union's political regime cannot be understood without bearing in mind that the original Community was conceived within a fundamentally intergovernmental logic. The 'Founding Fathers' were not idealistic federalists, but realistic politicians (Milward 1992). Their ambition was not to build a federal state that would gradually subordinate the member states, the way Washington imposed itself upon the American states. True, in his famous *Manifesto di Ventotene* of 1943 the

Italian activist Altiero Spinelli wrote that a European federation should replace the old system of sovereign states. But those in command had more realistic views: the Italian statesman Alcide De Gasperi was primarily moved, after 1946, by a desire to 'reassert the role of Italy in the European and world order, and a clear understanding that welfare and the promise of economic security were the vital steps to national reassertion' (Milward 1992:333). The same holds true, *mutatis mutandis*, for the other five Founding states. The Belgian federalist Fernand Dehousse pleaded for 'integral federalism' as a solution to Belgium's internal and external challenges. But he had no influence on his socialist colleague Paul-Henri Spaak, who supported 'the American wish for political integration in Western Europe ... because it would be the best available guarantee of Belgium's economic and military security' (ibid.:324). In France, for Robert Schuman 'as for Spaak, the idea of European integration became dominant when he was called upon as a foreign minister to grapple with the problem of national security' (ibid.: 325). Even the German case was not really different. It is difficult not to follow Ernst Haas when he underlines that 'the triptych of self-conscious anti-Nazism, Christian values and dedication to European unity as a means of redemption for past German sins has played a crucial ideological role' in the Europeanization of his country (Haas 1958:127). But even the most ardent defenders of idealist readings of the EU (or so-called constructivist explanations) acknowledge that this concern was merely a rhetorical argument: 'Interests and identity coincided, since Adenauer used his firm belief in Western institutions to regain national sovereignty for West Germany' (Risse and Engelmann-Martin 2002:296). In the six Founding states, cooperation was deemed a necessary condition for and/or guarantee of national sovereignty. Jean Monnet, like Paul-Henri Spaak, Konrad Adenauer and Robert Schuman, believed that the states were and would remain the mainstay of European politics. They meant to oblige them to cooperate, not to dismantle them by transferring their sovereignty to a superior power.

According to those who inspired it, the core of the Community method lay in the instruments which, while leaving the states with their basic functions, would encourage them to go beyond diplomatic negotiation. The *raison d'être* of European integration was not to replace intergovernmental negotiation by something else, but to make it work better. Reflecting on the collapse of the Third French Republic, Monnet had learned two political lessons, which are behind his proposals. Within the state, he thought, the parliamentary regime gave too much power to party forces, favouring particularist interests and the short term. The regime needed to be corrected in such a way that it could transcend these divisions and adopt long-term policies. It is in this spirit that Monnet conceived the 'Commissariat au Plan' (Planning Commission). Without substituting for policies, this organ – meant for studies and proposals, and made up of high-ranking civil servants and experts – was to encourage the government to bring out a global and lasting strategy, which could counterbalance political pressures of the moment. To a very large extent, it is the same intuition which inspired Monnet and his friends when they conceived the 'Community method'. At the external level, diplomacy has the same defects as parliamentary life: it is undermined by the protection of the states' particular interests, the obsession with the short term and the lack of a shared view. In order to give European cooperation a stability unknown until then, what needed to be invented was an institutional technique to correct the failings of classic diplomacy. In other words, their aim was not to eradicate the intergovernmental method, but to perfect it.

In order to do this, two mechanisms sufficed. It would first be advisable to reduce the use of the right of veto: unanimity would remain necessary for the negotiation of treaties and for major commitments, but it should be put aside for ordinary decision-making. The system of voting by qualified majority is due to this conviction. In addition, intergovernmental negotiation had to be channelled so as to avoid its getting stuck in the prewar rut of diplomacy. Until then, the work of governments had to be prepared by a 'neutral' organ which, like the French 'Commissariat au Plan', would give governments long-term perspectives and a common vision. Such would be the main function of the High Authority, the Commission's precursor. Afterwards, verification that the governments had fulfilled their obligations was necessary, if the diplomatic tradition which consists in making formal commitments (which, more often than not, go unheeded) was to be broken. A Court of Justice, supported by the High Authority, would be the 'guardian of the treaties'.

These mechanisms give life to the 'supranational' principle: the qualified majority reduces the weight of the veto, the mediation role of the Commission facilitates compromise-making, the Court's control ensures that commitments are fulfilled. Thus conceived, supranationality is not meant to replace intergovernmental cooperation, it aims to make it possible.

This 'improved intergovernmentalism' has remained the core of the 'Community method'. From the outset, the Union's political regime has gone through many revisions. The Court itself has strengthened its powers, so as to make private individuals the most vigilant guardians of Community legality. The European Parliament, originally composed of national MPs and confined to a vague mission of 'deliberation', is now elected by direct suffrage and has acquired a wide range of legislative and budgetary powers and political control. A European Council, made up of heads of state and governments, was created in the 1970s to provide the Union with the 'necessary impetus'. New organs have frequently been set up to give other actors a voice. In addition to the Economic and Social Committee representing trade unions and employers from the beginning, a Committee of the Regions and a Conference of European Affairs Committees, made up of national MPs, have been set up. A Court of First Instance, a Court of Auditor, an Ombudsman, and organs for the fight against fraud have recently been established, to meet concerns that there should be a constant improvement of the European institutions' accountability. In parallel, independent agencies have been formed to improve the institutions' information or to regulate specific areas.

The Union's institutional system has thus constantly developed to meet the preoccupations of each era. But the heart of the regime has not changed fundamentally. European political decision-making remains mainly based on dialogue between the Commission and the governments gathered within the Council. Only the European Parliament's growth constitutes a real novelty in relation to the original model. But we will see in Chapter 6 that its influence should not be overestimated: it remains excluded from large spheres of the Union's activity, and where governments have entrusted it with a legislative power, it, too, is forced to manage national interests and enter into dialogue between the Commission and the Council.

The governments' omnipresence

In a union of states, even more than in a classic federal system, the participation of national organs in joint decision-making is one of the regime's basic functions. The governments are directly represented within the European Union at three different levels, corresponding to the three strata of power of the executive branch of government (Hayes-Renshaw and Wallace 1997).

Providing impetus and settling big issues: the European Council

The highest level of this 'pyramid of negotiation' is the European Council, which consists of the heads of state or government as well as the President of the Commission. This institution, which was only recognized by the Single European Act of 1986, did not belong to the original Community model (Taulègne 1993). It was only in the early 1970s, with the stagnation of integration, that it seemed necessary to involve the top executive level of national power directly in European decision-making. French President Valéry Giscard d'Estaing and German Chancellor Helmut Schmidt, prompted by the desire to revive the dynamics of integration in 1974, suggested to their counterparts in other member countries that they should meet regularly to take stock of the Union's situation, to coordinate big political commitments and to plan new areas of cooperation. Those defending the 'Community model', such as Jean Monnet, supported this institutional innovation, which they expected would re-launch the dynamics of integration – very likely to be paralysed, otherwise, by the enlargement to include the United Kingdom, Ireland and Denmark and by economic stagnation.

Since then, the European Council has been the real driving force of European integration, and it was only when it could rely on a consensus among the heads of state and government, that the Commission was able to contribute towards orientating the dynamics of European integration. Meeting two to four times a year, the very top European leaders put forward 'conclusions' which set the course for middle- and long-term joint action. Long-awaited by the other institutions, these political declarations make a 'collective head of state' out of the European Council, giving a broad outline of the Union's policies and marking out the Commission's work, as well as that of the Council of Ministers and the European Parliament. It is at this level of power, for example, that it was decided to start cooperation regarding crime prevention in the 1970s, to think about an Economic and Monetary Union in the 1980s, or to enlarge the Union towards the east in the 1990s. Over the last decade, the heads of state and government have, furthermore, increased thematic European Councils intended to outline new processes of cooperation or to strengthen former regulations. Thus they decided in Luxemburg (December 1997) to intensify the coordination of economic policies, and they defined the foreign policy tasks in St Petersberg (February 1999). The European Council of Cologne (June 1999) created an organ intended to draw up the Union's Charter of Fundamental Rights, the one in Tampere (October 1999) increased cooperation in criminal matters, the one in Lisbon (March 2000) established a coordination process of social and employment policies, and the one in Laeken (December 2001) set up the Convention on the Union's future. European jargon is now peppered with town names to which these great undertakings correspond. In European circles, one commonly speaks of the 'Lisbon process', or the Barcelona one, the 'Declaration of Laeken', the 'St Petersberg tasks' and so on.

The European Council does not content itself with beginning new undertakings. The treaties also assign it its own decision-making powers regarding certain policies (economic and employment matters, foreign policy and security) and the appointment of top EU organs: the appointment of the Commission's President, the High Representative for Foreign Policy and members of the board of directors of the European Central Bank are still matters for the heads of state or government. What is more, the European Council has asserted itself, as time goes by, as the place where the most sensitive political conflicts are resolved, and notably those dealing with the Union's budget. Consequently, it can have an extremely heavy timetable. In March 1999 in Berlin, for example, its meeting ended in both an agreement on the budget for the 2000–6 period, and the appointment of Romano Prodi to the Presidency of the Commission, and it issued two declarations, one relating to Kosovo and the other to the Palestinians' right to a state.

The Union's draft constitutional treaty indeed consolidates this institution – in the chapter on institutions of the constitutional treaty, the European Council is the second institution listed, indicating its political importance. Reasserting its role, it plans to provide the European Council with a permanent chairperson, elected by a qualified majority of its members, for a two-and-a-half-year mandate, renewable only once. This position (which the media are bound to call the 'President of the Union', even if the holder is only the chairperson of one of its institutions) will have relatively limited but symbolically important functions: presiding over and leading the European Council, seeing to its cohesion, and representing the Union in matters of foreign policy in meetings gathering together heads of state and government. This innovation gave rise to extensive debates within the European Convention in 2002–3: the representatives of small countries feared that the European Council Chair would favour the interests of the bigger states, which were the main advocates of this reform, while those supporting the Community method feared competition between this new 'President' and the Commission's one. In spite of these reservations, the members of the Convention accepted this innovation, while at the same time precisely defining the functions of the President chosen by the governments. Some also considered that, in the long run, the same person would carry out the two functions: the constitutional treaty does not, in fact, preclude the President of the Commission from being elected Chair of the European Council. In this case, unlikely in the short term, the Commission would gain more authority and would emerge as the central piece on the Union's institutional chessboard. In the meantime, competition between the two executives (which is somewhat reminiscent of the semi-presidential configuration of the Fifth French Republic) will continue.

Making everyday decisions: the Council of Ministers

Below the European Council, the governments are also represented within the Council of Ministers. From the outset, this central institution has been the place where all 'ordinary' decisions linked to the Union's policies are made.

The Council's most striking characteristic is its variable composition. Unlike a Senate, it is not made up of permanent members elected to that end; unlike the German Bundesrat, not all matters are within the competence of its members. The Council meets in ten different configurations, regrouping ministers qualified to deal with the matter in question. In certain areas which are at the core of the Union's competencies, these councils (dealing with agriculture, economic and financial affairs) meet every month; thus the ministers of foreign affairs and their colleagues in charge of the economy spend almost as much time with their European counterparts as with their national colleagues. In other sectors, linked to more recent European policies, and where the Union completes and coordinates the action of member states more than it substitutes for it, the ministers do not meet more than three or four times a year. The inevitable consequence of this is to open up an implicit hierarchy between the 'great' councils and those carrying a smaller load. Faced with the tendency of the ministers of economy and finance to take on a wide range of problems – covering, for example, public expenses or retirement schemes – their colleagues in charge of the budget or social services, which meet much less often, may feel marginalized.

The General Affairs Council, which assembles ministers of foreign affairs, is supposed to ensure the coordination of these sectorial configurations. In practice, the Council's secretariat, whose members are diplomats and high-ranking civil servants appointed by the governments, ensures the permanent monitoring of issues and their coordination. It should be remembered that the Commission takes part in Council meetings. When it is a question of passing European legal acts or coordination programmes, the Commission members who took the initiative take part in negotiations, where they defend the proposals they have made. This interpenetration between the two executive poles allows the Commission to maintain its role of mediation.

Below the tip of the iceberg: the Committee of Permanent Representatives

Finally, before these political meetings take place, national governments are also present in the preliminary structures, where the diplomats and national civil servants work. In reality, this is where the main part of the work is carried out. The Committee of Permanent Representatives (COREPER), made up of diplomats, meets every week. COREPER II, made up of permanent representatives (ambassadors to the Union), prepares the work for the ministers of foreign affairs: it coordinates the actions of different councils, and ensures the monitoring of foreign relations. COREPER I, consisting of deputy permanent representatives, studies all the cases that are to be submitted to the other configurations of the Council. Almost 85 per cent of these cases end in an agreement at this stage, and are submitted to the Council merely for ratification. So, it is in this discreet and little known sphere that most of European politics is carried out. Here too, the Commission representatives take part in debates and negotiations.

All major decisions affecting the Union's institutional organization, new commitments and resources thus come under an intergovernmental logic. All appointments to key posts are decided by the governments of the member states. In ordinary decision-making, the national executives are still the cornerstones of negotiation, both when it is about coordinating national policies and when common norms are adopted. The governments are the only elements of the Union's regime that must be present at all levels of administration, and in all areas of competence – with the partial exception (we will come back to this) of what comes under the heading of the Court and the Central Bank. The area covered by the Council is one of the elements distinguishing the Union most clearly from classic federal organizations. German federalism no doubt allows the *Länder* governments to be represented, through the Bundesrat. But the comparison stops here. The principle of participation, which guarantees the representation of states in federal organs, finds an unequalled intensity in the EU.

The governments' central position in the Union's regime is not its only feature. The presence of another executive, named by the governments but largely shielded from their influence, is the most innovative element of the European model. If the Union can rely so much on the governments, it is also because the Commission facilitates their cooperation.

Why the Commission cannot be a European government

Aware that, left to their own devices, they would not exceed the results of prewar diplomacy, the originators of the 1951 Treaty of Paris accepted that some form of supranationality would be needed to make their cooperation work. But they did not see this innovation as a breach of their sovereignty. The treaty, setting clear and precise targets, was more similar to a 'law' than to a 'constitution'. In this context, the governments had no reason to fear this specialized executive: since they took the most important decisions, the management of the ECSC's policies could be entrusted to a supranational organ made up of competent civil servants and protected from government pressure. The High Authority had autonomous decision-making powers, but within a context strictly defined by the governments, and where they remained present. Moreover, it was decided that the Commission would have nine, and not five members as Jean Monnet had wished, so that each of the member states was represented. (The smaller states would each appoint a commissioner, and the three larger states – the Federal Republic of Germany, France and Italy – would appoint two.)

The negotiation of the Treaty of Rome, five years later, came to confirm this Community matrix, while at the same time adapting its general configuration to suit the new commitments. Unlike the previous treaty, this one was more a 'framework treaty' than a 'framework law': precise in some of its arrangements, it contented itself, elsewhere, with setting general objectives and envisaging the creation of common policies. Consequently, the significance of the executive function changed: it was no longer only a matter of adopting and implementing measures within the framework of precise commitments negotiated by the governments, but often, as for the common agricultural policy, it involved defining the scope of these commitments themselves. In these circumstances, the governments were more concerned than ever with preserving their power – all the more so, since experience of the High Authority had taught a lesson to the more distrustful of them, who now perceived in concrete terms the meaning of 'supranationality'. The compromise of the Treaty of Rome, while confirming the collaboration between the supranational Commission and the intergovernmental Council, redefined its terms. It was now up to the governments to decide matters and, if need be, to entrust the execution of their decisions to the Commission; intergovernmental logic was clearly reasserted.

But at the same time, the supranational principle was preserved. Far from being just an organ for the execution of decisions made by the governments, the new Commission had to encourage their collaboration. The essence of the 'Community method' lies in this distribution of tasks between the two organs, and this, in practice, requires them to cooperate. Although the Council of Ministers can decide matters on its own, according to the decisionist doctrines of the time, this power is subject to the supranational organ: the Commission enjoys a monopoly of initiative: it alone can suggest that governments adopt norms, and require them to submit proposals to it. It thus holds the key to fixing the political agenda. This original procedure preserves the formal principles of national sovereignty: legally, the governments remain in control of decisions. But at the same time, it escapes a pure logic of international negotiation: the Commission's influence can spread through its right to take initiatives as well as through the control it exerts after a decision has been made.

Thus the Commission is generally considered the most original of the Union's institutions (Ross 1995; Cini 1996; Nugent 1997; Spence and Edwards 1998; Nugent 2001; Joana and Smith 2002). Its uniqueness also explains why the Commission's role has long been, and sometimes still is, misunderstood. Some, following the outlines established by de Gaulle, continue to perceive it as a technical instrument, a secretariat, subordinate to the Council of Ministers. Others see it as the potential government of a federal union. In fact, neither of these two contrasting visions is unfounded. Like the secretariat of an international organization, the Commission sets out the Council's decisions and follows up their execution when requested to do so. Furthermore, its members are individually appointed by the governments. On the other hand, the Commission is a collegial organization, approved by the European Parliament and organized on a governmental model, whose proposals are voted on by two 'chambers', and which can be dismissed by one of them. What is more, the Union's constitutional treaty is prepared to grant more powers to its President and to make it more dependent upon the results of European elections. Half council secretariat, and half federal government, the Commission escapes established categories. Its appointment, and the way it influences the political profile of its members, are the best illustration of its hybrid nature.

Appointing the Commission: intergovernmental negotiations vs. party politics

The appointment of commissioners has long remained the jealously guarded privilege of the governments. Appointed 'by common accord', according to the treaty, they have in fact been chosen individually by each of the member states. Only the choice of the Commission's President was the subject of a negotiation between governments, which, without ever establishing a system of strict alternation, made sure that they maintained a certain balance between nationalities and political tendencies. Because of its multinational character and the way its members are appointed, the College of Commissioners – composed of 9, then 13, 14, 17, 20 and today 25 members, following the Union's enlargements – was more a collection of top individuals than a 'team' held together by a political project and ideology.

After being elected by direct suffrage in 1979, the European Parliament undertook to get involved in this intergovernmental procedure. Arguing that they directly represented the European citizens, the majority of MEPs claimed that the Union's executive would suffer from a deficit of legitimacy as long as its appointment was not approved by the Parliament itself. And although the treaty was silent on this matter, they took the initiative in 'confirming' the Commission presided over by Gaston Thorn in 1981. Concerned to avoid conflicts, and probably hoping to pacify the most vindictive MEPs, the governments then gave the Parliament secretariat the right to offer an opinion on the appointment of the next President. Unsatisfied with this modest concession, the Strasbourg deputies continued to vote for the 'appointment' of Commissions throughout the 1980s. Finally the governments, perhaps prompted by a parliamentary tropism, 'constitutionalized' this process by including it in the Maastricht Treaty. Later, the treaties of Amsterdam and Nice again (at its prompting) increased the Parliament's power in this procedure. The Commission's appointment is now carried out in two phases: in the first, the governments appoint its President by qualified majority, and the Parliament gives its approval. In the second stage, each government designates its commissioner, the President allocates portfolios, and the Commission is finally approved by the European Parliament (EP) as a college. Since the mid-1990s, the EP has, in addition, taken the initiative in organizing hearings with the nominee commissioners in the framework of the competent EP committees, before giving its approval to the College as a whole.

Choosing the President

The draft constitutional treaty, which will be applied to the apointment of the Commission in 2009 at the earliest, confirms this mechanism, while at the same time requiring future governments to take 'into account the elections to the European Parliament' and to carry out 'appropriate consultations' (by which the treaty means consultations with party groups). Under these conditions, it is theoretically possible to further personify and politicize the European elections, and thereby strengthen the Commission's leadership: if they wanted to, the European party federations could indicate, before an election, which candidate they would support as President of the Commission, in the event of their winning the election. The voters would better understand the issues of a campaign which brought into contention supporters of, say, Giuliano Amato for the Socialists, Jean-Luc Dehaene for the Christian Democrats, Guy Verhofstadt for the Liberals, Joschka Fisher for the Greens, and so on. Election campaigns would not take a bipolar turn in spite of this: unlike French presidential elections, the European mechanism is not a double-ballot system forcing the parties to group into two camps; and unlike British, Spanish, German or Italian parliaments, the European party system is not clearly organized around two dominant poles. As a result, the Party of European Socialists (PES) and the European People's Party (EPP), unable to form ideologically coherent majorities, were constrained until 1999 to support the same candidate. The President of the Commission was thus elected by a near consensus, enjoying a very large parliamentary majority; he was not the representative of a camp clearly placed to the left or to the right.

The Commission therefore remains very different from a classic parliamentary government. The MEPs' ability to influence the selection of the Commission's President is weak: as they only intervene after the governments have appointed their candidates, the MEPs can, at best, make their discontent heard. Thus, in 1995, many of them voted against Jacques Santer, who was appointed by the governments, so as to counter the veto exercised by the United Kingdom regarding the candidacy of the Belgian prime minister, Jean-Luc Dehaene, which the larger groups in the Parliament supported. In 1999, the German Christian Democrats voted against the College as a whole, because Gerhard Schröder's government had appointed two candidates close to the majority (a Social Democrat and a Green), while the Conservative opposition had won the European elections. Nevertheless, these protests could not prevent the Commission from being mainly centre-left (half of the twenty members of the Prodi Commission were close to the PES, 7 to the EPP, 2 to the liberal group, and one of them was a former Green minister), reflecting the governmental majorities, while the elected Parliament in 1999 was inclined to the centre-right. The Prodi Commission was nevertheless approved by 70 per cent of the votes cast, a little less than the College run by Jacques Santer five years earlier (71.9%) and the one presided over by Jacques Delors in 1993 (73.6%).

The election of Jose Manuel Barroso in July 2004 partly broke with these traditional alliances. The conservative group, sure to be the largest group after the European elections of June 2004, had announced that it would reject a candidate from another group. Parliamentary logic implied, they argued, that the President of the Commission should be of the same 'colour' as the dominant group. Yet it would be misleading to think that this explains the European Council's decision to nominate Barroso. In fact, the former Portuguese prime minister was chosen only after a heated confrontation between governments, where party politics played only a minor role. Initially, France and Germany supported the liberal Belgian prime minister Guy Verhofstadt – thus ignoring the EPP's warnings. It was only after the British government rejected Verhofstadt's candidacy (because of his role in the coalition against the war in Iraq a year earlier, much more than because of his party affiliation or his federalist reputation), and after many other names had been circulated unsuccessfully, that Barroso's name was put forward for the Presidency. The governments may have thought that they risked being disavowed by the European Parliament if they chose a liberal or a socialist candidate, but this was only one element of a much more complex negotiation. This choice nevertheless gave rise, for the first time, to some form of party polarization within the European Parliament. As in the past, the Eurosceptics, the Communist left and the Greens voted against the President designated by the European Council. What was new was the attitude of the socialist group. While, in the past, they had voted with the EPP, they decided to break this alliance. Apart from the conservative group, only the liberal–federalist group widely supported Barroso. The vast majority of the socialist group voted No, so that Barroso only got a centre-right majority of 58 per cent. The polarization was nevertheless far from perfect: the British Labour MEPs voted against their group, following the instructions given by their national party. The Spanish Socialists did the same – in accordance with an intergovernmental bargain which had given Spain the post of High Representative for the Common Foreign and Security Policy.

Selecting the commissioners

If the influence of the MEPs on the choice of the President of the Commission seems to be growing, their role in the selection of the other commissioners is much weaker. Until now, the governments have each appointed 'their' commissioner. Formally, they consult the President of the Commission, but it is hard to imagine the latter, freshly elected, refusing the commissioner proposed by a government. In reality, neither the President of the Commission nor the political groups of the European Parliament have any influence on the formation of the College, which remains the governments' privilege. Until 2004, the debates to which the European Parliament took the initiative of subjecting future commissioners were scarcely more influential. Inspired by the practice of the American Senate, these 'hearings' held within the parliamentary committees show that the Parliament is aware that the Commission mainly issues from the governments: like their American counterparts, MEPs question future commissioners more on their technical skills and on their integrity than on their political intentions, thus paying unintentional homage to the separation of powers and the Commission's ideological 'neutrality'. When they threatened not to appoint the Barroso Commission in 2004, this was not because a majority disagreed with the political positions of the commissioners, but because some of them were deemed incompetent or not impartial enough.

The individual profile of the commissioners is also marked by this procedure. As their appointment mainly depends on the governments, long careers within the Commission are rare. Even a talented commissioner who enjoys wide support within the Parliament, has little chance of being appointed again after a change of government in his native country. If four commissioners have weathered the decade of the 1990s (the Spanish Socialist Manuel Marin, the Belgian Socialist Karel Van Miert, the British Conservative Leon Brittan and the German Christian Democrat Martin Bangemann), the other members have rarely served more than one term, and from one Commission to another, renewal affects between half and four-fifths of the members (MacMullen 1997).

Since the early 1990s, the Commission's profile has tended to become more politicized. In the first few years, half the Colleges were made up of former ministers, and the other half, of diplomats or high-ranking civil servants. Since the late 1980s, 'politicians' have constituted by far the greater part – whereas diplomats made up only one-sixth of the members (Joana and

Smith 2002). Their previous career was generally spent within the national context: only 15 per cent on average of the College members have been MEPs beforehand, while half or two-thirds of them have exercised ministerial functions, and almost three-quarters have been members of the assemblies in their native state. The Barroso Commission accentuates this politicization: only two of its 25 members have not exercised ministerial functions in their country (the former MEPs Viviane Reding from Luxemburg and Olli Rehn from Finland); four are former prime ministers, and the others exercised ministerial functions through which they were deeply involved in EU matters (foreign affairs, finance, economy and social affairs, agriculture ...).

The Commission is thus becoming a team of high-level politicians, with solid European experience. But at the same time, the rule governing their appointment entails that more often than not they only spend five years in Brussels, before going back to their home country. While being more politicized than the Colleges of the 1960s and 1970s, made up of junior ministers, civil servants and diplomats, the current Commission is also much less insulated from national politics.

Allocating portfolios

The distribution of portfolios within the College also responds to a system of bargaining between governments rather than a parliamentary set-up. Until 1999, this was purely an intergovernmental compromise. The Commission's President was associated with negotiations between governments, and the European Parliament had attempted (through the individual hearings of future commissioners) to influence assignments, but decision-making still mainly involved compromises between heads of state and government. The bigger states tried to obtain the most noticeable assignments or the ones with the biggest budgets, and those where the Commission's intervention is the most decisive (trade, competition, economic and monetary affairs, internal markets etc.), and they generally proved successful. Distribution could sometimes take into account the candidates' personal competence, and their past experience within the Commission (in this way Belgium obtained the competition portfolio for

Karel Van Miert in 1994), and the small states could get portfolios linked to issues that were important to them (like humanitarian aid for Denmark, or the environment for Sweden, in 1999). But the most strategic positions were the object of heated bargains largely dominated by the bigger states.

The rules of the Treaty of Nice have in part broken with this pattern of negotiation. Until then, the President was but a *primus inter pares*, deprived of any formal power over 'his' commissioners. As a result, he could not impose sanctions on commissioners who had breached their obligations. This had been one of the major causes of the fall of the Santer Commission in 1999: faced with a threat of parliamentary censure, but unable to compel commissioners accused of fraud or maladministration to resign, the President had been forced to decide on the collective dismissal of his College. To avoid a repetition of these events, the governments agreed to give Santer's successor – the Italian prime minister Romano Prodi, nominated in 1999 – more powers over his colleagues. One year later they 'constitutionalized' these mechanisms by including them in the Treaty of Nice. The leadership of the Commission's President is now, on paper, clearly asserted. The treaty states (TEC, article 217) that the Commission 'shall work under the political guidance of its President, who shall decide on its internal organisation'. This principle entails that the Commission's tasks 'shall be structured and allocated among its Members by its President', who may 'reshuffle the allocation of those responsibilities during the Commission's term of office'. The members of the Commission must also 'carry out the duties devolved upon them by the President under his authority', and in the case of conflict, they 'shall resign if the President so requests, after obtaining the approval of the College'.

In July 2004, the President of the Commission, nominated by the governments and approved by the EP, made extensive use of these powers. Jose Manuel Barroso chose to follow an openly political logic: while giving important portfolios to the commissioners designated by the governments which had supported him (Trade to Britain, Regional Policy to Poland, Justice and Security to Italy, Competition to the Netherlands, Economic and Monetary Affairs to Spain etc.) he deliberately ignored the pressures of other governments which weren't among his strongest supporters (France only got Transport Policy, and Germany, Enterprises and Industry). Whether he will manage to preserve the confidence of those countries which were disappointed by his decision, notably the Franco-German axis, remains to be seen.

What does the Commission do?

The Commission's hybrid nature is illustrated not only by the way it is appointed, but also by the functions it is allocated. Some of them are similar to a government's tasks, but others are closer to the role played by an administration or a regulatory agency.

As was seen in Chapter 3, the Commission is, above all, the 'guardian of the treaties'. It is the Commission which checks that the states have transposed and implemented the commitments that they have also subscribed to at the European level. On a close examination of national legislative acts and administrative practices, it may find it necessary to investigate recalcitrant states and to refer matters to the Court. As such, it exercises an almost judicial function, which makes it similar to the United States' Attorney-General. Beyond this role of general control, the Commission's functions resemble those in federal states pertaining to the government and its administration.

Indirect leadership

The most visible part of its work, which is also the most 'political', comes from its fundamental power of initiative. Formally, the Commission alone is authorized to submit decision-making proposals to the Council and the Parliament. Since Maastricht, the Parliament can only request the Commission 'to submit any appropriate proposal' (TEC, article 192), which amounts to a right of indirect initiative.

In reality, the Commission's 'monopoly' is limited. The statistics that it has established show that barely 15 per cent of the proposals are genuine initiatives (European Commission 2001). Often, the

Commission is compelled to bring in a written proposal, as a result of international agreements (30%), or to adapt the existing legislation (32.5%). Furthermore, many of these proposals are in response to requests from the Council, the Parliament or third party organizations (22.5%). Over the last ten years, the European Council's political stance forced the Commission to start huge legislative programmes in sectors that it had not itself recognized as priorities. If it remains in control of the content of proposals, the decision to intensify cooperation in criminal or immigration matters, for example, in fact pertains to the accord between governments. In this respect, the Commission finds itself in a position rather like that of a government compelled to follow tendencies determined by the head of state in a semi-presidential regime such as the Fifth French Republic.

The fact remains that, within this general political framework, the Commission continues to perform an essentially political function, very close to that of a government. It is the Commission that establishes the Union's legislative programme and has its administration draw up new laws; it is also the Commission that consults interested parties and state representatives, presents and defends its draft legislations before the Council and the Parliament, and acts as an arbitrator between the two 'chambers'. What is more, the Commission also has a role of representation and negotiates on behalf of the Union on the international scene, in sectors linked to EU competencies. Within international commercial forums, the World Trade Organization in particular, it is the Commissioner for Trade who negotiates on behalf of the Union, on the basis of the mandate outlined by the governments. The Commissioner in charge of external relations carries out negotiations leading to the adoption of association agreements, while the Commissioner in charge of enlargement works directly with the authorities of candidate countries in order to prepare their membership.

Managing policies

If, in these key sectors, it conceives and conducts the government policies of the Union, elsewhere the Commission acts more like an administration or regulatory agency. The governments can in fact decide to trust the execution of the Union's policies to the Commission rather than to their national administrations. The extent of this delegation varies considerably from one area to the next. Sometimes, governments have found it necessary to grant the Union a wide executive power. Such is the case, particularly, for competition policy. The treaties of Paris and Rome already included precise measures in this respect, aimed at controlling agreements between companies, and state aid, and to prevent abuses of dominant positions. The Community system requires the Council to adopt norms which specify the scope of these principles, and the Commission to ensure that they are respected. Since the inception of this policy, the governments have constantly reinforced the Commission's means of surveillance and control. It is the Commission which receives complaints, leads investigations (enjoying, to this end, very extensive powers of investigation), negotiates with the governments and, finally, makes decisions, which can be accompanied by sanctions. The impact of these measures is considerable: the Commission can prevent a government from granting public aid to a company, or prohibit a company merger, even if the companies involved are not based on European territory. This is, for example, how the Commission imposed a fine on Microsoft of almost half a billion euros in March 2004. In this key sector, the Commission acts like an 'independent regulatory agency': within the normative context defined by political authorities, it enjoys powers of investigation, decision-making and sanctions, and is largely independent of the governments which vested it with its powers – even if it carries on intense negotiations with the national administrations. Moreover, in these matters, as in any others, the Commission can bring in proposals aimed at extending the range of European regulation.

Competition policy is, however, an exception in the definition of the Commission's powers. In these sensitive matters, marked by the memory of the role the trusts had in precipitating the economic crisis of the 1930s, and then in Nazi Germany, the governments have concluded that their commitments would not be credible if they did not entrust them to the care of an independent regulator. They probably also considered it politically useful to transfer the often unpopular decision-making responsibility to a third party. In other sectors, however, they entrusted executive tasks to the Commission only sparingly, and made sure that it was strictly controlled. The daily functioning of the internal market is closely regulated. Each year, between 1,500 and 2,000 European regulations are adopted in matters relating to the importation and marketing of agricultural produce and industrial goods or services in the Union. Almost three-quarters of these norms are written by the Commission, which, in this respect, carries out the classic administrative functions. The governments are, however, concerned about keeping an eye on these decisions, whose impact on their firms and on consumption can be considerable. This explains why (since the 1960s) they have established 'committees' intended to control the Commission's statutory policy.

The function of these committees (whose number is estimated at over 500), made up of national civil servants and presided over by European civil servants, is to examine the regulation projects established by the Commission's services. Known by the barbaric name of 'comitology', this practice covers a wide variety of decision-making mechanisms (Christiansen and Kirchner 2000). Sometimes, the Commission simply has to consult groups of national experts, without being bound by their opinions. Sometimes, committees enjoy the right to refer back to the Council projects which are not supported by a majority. In this way, governments can make sure that regulations which could be against their national interests are submitted to them, depriving the Commission of its autonomous regulatory power. This mechanism, long criticized by the Commission (because it is a hindrance to its regulatory activity), and by the European Parliament (because it is largely outside the control of MEPs), regulates ordinary decision-making in vast domains like the mobility of the workforce, the regulation of services, harmonization of products, the common agricultural policy, etc. 'Comitology' is a miniaturized form of the 'Community method': just as it is the Commission which proposes the adoption of European legislation by government representatives, the regulations are the subject of continuous negotiations between national and European civil servants. These arrangements also tend to expand with the passing of time. The new policies established by the treaties of Maastricht and Amsterdam have all led to the creation of committees made up of members from national and European administrations, with the intention of influencing the Council's decisions. The Economic and Financial Committee within the framework of the Monetary Union, the Employment Committee, and working groups in areas such as immigration and asylum, all contribute to this move towards interpenetration between the national and European administrative spheres – members of national administrations who work within this nebulous executive are today estimated at almost 25,000 (Roemetsch and Wessels 1996).

The latent competition between the Commission and the Council, present at all levels, is probably the most distinctive feature of the EU's regime. Despite its formal resemblance to a government, the Commission is not the centre of the polity. Appointed by the governments, the commissioners are not completely impervious to the interests of their states. As we will see in coming chapters, the persistence of this international dimension is observable elsewhere: MEPs, elected from a national list of candidates, are also the embodiment of national realities; and even if they are supposed to act independently, the judges of the Court and the members of the Central Bank's board of directors are appointed by the governments, as are the members of the Committee of the Regions and of the Economic and Social Committee. Not one federal system accords such a central place to the executives of constituent entities. None, not even the Swiss system, establishes such a complex system for the balance of votes and the distribution of leadership functions.

In a certain sense, the Commission can appear weaker than a parliamentary government. It does not control the majority of the Parliament and Council which vest it with powers and vote for the 'laws' it proposes. It is therefore compelled to negotiate support for its projects on a case-by-case basis, as does the President of the United States in Congress. But this supposed weakness is also its strength. History teaches us that where an executive controls the legislative chambers through political parties, it in turn becomes dependent upon them. A majority asks for guarantees. The government loses in autonomy and in impartiality what it gains in stability. Insofar as it has not obtained a fixed mandate from them for a given project, the Commission is not bound to the European Parliament and Council. It thus keeps its capacity for autonomy in regulating areas entrusted to it, and the power to act as an arbitrator between the two other extremes of the institutional triangle, with regard to which it ensures that it maintains an equal distance.

Chapter 5

Building Compromise in a Divided Polity

We have seen in the previous chapter that competition for leadership is a central feature of the European Union. The permanent rivalry between the Commission – supposed to promote general European interests – and the Council, representing the governments' preferences, helps preserve the balance between the states' and the Union's powers. We will now see how these two central institutions cope with their own internal diversity. Consisting of government representatives, the Council is, by definition, riddled with tensions between states. Despite its formal independence, the Commission – whose members are appointed individually by the same governments – faces a similar situation. The two executives nevertheless manage to compromise, in part because they are forced to do so to promote their own interests vis-à-vis the other institutions, but also and primarily because of their own culture of negotiation. We will see in the next chapter that, in its own sphere, the European Parliament faces similar problems with comparable solutions.

The Council and the logic of conflict avoidance

If one feature should characterize the Council, it is its strong propensity to avoid confrontations. Head-on opposition is very rare in the Council, where almost all decisions are made by consensus. Sometimes the treaty compels it: the rule requiring a unanimous vote remains in force in certain areas such as foreign and security policy, fiscal and social policies and the sensitive aspects of policies for economic cohesion and commercial policy. Moreover, even in areas where they have agreed to decide by qualified majority, the governments remain marked by a spirit of unanimity. Since the mid-1990s, between 75 and 85 per cent of the decisions within the Council have been made through a unanimous vote (Mattila and Lane 2001). In other words, only 40 to 50 of the 200 texts that the Council examines each year give rise to opposition between the governments.

Several essential features of the Union's political regime explain this attitude. First, as in other international organizations, preparatory organs, made up of diplomats and national civil servants, help reduce the scope for potential conflicts by removing the largest part of negotiation to private forums. Moreover, the functional nature of the Union helps to sort out problems. The complex system of weighing votes in the cases where qualified majority applies is a third element favouring conciliatory behaviour. Finally, mutual trust and respect are conveyed by the Council's rotating presidency.

The legacy of diplomacy

We have seen in the previous chapter that about 80 per cent of the decisions that are supposed to be taken by the Council are actually reached at the level of COREPER, which is composed of the governments' permanent representatives. The rare studies of this echelon of power in the Union show that the continuous and discreet nature of this joint work allows for the construction of a 'negotiation culture' between diplomats (de Zwaan 1995; Kassim et al. 2001; Bestock 2002; Lewis 2002). If the permanent representatives, and about fifty collaborators assisting each one of them, stand by the interests of their countries, they are also often capable of influencing their governments' stances. When the instructions they receive are unacceptable to their partners, they can attempt to interpret them in a flexible way or try to persuade the ministers to come round to their point of view. Finding themselves all in the same position – one of subordination to politics – they exhibit mutual understanding. These permanent representatives know that they cannot oppose a large majority on a long-term basis without running the risk of being marginalized. A spirit of collegial negotiation, strengthened by the informality and privacy of these negotiations, and by the representatives' long experience together, contributes towards alleviating conflicts.

A comparable spirit can be observed at the highest level of the Council's pyramid of negotiation, that of the European Council. Observers emphasize that it is the very informal nature of these meetings which guarantees its efficiency (Schoutheete 2006). Prepared by whichever government holds the Union's Presidency, with the support of the Council's secretariat and in close cooperation with the states' permanent representatives, these meetings keep to the simple form of direct and intensive confrontations between a small number of key political leaders. Only the heads of state or government and their ministers of foreign affairs participate directly in these debates and negotiations. Alternating formal sessions, dinners and informal bilateral discussions, these meetings play an essential role in the mutual understanding of European leaders. Symbolically speaking, the 'family photos' grouping all the very top European leaders and the President of the Commission have become a ritual meant to show the spirit of cooperation between the governments.

Compared with politicians, diplomats have a double advantage. That of continuity to begin with: whereas the ministers only meet in Brussels for a few days a month, or even a few days a year, the representatives are there permanently. Then that of specialization: the diplomats based in Brussels only deal with European policies, which are, for government members, only one of many tasks. Yet, we should not artificially oppose the climate of consensus governing diplomatic negotiations, and the hard bargaining between governments. In reality, the Council's work is also dominated by the search for wide compromises.

Dividing issues

The very nature of the Union's competencies largely contributes towards reducing the intensity of the conflicts. The detailed norms submitted to specialized ministers are, in themselves, less contentious than the large fiscal projects or large school or penal reforms which make up the gist of governmental work within the states. In the Union, we also observe that tensions are focused on a few sensitive matters, particularly those with strong budget implications, like the agricultural policy.

The Council's sectorial organization also facilitates compromise. For example, when ministers for environmental or social affairs meet in Brussels, they may feel a certain 'corporatist' solidarity: dealing with the same matters, often with similar political tendencies, and finding themselves in comparable positions within their respective governments, they may feel as close to their counterparts from other countries as to their national colleagues. Some observers have gone as far as considering that the spectacular development of environmental policies in the Union was explained (at least partly) by the complicity of ministers in charge of this matter, and by the opportunity they got in Council meetings to escape the constraints that they are subject to in their respective governments. Particularly in a coalition government, a socialist minister for social affairs can be tempted to seek an alliance within the Council in order to advance a policy that his conservative partners are blocking at the national level. More broadly, the logic of the institutional triangle favours the formation of horizontal networks of political actors. The presence of the corresponding commission members during Council meetings, and the heavy negotiations with the presidents of the parliamentary committees in charge of the same subjects, can produce, in the long run, a 'community of actors' specializing in a given public policy.

Avoiding confrontation: the logic of qualified majority voting

The Council's voting rules are also designed so as to maintain the spirit of consensus. Qualified majority is based on a complex system of weighed votes: each government has a certain number of votes, according to its demographic influence, and the majority is acquired when a very wide proportion, touching on two-thirds, is gathered together. In other words, the normal level of decision-making within the Council far exceeds a simple majority, and approaches the specific majorities required within the member states to modify the constitution. This goes a long way to explain the spirit of consensus governing the Council's work: in Christopher Lord's words, 'Preferences and assessments that are formed collaboratively are ... more likely to conclude with consensus decisions than those which are bargained competitively' (Lord 2004:107).

In practice, the decision-making logic does not so much consist in forming a majority, as in making sure a 'blocking minority' is not formed. At the time of the six-member Europe, a decision could be blocked by two big states, or by one big state and a medium-sized state (Belgium or the Netherlands). As enlargements have continued, the configuration of the 'blocking minorities' has become more complicated, but the principle has remained the same. Today, under the rules of the Nice Treaty, a decision cannot be imposed against the position of the four big member states, or three big states and one medium-sized one, or six to seven medium-sized and small states. Inversely, in the event that the four biggest states (which alone account for more than half the population in the 25 countries of the EU) should agree to establish a norm, they would still have to persuade at least seven other governments to follow them.

This system is apparently a guarantee for the least populated states. As Table 1 shows, whilst the Federal Republic of Germany has 29 votes for a population of almost 82 million inhabitants,

Table 1. *Qualified majority voting (Treaty of Nice)*

States	*Number of votes held by each country*
Germany, UK, France, Italy	29
Spain, Poland	27
Romania	14
Netherlands	13
Belgium, Portugal, Greece, Czech Republic, Hungary	12
Sweden, Austria, Bulgaria	10
Denmark, Finland, Ireland, Slovakia, Lithuania	7
Luxemburg, Latvia, Estonia, Slovenia, Cyprus	4
Malta	3
Total	345
Qualified majority	255

Luxemburg has 4 votes for a population of 400,000 inhabitants (in the balance such as it was established by the Treaty of Nice). The smallest country is thus thirty times 'better represented' than the largest. The imbalance remains strong if the extremes are left out. With 12 votes, Belgium is three times 'better represented' than the United Kingdom.

But these are only abstract considerations: the important thing for the governments is to be able to form a coalition as easily as possible, so as to block a decision they would be unhappy about. This explains why, although formally under-represented, the big states have put up with this system for so long. In the way it was conceived by the system, the qualified majority makes them pivotal players in building a blocking minority. This is confirmed by the facts. Governments resort very little to the opposing vote – in only about fifteen decisions a year. Sometimes, when a decision is sharply contested by a large member state, the proposal is simply not put to a vote. The small states' capacity to block a decision is much weaker: for example, Belgium could not prevent a vote on a directive related to the composition of chocolate in 1999, while at the same Council meeting Germany and Britain could make sure votes were not taken on proposals they disliked. Moreover, small states use negative votes only with infinite prudence (Mattila 2003). The Federal Republic of Germany cast 11 opposing votes in 1998, yet Luxemburg and Finland did not resort to them at all in the same year. On average, between 1995 and 2000 Luxemburg only resorted to the opposing vote 0.3 times and the Federal Republic of Germany 3.3 times half-yearly.

The studies carried out since votes in the Council were made public (1994) show that, beyond size, the opposing vote is explained by three barely surprising factors: first, the governments of the most Eurosceptic countries are more aggressive than others; secondly, conservatives block European decisions more frequently than do the Social Democrats; thirdly, the countries which are net contributors to the European budget are more reticent than the beneficiaries (Mattila 2003). Here we find a classic vote logic, where political forces in favour of joint regulation are mainly recruited from the left wing and in the least developed regions. So far, however, these positions are not fixed. If relatively stable power balances can be detected in certain areas like the agricultural policy, coalitions continue to fluctuate on the whole. They vary from one field to the next, and are constantly restructured by changes of majority within the states. The complexity of political cleavages in the Union, and the lack of a regular electoral rhythm, makes a freeze in oppositions virtually impossible.

Reforming voting methods was at the centre of one of the most lively disputes of the latest treaty reform. Within the European Convention of 2002–3 and the intergovernmental conference (IGC) that followed in 2003–4, there were many representatives who considered that the present system (adapted to the dimensions of a European Union comprising 25 member states through the Treaty of Nice of 2000) was too complicated, and that it should be replaced by a simpler dual standard: a majority would be acquired if it comprised both a majority of states and at least three-fifths of the population. This proposal was supported by only the bigger states, since a more proportional system would give them more weight than the established system of weighed votes, which over-represents the small states. Other governments (headed by Spain and Poland) rejected this reform, because they refused to give up what they had won at Nice – the Treaty of Nice gave these 'quasi-big' states a weight almost equivalent to that of the four big states (27 votes for 40 million inhabitants each, compared with 29 votes for the Federal Republic of Germany, whose population is greater than that of these two states put together).

The Convention carried on regardless of the opposition of these two medium states, and advocated changing to the double majority by playing for time – as a concession, the weighing of votes as it is defined by the Treaty of Nice would remain in force until 2009. Yet these two governments were not satisfied with this 'compromise' and threatened to veto the new constitutional treaty if their partners did not renounce this reform. The intergovernmental conference thus came up with a seemingly insoluble opposition between governments. While Germany and France firmly insisted on the double majority, Spain and Poland categorically refused to relinquish the advantage they had so recently acquired. In the end, after a year of tricky negotiations, and a change of government in Spain which made compromise possible, the intergovernmental conference reached a complex agreement, giving something to each party. The constitutional treaty preserves the principle of the double majority, while raising the threshold, to meet the opposition of the two quasi-big states: when this treaty comes into force, a qualified majority will be defined as 'at least 55 per cent of the members of the Council' comprising 'at least 65 per cent of the population of the Union' (article I: 24). But this compromise was not enough to reassure all the parties, so it was flanked with complementary rules to meet the worries of other states. First, to make sure that a large number of states cannot be put in a minority, the treaty adds that a majority of 55 per cent of the member states must comprise at least 15 of them. (This is a somewhat redundant condition since this rule will not come into force before 2009, and in the meantime Bulgaria and Romania should become members of the EU, so that 55% of the number of states will always comprise at least 15 states.) Secondly, to avoid giving too much weight to the big states in this more proportional system, the treaty states that 'a blocking minority must at least include four Council members'; in other words, even if the three largest states are demographically able to form a blocking minority, they will have to find a fourth ally. Thirdly, a safeguard clause inspired by a mechanism adopted in the mid-1990s (the so-called Ioannina compromise of 1995) was added: in cases where members of the Council representing 75 per cent of the level of population or of the number of member states necessary to constitute a blocking minority indicate their opposition, 'the Council shall discuss the issue' with a view to reaching a satisfactory solution to address their concerns. In other words, when a group of states is nearly in a position to form a blocking minority, it may slow down the process to try and get more concessions.

This intricate compromise illustrates the centrality of intergovernmental bargains in the EU. Even if, in practice, votes are rare, the member states try hard, when they renegotiate the rules of the game, to maximize their weight in the decision-making procedures – and in particular their capacity to block a decision they dislike. Although they are rarely used, these rules are an essential element of the 'spirit of consensus' in the Council: giving each party a fair share in the collective capacity to decide is necessary to preserve the mutual trust without which the Council wouldn't work.

Rotating leadership

Beyond these very precise decision-making mechanisms, making compromises within the Council is also favoured by the process of rotating presidencies. Rather than entrusting a permanent organ with the Council's coordination, the governments initially chose to preside over it themselves in turn, by alternating every three months and then every six months. In concrete terms, the European Council, the Council's configurations and COREPER are presided over by one of their members. This mechanism has proved very important in the construction of the Council's praxis. On the one hand, by not granting the Commission this tricky task, the rotating system allows the College to play its mediatory role to the full. On the other hand, a rotating system creates a spirit of mutual respect among member states. The government finding itself in this position is torn between two standpoints: as a Union member, it is inclined to defend its national interests, but in exercising the presidency it must show its efficiency by bringing decisions to a successful conclusion. In practice, governments holding the presidency resort to a functional splitting in two. They give themselves a double representation within the Council, one defending the national interest and the other coordinating the whole thing. Some presidencies manage to reconcile these two requirements better than others. On the whole, the second inclination prevails over the first. The governments know that for six months they are at the centre of their partners' and the international media's attention. If their presidency is a success, their reputation and their credibility will come out of it stronger. In the event of failure, they will, for a long time, drag around the negative image of a biased and inefficient partner. This subjective constraint explains why the governments devote a lot of energy to bringing cases handed over by their predecessors to a successful conclusion. The presidency thus plays a mediation role complementary to that of the Commission – and often better accepted because it comes from a peer.

This mechanism has also given rise to long debates in recent years. Some commentators have stressed its virtues. Rotation has allowed for the preservation of equality between states, it favours the socialization of national bureaucracies directly involved in the Union's coordination every five or six years, and creates a 'European moment' in the states' political life when it is their turn to preside over the Union. Others have underlined the limits of this process. The rapid change in presidencies generates problems of continuity – even if a *troika*, associating the countries preceding and following in the order of rotation, ensures a smooth passage, and if the Council's secretariat continues to follow up on cases. Deprived of a 'face', the Union also lacks visibility, both in the member states and on the international scene. Moreover, rotation leads to certain outbidding tactics: each government tries to leave its mark and to make progress with the cases important to it, contributing towards obstructing the timetable. Despite a strong wish by many governments to abolish this system, the Union's draft constitutional treaty partly preserves it. Electing a permanent Chair of the European Council, and creating a Union ministry for foreign affairs, will limit the tasks of the presidencies in the future. The latter will only be in force in the other configurations of the Council. There, presidencies will be exercised for a period of 18 months by pre-established groups of three member states – with groups being made up 'on the basis of equal rotation among the member states, taking into account their diversity and geographical balance within the Union'. In practice, one member of the group will chair all configurations of the Council for six months – assisted by the other two members, as in the past.

The internal organization of the Council thus exhibits a large set of sophisticated techniques designed to avoid confrontation, to convey a spirit of fair negotiation and to make compromise possible even when the states' interests may seem incompatible at first glance. We will now see that the Commission, despite its supposed neutrality, also faces internal tensions. But it copes with them differently: because it is not supposed to represent the member states, it cannot resort to techniques of conciliation based on the weighing of clearly identified interests.

The Commission's spirit of collegiality

Unlike the Council, the Commission is supposed to 'forget' national interests. The treaty lays down in principle that commissioners must be chosen 'on the grounds of their general competence' and from among persons 'whose independence is beyond doubt'; in exercising their powers, 'they shall neither seek nor take instructions from any government or from any other body'. As for the member states, they undertake 'to respect this principle and not to seek to influence the Members of the Commission in the performance of their tasks' (TEC, article 213). Clear though it is, this principle is far from obvious. At first sight, the Commission seems to accumulate difficulties. Might not its political nature affect the impartiality of its control? Inversely, is there not a risk of the spirit of neutrality and formalism corrupting political negotiations? Moreover, how does one give a European unity to an organ whose members are appointed – and may be re-appointed – by the governments? And how does one preserve the impartiality of an organ which is approved by party groups in a directly elected parliament?

Recently, the Commission has indeed experienced serious internal crises. The Committee of Independent Experts, created in 1999 by the European Parliament and the Commission itself to examine its internal functioning following allegations of fraud and corruption (Lequesne and Rivaud 2001; Constantinesco 2000), had issued a severe indictment against the College. After their inquiry, the five experts concluded that the Commission was suffering from an acute crisis of administrative and political cultures: 'The studies carried out by the Committee have too often revealed a growing reluctance among the members of the hierarchy to acknowledge their responsibility' (Committee of Independent Experts 1999a:146). The authors were also worried about the top hierarchy's lack of interest in tasks of management and control, and denounced 'the existence of as many feudal systems as commissioners', their 'incapacity to anticipate' (ibid.:143), the poor functioning of internal control mechanisms and the late, slow and rash nature of sanction procedures. Their second report, submitted in September 1999, was no more lenient. It considered that 'unhealthy national allegiances ... cut across the formal structures of the Commission', resulting in the creation of 'national fiefdoms'; it denounced 'cabinets [that] often act as screens and fences, impeding direct communication between commissioners and departments', and the rules and procedures that officials must follow, which 'are used to install a conspiracy of silence' (Committee of Independent Experts 1999b:5). Very poorly accepted within the Commission, this report has nevertheless raised awareness, which has speeded up reflections on its internal reform and, more broadly, a debate on the improvement of 'European governance'. Despite the threatening tone and the definite condemnations of this report, largely influenced by the context of the crisis of that time, we must not get the impression that the Commission is fundamentally paralysed by internal and external conflicts. Observers agree, on the contrary, that in the long run the Commission manages to function in spite, or even because, of tensions affecting it.

Why politicization does not harm the Commission's neutrality

One might think, *a priori*, that a College whose members are nominated by the governments, and which is approved by the European Parliament, will be so politicized that it will lose its impartiality (Majone 2001b). Yet the paradox of the Commission is that it is subject to so many pressures that it actually manages to ignore them to quite a large extent. Playing on the rivalry between its 'principles' and those who control it, the College remains somewhat insulated from the short-term fluctuations of politics.

First, the appointment procedure prevents the Commission from defending a narrow party line. Insofar as the governments, by appointing their candidate, take their partisan affiliation into account, and since it is rare for the 25 governments to be of the same political colour, the Commission is always a very large 'political coalition'. Reflecting the majorities of the governments which appointed it, it sometimes inclines towards the centre-left (as in 1999), sometimes towards the centre-right (as in 2004). But the Commission does not experience any clear form of alternation. Since the mid-1980s, two-thirds of its members have always belonged to the two main European political families: the socialist parties and the Christian democrat and conservative parties. The Prodi Commission also included liberals and a commissioner from the German Greens, so that the four main groups of the European Parliament were 'represented'. The Barroso Commission comprised 9 members close to the EPP, 8 close to the PES, 7 to the liberal–federalist group, and a member of the Irish Fianna Fáil (which is a member of the Union for Europe of the Nations (UEN) group). As a result, only the Communist left, the Greens, the Eurosceptic group and the extreme right-wing parties were not 'represented'. The Commission's 'parliamentary surface' thus reached 79.6 per cent, that is to say a level nearing the one found in Switzerland, or in Austria in the 'big coalition' periods. In these conditions, it is simply impossible for the Commission to favour one ideological family at the expense of the others. The rules governing its appointment force it to search for broad compromises.

Why the representation of the states in the Commission does not alter its neutrality

Although the College is theoretically a neutral institution, whose duty it is to ignore government pressure, each of the states wishes to be represented. The debate on the reform of the Commission within the 2002–3 European Convention, and the IGC which followed, mainly focused on this issue. One might think *a priori* that this would threaten the Commission's independence, but in practice this is rarely true. The governments know that commissioners are, more often than not, unable to relay national interests. This presence remains important for them for other reasons. On the one hand, it guarantees that, during its discussions, the Commission can be 'enlightened' on the situation of a particular state by one of its nationals. It is a question not so much of reintroducing an intergovernmental logic within the key organ of supranational states, as of guaranteeing that it can make its decisions with knowledge of the facts. (This is symbolized by the habit members of the Commission have got into, when they are talking about situations in their own country, of calling it 'the country I know best', rather than 'my country'.)

On the other hand, in many states, the commissioner is the face of the Union in his state, the one who can explain European issues in the national arena. This 'representation' is seen, particularly by the smaller states, as a means of reducing the distance between their country and 'Brussels', by ensuring reliable information in both directions.

The Union's enlargement to include ten new member states in 2004, however, raised a heated debate over the Commission's composition. During preceding enlargements, the original system had been preserved, at the price of expanding the Commission, which might weaken its cohesion and lead to a still more dispersed distribution of the commissioners' portfolios. According to some, the size of the 2004 enlargement made the maintenance of the initial rule untenable. In a European Union with 27 countries, the Commission would have 33 commissioners. On the other hand, the big states were not prepared to give up their second commissioner. After endless quarrels, the governments agreed in June 2004 to reduce the size of the Commission in the future. The Commission appointed in 2004 consists of one national from each member state, and so will the Commission appointed in 2009 – so that the old and new members are put on an equal footing for at least a decade. But this is a provisional compromise. The draft constitutional treaty states that after 2014 the Commission shall consist of a number of members 'corresponding to two thirds of the number of Member states', which means 18 members after Romania and Bulgaria join in 2007 or 2008. Thus reduced, the Commission is supposed to find its coherence again. But to reassure the small states, which feared never being represented within the Commission, compensations were offered. The constitutional treaty provides for a rotation mechanism intended to ensure that the commissioners are not always from the big states: the European Council, in defining the mechanism of rotation, must adhere to the following principles (marvels of constitutional Byzantinism): 'the difference between the total number of terms of office held by nationals of any given pair of Member States may never be more than one' and moreover, 'each successive College shall be so composed as to reflect satisfactorily the demographic and geographical range of all the Member States of the Union'. Which confirms, if need be, the importance of state representation in the institution that is supposed to embody the Union's general interest.

In actual fact, although they are conveyors of national interests and partisan views, which bring them into conflict, commissioners rarely take the risk of jeopardizing the unity of the Commission. It is true that, in the second half of the Prodi Commission's term, tensions sharpened. In the course of 2002 alone, reform proposals for the fishing and agricultural policy put forward by Franz Fischler were publicly criticized, with unkind words from his Spanish and French colleagues; the Commission's official line concerning foreign and security policy was considered unrealistic by the Commissioner for External Affairs; and President Romano Prodi himself described the Stability Pact as 'stupid', arousing irritated reactions from the Commissioner for Economic Affairs as well as expressions of solidarity from the French commissioner in charge of trade. In the space of a few months, the Commission seemed to be transformed into an Italian-style government, displaying in the public arena conflicts which could not be resolved within it.

It remains to be seen whether this recent trend constitutes a turning-point in the culture of the Commission. Until recently, in fact, such public debates were rare. The commissioners in charge of agriculture and trade clashed with each other in 1990, with regard to their respective competencies within the framework of negotiations of the General Agreement on Tariffs and Trade (GATT). The so-called 'mad cow disease' had caused conflicts of the same type between British and Austrian commissioners in 1997. In these tense circumstances, the members of the College openly defended national interests, a partisan view, or positions of power. Such events nevertheless are the exception. Most cases dealt with by the Commission cut across national and ideological cleavages, preventing such conflicts from arising. Moreover, commissioners know that they cannot exploit these strategies of confrontation. If they were to defend their native country on a long-term basis, or constantly support an ideologically marked line, they would jeopardize their own credibility (Joana and Smith 2002).

The Commission's appointment procedure, combining individual national designation and collective approval by the European Parliament, thus creates a political configuration which in fact guarantees that its 'neutrality' will be set down as a legal obligation. Individually, the commissioners sometimes accept instructions, or at least let themselves be 'influenced' by parties or by the national authorities who appointed them – in particular when they are close to their country's political majority, and envisage returning to national politics after their term in Brussels. But collectively, taking in all the divergent national interests and different political tendencies, they are not in a position to favour one camp or the other in the long term. The different points of view represented within the Commission are the best guarantee of its independence. Two hundred years after Madison drew up the US Constitution, increasing the number of factions remains the best way of preventing one of them from dominating.

Permanent negotiation

Moreover, compromise culture and practices have been established within the Commission which allow for conflicts to be settled discreetly and peacefully more often than not. Each of the College members relies on a cabinet, one of whose functions is to follow up cases from the other departments; as in national coalition governments, the 'inter-cabinet meetings' are places where lines of agreement are established and where conflicts are defused even before the commissioners have to know about them. In addition, numerous issues are dealt with in writing, and only reach the College for ratification. This intense process of horizontal negotiations limits the pernicious effects of compartmentalization, and maintains the Commission's cohesion. The College, which meets once a week, is more the place where agreements are noted than the one where they are made.

Indeed, votes are very rare there. The details of the Commission's deliberation being secret, little is known about the College's functioning; but accounts reinforce the belief that Presidents only resort to voting in extreme circumstances, when two or three commissioners state a firm opposition (Nugent

1997; Joana and Smith 2002). The Presidents know that this instrument is two-edged: in resorting to it too often, they run the risk of alienating frequently defeated commissioners, or even stablilizing cleavages, which would ruin the collegial spirit. In the present Commission, where each member state has one seat regardless of its size, voting would be near nonsense: even if the commissioners are not supposed to represent their state, the legitimacy of a decision adopted by 13 commissioners from small states, against the will of their British, French and German colleagues, would be very weak.

In the end, the Commission's independence and its collegiality are merely guaranteed by the informality of its work. The College remains an institution with little hierarchical organization. Of course, commissioners from big states and handling important portfolios have an influence in proportion to the weight they carry. Of course, commissioners pertaining to the same ideological family tend to support each other. But no stable form of leadership or coalition has ever been established on a long-term basis. Formally, the treaties have largely increased the means of ensuring the President's authority over the College. In fact, however, this margin for manoeuvre is limited. The commissioners are also 'heavyweights' with long political experience, enjoying their own support networks in the capitals, in the European Parliament and in 'concerned circles'. Above all, the President of the Commission knows that any measure of authority with regard to one of its members could arouse hostile reactions from the government which appointed that member. The Commission gives the President a more important role in the government but, at the same time, individuals forming it are increasing their personal influence. The collegial administration consequently continues to depend on the *self-restraint* of members, as much as on the President's authority.

Chapter 6

Representation and Accountability: a Semi-parliamentary Regime

Of the three poles of the Union's institutional triangle, the Parliament is the most familiar. All European regimes have a parliament, which is their cornerstone: an assembly elected by universal suffrage is supposed to be a reflection of the people, the government's source of authority and 'the nation's grand forum' according to John Stuart Mill. What also makes the European Parliament (EP) familiar to us is its history, which reminds us of Westminster's: conceived at its beginning as a 'deliberative' organ without decision-making powers, composed of national delegations which only met occasionally, it was originally the deprived embodiment of the 'Community model'. But like state assemblies, it was able to use its weak powers and its organizational autonomy to assert itself as one of the key elements of the institutional system. This chapter will first explain the reasons for this 'success story' and stress its limitations: if the EP could impose itself as the third corner of the European Union's institutional triangle, counterbalancing the Commission–Council pairing, its influence could not be overstated. The second section of the chapter will show how this parliament accommodates its diversity: despite its deep heterogeneity, the EP has given rise to an original form of parliamentary deliberation, adapted to the essential features of a federation of states. The third section will explain how this transnational parliament interacts with the other poles of the EU regime through its most important function, legislative co-decision.

The rise and stagnation of the EU's Parliament

In retrospect, the progress of the European Parliament seems so spectacular that some read it as the story of an uninterrupted conquest, and predict that it will lead to the Union's complete parliamentarization (Corbett 1998; Westlake 1999). One day, they argue, the European elections might become the key moment of the continent's political life, leading to the establishment of an executive armed with a five-year political programme. Although it has been nurtured by federalist movements for a long time, this plan remains unlikely. It overestimates the European Parliament's ability to bring changes to the regime. It is true that in the 1950s and 1960s, the MEPs were able to invent methods of investigation to increase their control; that in the 1970s they used the budgetary powers they had been given so that they could interfere in the legislative process; that after being granted a right to be consulted on certain decisions, they used their room for manoeuvre to demand a real power of legislative co-decision; and that the initiative they took to participate in the Commission's appointment has been accepted by the governments, which have codified this procedure in the treaty.

But we must not lose sight of the fact that all this was only possible because the governments themselves accepted it. They were the ones who originally created a common assembly; who gave it the power to control the budget when they endowed the Community with its 'own resources'; who also granted diverse legislative procedures and gradually extended the area of application of the co-decision process through the revision of treaties. However, at each of these stages, if a significant minority among the governments had been hostile to the Parliament's reinforcement, it would not have been able to assert itself. In only two cases can it be considered that the European Parliament was really able to compel governments. The first concerns the Commission's appointment: after the 1992 Maastricht Treaty gave the European Parliament the power to approve the Commission's President, designated by the governments, the MEPs were able to use the threat of refusing this approval so as finally to be consulted on the College's appointment as a whole. The second case concerns their influence in the co-decision procedure, also created by the Maastricht Treaty. The MEPs managed to make the 'third reading' pointless – a procedure meant to give the Council the last word – by systematically rejecting any agreements confirmed by the Council against the MEPs' wishes. In Amsterdam in 1997, for both these cases, governments were to bring this practice, established by the Parliament, into alignment with the treaty (Hix 2002). But these are exceptions, which cannot be generalized. In many other cases, claims supported by the majority in the Parliament (approval of the appointment of judges, generalization of co-decisions, consolidating budgetary power, and so on) were not followed up by the governments.

The reasons why governments 'parliamentarized' the Union remain partly obscure. At first sight, we may be led to think that it is not in the interest of member states' representatives to share their legislative power, even less so to strengthen an institution which, in the long run, will become their rival. No doubt some governments have been prompted by strategic motives when they have supported the European Parliament's consolidation. For the Germans, long placed on the same footing as the French, the British and the Italians as regards the calculation of a qualified majority in the Council, now that, since reunification, they have 20 million more inhabitants than the other great powers, the European Parliament could be a compensation. In exchange for parity between the big states in the Council, the Federal Republic of Germany obtained more MEPs than the others.

Other governments, harbouring old suspicions with regard to the Commission, may have wagered that by strengthening the European Parliament, they would, in the long run, weaken the College of Commissioners. Obliged to negotiate with two organs, its influence has tended to decrease, while MEPs have increasing control over the Commission's administrative and executive action. Since the late 1990s, the attempt to use the European Parliament to put forward strictly national interests has also tended to grow in several states. In some member states, the United Kingdom and Germany in particular, the parties of the majority perceive the European Parliament's influence more and more clearly, and have tried to make government allies out of their elected members in Strasbourg. For a long time, this pressure has remained discreet (paying tribute to the European Parliament's autonomy), but since the end of the 1999–2004 legislature it has grown. In a televised speech delivered on the eve of the June 2004 elections, the French head of state Jacques Chirac openly regretted: 'that France's weight and influence within the European Parliament [is] not equal to the stakes for our country. I hope that the future French MEPs will be able to group together to make our nation heard more efficiently' (*Le Monde*, 30 April 2004). Some weeks earlier, the Hungarian prime minister went as far as suggesting that all Hungarian parties should form a single list of candidates, so as better to defend 'Hungarian interests' in Brussels. He withdrew this proposal because of a barrage of criticism and mockery from the opposition. These two anecdotes are symptomatic. They show that there is still an attempt to see a channel for the representation of national interests within the European Parliament parallel to that in the Council.

On several occasions, however, the choice made by governments to strengthen the European Parliament cannot be explained solely by strategic motives. It also pertains to a form of institutional mimesis: the political culture of European leaders leads them to think that, in order for this regime to be legitimate, it must be given the essential features of a parliamentary regime (Kohler-Koch 2000; Rittberger 2001). The mental framework of European political personnel is awash with a formalism which, combined with their desire to respond to critics of the Union's 'democratic deficit', almost naturally leads them along this line: if they have regularly extended the area of co-decision, it is more due to a concern with 'simplifying' and 'clarifying' an institutional system constructed by continuous adjustments, than to an adherence to a German-style federal parliamentary set-up.

This does not mean that this mimesis dominates all strategic motives. Aware that they do not have a hold over the elected members of opposition parties, and knowing that the elected members of their own parties can at times escape their surveillance, the governments make sure that they remain in control of the policies they regard as being more sensitive. Thus the

Strasbourg assembly continues to be kept in the background of the Union's vast areas of activity. Where there is a 'legislative' competence, that is to say in matters tied to the internal market and its regulation, the Parliament has become inescapable. Nowadays, in this area, it is rare to find norms that are adopted by the Council without approval from the MEPs. But beyond this central domain, governments prefer to coordinate their national policies without harmonizing them. In the fields of foreign and security policy, of defence, and of cooperation in criminal matters, the governments adopt only general political agreements, for which the European Parliament can, at best, give its opinion – an opinion which the governments are obliged to hear, but which they do not have to follow. Furthermore, this is not confined to 'intergovernmental' matters. In major fields such as the coordination of economic and budget policies and 'open coordination' of social and employment policies, the European Parliament is also relegated to a secondary role.

As legislative action has tended to be reduced, in the spirit of subsidiarity, and as the governments, since the mid-1990s, have more willingly chosen the option of coordinating national policies, the European Parliament's influence may stagnate or even diminish. Indeed, taking this evolution into account, members of the Convention on the Union's Future have called for the strengthening of national parliaments' involvement in European decision-making. The 'early warning' mechanism evoked in Chapter 3 will allow them to closely monitor respect for the principle of subsidiarity. Moreover, the draft constitutional treaty comprises a new protocol on the role of national parliaments within the Union, which aims at improving their information and capacity for control. Finally, even if they were associated with the work of the Convention on the Union's Future, and even if the Convention itself suggested that this method be used again when modifying the constitutional treaty in the future, we must bear in mind that treaty reform remains the jealously guarded monopoly of the governments. Difficult intergovernmental negotiations on the new treaty in 2003–4 have confirmed, if that were necessary, that the governments intended to remain in control of the treaties.

Forging consensus in a divided assembly

In spite of this context marked by mistrust, the Parliament was able to surmount the difficulties it was confronted with so as to be able to operate as an ordinary assembly. In areas where it enjoys real power, it established typically parliamentary structures and work methods and gained an influence that nobody would think of denying it.

At first sight, an assembly of this nature could appear to be ungovernable. The 732 MEPs are elected within the framework of national constituencies, on national parties' lists, and after campaigns which are hardly focused on European themes. Citizens have a poor knowledge of the assembly, and their vote is influenced more by internal political stakes than by the Union's policies. The result is a poor turnout at the polls and a strong split in representation. The assembly elected in June 1999 had no less than 129 parties, which was indisputably the world record. In June 2004, after the enlargement to ten new countries, and despite changes in national electoral systems aimed at reducing dispersion, 161 parties were represented in the EP. The Italians alone had sent representatives of 21 parties to Strasbourg, five of which were linked to the Christian Democrat family.

Elected on a national basis, the MPs are hardly encouraged to act within a European logic. If they want to be re-elected, they must comply with the national parties of their own country in the hope of figuring on the list of candidates again. What is more, since most political leaders continue to regard the Strasbourg assembly as a second choice, the renewal of candidates is very high. From one election to the next, more than 60 per cent of the MEPs are newcomers.

Since its election by direct suffrage in 1979, the presence within the institution of a majority in favour of European integration and of strengthening the Parliament has allowed the Parliament to overcome these handicaps and to set up a real European parliamentary practice. From the outset, the MEPs have been organized in a standardized way, imitating the practices of national parliaments. The essential part of their work goes on within the framework of party groups and parliamentary committees, which are their two main work structures.

Managing diversity: the role of party groups and committees

These choices were laid down very early. During the inaugural session of the ECSC's common assembly in September 1952, the MEPs chose to gather as political groups rather than as national delegations to hold the election of their president. The following year, they gave these groups a formal foundation by including them in the Assembly's rules of procedure. At the same time, they drew up the first seven parliamentary committees. By doing so, they showed their desire to get away (at least in part) from the confrontation of national interests.

Over the decades, the impact of these two forms of organization has never stopped growing. Today, the Parliament has twenty permanent committees, which very broadly cover the subdivision of the Commission's tasks as well as the Council formations. These internal organs constitute the main site of legislative activity. This is where texts prepared by the Commission are examined, where the debate between political groups is conducted and where amendments are made. The further the EU competencies are extended, the more widespread the Parliament's power of co-legislation is, and the more the committees tend to be strengthened.

The initial choice of forming transnational political groups has never been called into question. MEPs have always kept their national origins in mind, but it is within party groups that they have taken most of their stances (Raunio 1997). No doubt, the assembly's partisan structuring remains more fluid than that of most national parliaments. European representation, which is subject to national electoral evolutions, still fluctuates from one election to the next. But the party system inside the European Parliament has tended to become institutionalized with the passing of time.

Today, the assembly has seven political groups, three of which were constituted from the beginning and have representatives from all, or almost all member countries (socialists, Christian Democrats–conservatives and liberals–federalists). The European People's Party and European Democrats (EPP–ED) is by far the largest group (36.6% of the seats), gathering MEPs elected on

44 different lists in the 25 member states. The grouping of Christian Democrats and Conservative parties is dominated by the 49 members of the German CDU–CSU. The socialist group in the European Parliament (PES) is somewhat smaller (27.3% of the seats) and somewhat more homogeneous. It nevertheless suffers from tensions between its largest delegations: the French socialist MEPs form the first sub-group (with 31 out of the 200 members), followed by the Spanish (24), German (23) and British (19) delegations. The third classic group, the Alliance of Liberals and Democrats for Europe (ALDE), experienced major evolutions after the June 2004 elections: a coalition of the liberal historical core with centrist MEPs from France and Italy who left the EPP–ED because they criticized its ever more conservative and Eurosceptic line, it remains a rather small group (12% of the seats), but with a pivotal position between the socialist left and the conservatives. Two other groups have become stabilized since the early 1990s and include elected members in about two-thirds of the member countries: the Greens–European Free Alliance and the European United Left–Nordic Green Left, with less than 6 per cent of the seats each. The last two groups, both of which were formed in 1999, are more heterogeneous and malleable coalitions. The Independence and Democracy group (IND/DEM) (5% of the seats) is a federation of Eurosceptic MEPs, dominated by the members of the United Kingdom Independence Party (UKIP) (11 of the 37 seats). The Union for Europe of the Nations group (3.7% of the seats) gathers conservative MEPs who refused to join the EPP–ED because their rivals on the domestic scene were already members of this group (like the Irish MEPs of the Fianna Fáil who could not be with the Fine Gail, and the Italians from Alleanza Nazionale who wanted to differentiate themselves from Berlusconi's Forza Italia). The remaining 4 per cent are MEPs elected by extreme right-wing and reactionary parties, who could not form a group and are known as the 'non-attached members'.

The two most powerful groups (the EPP and the PES) have always agreed to encourage this structuring, which they thought necessary for the effectiveness of parliamentary work (Costa 2001a). Through the Parliament's rules of procedure, they established conditions for the formation of groups encouraging the union of parties on a transnational basis (Kreppel 2002).

Today, a group must have at least 19 MEPs from one-fifth of the member states. Since political groups make up the main vector for distributing resources within the assembly, the members are strongly encouraged to organize themselves in that form. Committee presidencies, appointments to key posts (presidency and vice-presidencies, board, treasurers), the allocation of offices, collaborators and finance, the attributing of reports and allocating time for speaking – all this corresponds to a logic of proportional distribution between groups. Isolated MEPs, or those too few to form a group, are rendered virtually powerless. This explains why they sometimes seek to form 'technical' groups, with no partisan foundation. The agreement made in 1999 between the French (Front National) and Belgian (Vlaams Blok) extreme-right parties, the Lega Nord and the Italian Bonino list, broke apart during the legislature after the Court of Justice, to which the matter had been referred by other political groups, had ruled that a political group could not be established on a strictly technical basis.

In addition, the two largest 'parties', the EPP–ED and the PES, are involved in constant competition for first place. Originally composed of Christian Democrats, the EPP–ED group has opened up to a vast panel of other conservative formations since the mid-1990s in order to rob the socialists of their primacy. Today it assembles 44 parties, many of which are far from the original Christian Democrat line, like the Gaullists, the Irish Fine Gael, the British Conservatives or the members of Forza Italia. This strategy has allowed it to assert itself as the first party. But this choice had a price. The more and more heterogeneous group, the EPP–ED has seen tensions stirred up between its Christian Democrat centre and its Conservative right. At the end of the 1999–2004 term of office, British Conservatives obtained a 'dissident's right' which enabled them to dissociate themselves from their more federalist colleagues during debates on the Union's institutional future. A few months later, French Christian Democrats (concerned about marking their difference in relation to the Gaullists, with whom they are allies on the French scene) and some of their Belgian and Italian colleagues formed a centrist group, allied to the Liberals. The partisan scene of the European Parliament is therefore probably not fully stabilized.

Despite this strong internal heterogeneity, and the relative instability of the partisan scene, the European Parliament groupings have acted as relatively disciplined apparatuses. Since the implementation of the Maastricht Treaty in particular, which gave the Parliament a real power of co-legislation, the MEPs have very largely followed the voting instructions fixed within their group. During the 1994–9 term, the level of cohesion rose to 90.2 per cent for the EPP, 89 per cent for the PES, 85.2 per cent for the Greens, 83.8 per cent for the Communist left and 80.1 per cent for the Liberals (Hix and Lord 1997). During the 1999–2004 term of office, the two largest groups were slightly less disciplined (84.8% in the PES and 81.1% in the EPP), showing their growing heterogeneity. In the small conservative groups, whose existence is justified by organizational necessities more than real ideological similarities, the cohesion level is a lot weaker (58.3% for the UEN group and 40.5% for the Eurosceptic group). Within each of these groups, the British are the most undisciplined. The Conservatives vote against the EPP line in 31 per cent of cases and the Labour Party against the PES in 13.5 per cent of cases. Within the Green–Regionalist coalition, the elected members of Plaid Cymru go against the group's position in 17.5 per cent of cases and their colleagues from the Scottish National Party in 26.2 per cent of the votes (Hix 2000). On the whole, the coherence of partisan families nevertheless remains strong. No doubt the groups are more fluid than their national counterparts (where the level of discipline is generally close to 95%) but they are a lot more disciplined than the parties of the American Congress, whose cohesion varies between 25 and 60 per cent.

This result is even more spectacular as the groups have very few means with which to discipline their members. Unlike the national parties, they can promise neither appointments nor other remunerations. Nor can they threaten with sanctions when the lists are being prepared, as these remain the monopoly of the national parties. The groups are therefore obliged to bet on more flexible means of conviction. In the absence of a stable leadership, their line is formed in the continual interaction between group members. The MEPs spend most of their time in their political group examining bills, confronting viewpoints and seeking compromises. When they return to the committee or plenary session, they generally tend to respect the position fixed on by the group, because it has not been imposed on them by an authoritarian leadership, but is the fruit of a negotiation where all parties were able to make themselves heard. The MEPs tend to seek wide compromises (even if it means giving up clear-cut positions) rather than imposing a majority discipline. Insofar as group leaders know that they cannot easily impose sanctions on their members in the event of disobedience, they seek to obtain their consent rather than their submission.

All this explains why a majority trend is rare within the assembly. The flexibility of groups, combined with the voting rules, makes the formation of a stable majority impossible. The normal rule for decision-making is that of a simple majority of voters, but in many important matters (amendments to the budget and to the legislation in a second reading of joint decisions or assenting opinions) an absolute majority is required. In the Parliament's present configuration, obtaining 367 out of the 732 votes is no easy task – first of all because absenteeism remains significant. At the beginning of the 1999 term, voter participation varied between 58.9 per cent for the Italian MEPs and 82.6 per cent for the Dutch (Hix 2000). In these conditions, 367 votes represent about two-thirds of the members present. None of the groups is able to raise such a large proportion of votes. Even when the rule for decision-making is less strict, and even when there is a high rate of participation by the MEPs, homogeneous majority coalitions are virtually impossible. Alone, the EPP is very far from the number needed. Combined with the liberal–federalists, it still needs 11 votes to form a majority. As for the PES, even if it manages to form a 'plural Left' coalition with the Greens and the Communist left, it will only reach 38.7 per cent of the votes. In other words, the European Parliament (in its present configuration) is condemned to govern from the centre. The party system dominating it is similar to the 'polarized pluralism' defined by Giovanni Sartori: a relatively strong fragmentation of the political space, combined with ideological polarization, leads to a government by centrist compromise (Sartori 1976).

In practice, until recently, most of the votes have been obtained through a 'big coalition' between the two most powerful groups, the PES and the EPP. Until 1999, almost three-quarters of the votes were backed up by a super-majority of this type, the others being divided equally between unanimous votes and left–right oppositions (Hix and Lord 1997). The first studies carried out since the June 1999 elections show that standpoints were more polarized during this legislature. While 12 per cent of the votes remained unanimous (Hix, Kreppel and Noury 2003), the 'big coalition' only functioned in 48 per cent of cases. For 13 per cent of the votes, the EPP was allied with the Liberals and the Conservatives of the UEN group, in a centre-right configuration. In 14 per cent of cases a centre-left majority was formed around the PES, joining the Liberals, the Greens and the Communist left. The Liberals, which have only 8.5 per cent of the seats, have thus tended to set themselves up as a pivotal party in certain matters where Socialists and Conservatives cannot agree, and where the rule of the simple majority prevails – a privilege which also explains why some Christian Democrats decided, in June 2004, to break away from the EPP Conservatives in order to place themselves at the centre of the political scene.

These constraints have entrenched the culture of compromise within the European Parliament. Many observers (and MEPs themselves) are completely thrown by it. If the votes crossing the left–right divide do not astonish the elected members of the Benelux countries or their Finnish or Austrian counterparts, who are used to these 'consociative' practices, they clash with the traditions and references of those from countries where the political space is predominantly divided into two camps. In many cases, the formation of heterogeneous majorities is facilitated by the 'technical' nature of the norms debated, which in themselves do not give rise to any ideological polarization. With the Union having no fiscal powers and very few resources to adopt redistributive policies, it is rare for the interests of the Left and the Right to be clearly opposed. But this spirit of compromise also tends to subsist in matters where the elected members' positions are nevertheless very contrasted.

The logic of co-decision

The European Parliament's missions cover the whole range of standard parliamentary action. They hold hearings to interview members of the Commission and of the Board of Directors of the Central Bank before they are appointed; they debate numerous reports they receive from other institutions; they conduct their own inquiries to ensure the scrutiny of each of the institutions and of the nebulous sphere of 'committees' made up of national civil servants who assist the Commission in its executive tasks; they discuss the budget, try to amend it, grant or reject the rebate; they send delegations to the four corners of the world and discuss major issues troubling the planet (including those which do not affect the Union's powers or only affect them from a distance) and adopt numerous resolutions on these matters. But no activity takes up more of the MEPs' energy than the examination of the Commission's legislative proposals. Since they have obtained a real power of legislative co-decision, it is to this that the MEPs devote most of their energy. This relates to a deliberate choice: the European Parliament could have followed the inclination of national assemblies, most of which content themselves with ratifying bills proposed by their government and focus on tasks of political control. But aware of the opportunities that the European Union's political regime offers, they have resolved to set themselves up as true legislators.

Co-decision, which is now the primary mode of adopting European 'laws', is the procedure that best embodies the peculiar balance of a federation of states. It aims at compelling the three poles of the institutional triangle to work together, without one of them ever being able to dominate the other two. This process also places the Commission in a key position by giving it the monopoly of initiative and a constant right to revise its proposals in the course of political negotiations. It sets the Parliament and the Council on an equal footing at all stages of the procedure, from initial proposal, to amendments, to formal adoption. The mechanism is conceived in such a way that none of the three institutions can impose its point of view, and that each has the power to oppose any feature which does not have its consent.

This balance was not established in one go. Initially, the governments only granted the European Parliament the right to give its opinion, which, according to the Court's jurisprudence, they were obliged to consider but free to ignore. Later, the cooperation procedure established by the Single European Act of

1986 increased the MEPs' power of influence: a 'second reading' allowed them to propose amendments and even to reject the bill, in which case the Council could only adopt it unanimously. Co-decision, established by the Maastricht Treaty and simplified by the Treaty of Amsterdam, was the last stage in this legislative progression. It had long been called for by MEPs as a symbol of their power and a source of real influence. Its main innovation lies in the so-called 'conciliation' third phase, which aims to go beyond the deadlock of the pure and simple rejection of a text by seeking a compromise. (In the initial procedure established by the Maastricht Treaty, the Council could unanimously adopt a bill rejected by the MEPs, who were able to reject it in turn. Thus the MEPs only had a right of veto, whereas the ministers gathered within the Council had the power to confirm their position, despite the Parliament's refusal. The MEPs having announced that they would systematically reject the bills adopted by the Council against their opinion, and having confirmed this in practice, the originators of the Treaty of Amsterdam deprived the Council of this power of 'confirmation'. Since then, the two 'chambers' have been well and truly playing on equal terms.)

Ten years of practising co-decision (whose field has been extended by the Treaties of Amsterdam and Nice, and will continue to expand when the constitutional treaty comes into force) have shown that this system works, and have established it at the heart of European legislation. Since the mid-1990s, about thirty acts of a relatively wide scope have been adopted each year using these methods, with no major clashes.

Schematically, the process can be divided into five phases. Formally, by virtue of its monopoly of initiative, it is up to the Commission to start the legislative work. We must recall that this power to set the agenda is relative. To begin with, the Commission can only act within the framework of competencies established by the governments. If, at one time, it was able to try to adopt new policies by widely interpreting the foundations laid out by the treaties, or by resorting to an additional legal basis which would allow it to act when a competency was not formally defined, this power has been reduced in the past decade. As has been said, the governments have given in to the temptation to direct the legislative programme through the

European Council's conclusions. Concerned with avoiding set-backs, for its part, the Commission has agreed to negotiate an annual 'legislative programme' with the other two institutions. The spirit of subsidiarity also encourages it to resort to the legislative instrument only sparingly, so that the power of indirect initiative given to the Council and Parliament, as well as the obligations which flow from international commitments or previous legislation, have resulted in only one project in five being a genuine initiative of the Commission. Moreover, the College members practise self-censorship insofar as they make sure they anticipate the reactions of the other two institutions, as well as outside pressures which they are likely to yield to. By publishing the 'green papers' and 'white papers' on questions for which it envisages proposing new standards, by seriously consulting the 'concerned interests' or even by directly contacting government representatives and influential members of the parliamentary committees in question, the Commission sizes up potential reactions and adapts its own preferences. More often than not, a proposal brought before the Parliament is the result of an already lengthy process of informal negotiations. The fact remains that the power it has is not insignificant: the Commission controls the calendar and the terms of its projects.

Next comes the phase where the bill is examined by the two 'chambers'. Having been brought before the Parliament, it is transmitted to the relevant committee, where most of the analysis and amendment work is carried out. At this stage of the procedure, the MEPs are already endeavouring to set out their positions in the form of precise amendments. The terms of these are fixed in committee and confirmed in the plenary session. As the originator of the proposal, the Commission retains a certain degree of control over its bill. From this moment, it indicates which amendments it accepts and those which appear to misrepresent its proposal. In its turn, the Council of Ministers then examines the project. Within COREPER, each of the permanent representatives analyses the Commission's lines and the modifications proposed by the MEPs, in collaboration with 'his or her' minister. Within the Council itself, the ministers negotiate the more difficult cases, and ratify their representatives' positions in the other cases before making their position known to the other two institutions. At this stage, the Council can accept the Parliament's position and close the procedure by passing the bill.

This exploratory phase already includes extensive political positioning. Parliamentary debates go hand in hand with parallel and informal meetings between permanent representatives, MEPs and the team of the commissioner who has elaborated the proposal. In order to forge compromises, the MEPs take their stances through three complementary channels. First, they often take the initiative individually to consult organized interested parties, NGOs or associations active in the sector concerned with the legislation. Generally speaking, the Parliament is very open to 'lobbies' and associations: enjoying relatively meagre resources (at least compared with those of their counterparts in the American Congress), the MEPs find a precious source of expertise and information by consulting interested circles. The nature of the MEPs' interlocutors varies largely according to their field of specialization and political tendencies. Left-wing members are closer to civic associations and trade unions than their right-wing counterparts, who more willingly maintain relations with the industrial sector. But the networks are not fixed: the technical complexity of many bills and the flexibility of political alliances favours the mixing of types. It is not rare to see an elected Socialist dealing with industrialists, or a Conservative taking the opinion of trade unions or NGOs.

Besides this fluctuating channel of relations with 'civil society', MEPs resort to working as a political group to form their positions. On the occasion of weekly meetings, they endeavour to find a common position beyond national divergence and sectorial compartmentalization. The political group has an essential place in parliamentary life, because it allows compromises to be set in motion before the plenary session. Elected members who share the same political sensitivity try hard to reconcile their points of view in spite of diverging national interests, so as to carry weight in the final vote. Within the political group, MEPs also try to coordinate the work that they carry out in the different specialized committees. Each one explains his committee's stakes on the subject and ascertains that the position he intends to defend will be well supported by his friends during the vote in the plenary session.

The committees are the third site of negotiation: they are miniature versions of the Parliament itself, but as they are made up of MEPs with specific competencies and preoccupations, they are often more homogeneous than the EP itself. Despite their national and ideological divergences, the MEPs belonging to the same committee share an expertise and an interest in given subjects, which also allows for the initiation of compromises.

No stable schema can fully account for the smooth running of these negotiations. Sometimes national solidarities prevail. At other times, political groups manage to form united fronts. Elsewhere again, sectorial interests dominate. More often than not, these constraints combine in such a way that none of them can dominate. With the exception of matters where the consequences of political choices are very marked territorially (like everything affecting distributive policies, and in particular regional aid), national sensitivities are sharpened. On the other hand, when the effects of a decision are more diffuse (as they are for most directives regulating respect for the environment, public health, or the consumer), conflicts tend to slip into ideological references. It is the ever-changing combination of these constraints which gives parliamentary work its malleability and which surprises novices used to strict partisan discipline.

The third phase of co-decision opens with a second examination by the MEPs of the draft text (accompanied by comments from the Commission and the Council). At this stage (that is to say, generally less than six months after the formal commencement of the procedure), about half of the bills are approved by the Parliament. The other half are the subject of a second round. Theoretically, at this stage the MEPs can also reject the bill, in which case the procedure ends in failure. In practice, this happens only very rarely, so much do the other two institutions want to make sure that the elected members are treated with tact. The second reading does not differ from the first. The MEPs retain the right to submit amendments, which can be endorsed or rejected by the Commission before the Council gives its decision, in turn. The Council of Ministers can only unanimously adopt parliamentary amendments rejected by the Commission, which enables the latter to protect its proposal from attacks by the two 'chambers'. One-third of the bills which have not passed in the first reading succeed at this point.

The others, that is to say one-third of all the bills presented by the Commission, are the subject of an attempt at 'conciliation', which is the fourth stage of the procedure. Inspired by German legislative practice, this mechanism consists in creating a direct confrontation in private between a representative sample of each of the three organs. The Commission is represented here, the governments all delegate a representative (more often a civil servant or diplomat than a politician), and the MEPs have the same number of representatives, that is to say, 25 members since 1 May 2004, designated by the political groups on a proportional basis. For six weeks at the most, these emissaries try (behind closed doors) to come to a compromise acceptable to all the parties. On important bills, the ministers and commissioners themselves take part in these negotiations, and at the same time increase informal meetings in parallel – bilateral meetings of ministers to remove obstacles within the Council; trilateral confrontations between the commissioner, the president of the parliamentary committee and the Council member whose country holds the presidency, and so on. Most of the time, an agreement can be found at this stage.

In a fifth phase, the two 'chambers' only need to ratify the previously fixed position. A compromise reached in the conciliation committee may still be rejected afterwards, but in practice this is rare. The Council's presidency ascertains the support of each of the members before taking a vote. The presidents of the political groups follow suit in Parliament.

The spirit of compromise

Even if co-decision covers only part of the European policies (those where the law is made), it symbolizes the Union's political balances. In institutional terms, it makes up the most complete form of the institutional triangle. Through it, the Commission is supposed to embody a 'European interest', which comes up against state interests defended by the Council, the MEPs' partisan views, and the sectorial designs of groups putting pressure on the three organs. More than the expressed position of an unlikely majority, European norms are the result of a long confrontation of diverse forms of political expression. As far as attitudes are concerned, co-decision shows the willingness of the three poles to make the Union function. Each one tries at length to reach an internal consensus. When they then confront their differing positions, the representatives of the three poles again try to reach compromises, reduce conflicts, and avoid head-on clashes or an acknowledgement of failure. The decision-making pace is that of a series of gradual adjustments and continual compromises.

This culture of negotiation is favoured by the fluidity of European divisions. The opposition between the Left and the Right is superimposed on divisions between states and on divergence between integrationists and sovereignists. The three organs are permeated by these cleavages, which are never frozen on a long-term basis. Such a configuration of forces enables partial agreements and exchanges of complex concessions to be made. At best, political polarization is only relative and sporadic. The efficiency of the community method is due to this. Despite reservations, clashes of interest and impediments, the Union manages to produce laws. But this decision-making effectiveness has a drawback. It causes European decision-making to lack clarity. Political stakes are often segmented, very technically dealt with; the political stances of governments and MEPs are complex and changeable. The procedure as a whole is not in question: in Germany, the legislative process is just as complex without making it impossible for politicians to display clear positions, and for citizens to perceive them. In the Union, what confuses the issue is the decision-making style, the culture of consensus encouraged to manage the divergence of many interests.

Although the trio that make up the Union's institutional triangle differ in their composition and as to the functions they carry out, they have a certain number of points in common. First, we have seen that all three of them are very segmented: Council formations, Directorate-Generals within the Commission, and the parliamentary committees reflect the functional nature of the Union, whose competencies have developed slowly and in a very compartmentalized way. They are also the sign of specialized decision-making work, where big political moments and major stakes are rare. Moreover, in the three poles, informal negotiations between participants override public deliberations. There is nothing very original in this. For over twenty years, political science has shown that most decisions are made in very specialized 'policy networks' of which the public knows little.

Between the Union and parliamentary democracies, there is still a major difference however. While, within the member states, conflicts are staged through political life, which simplifies and personifies the stakes, in the Union they appear unvarnished. Compromise is not only a 'behind-the-scenes' practice, concealed by the power game, it is the essence of the power game. In each of the three sections, the actors do their best to reach extensive agreements, far exceeding simple majorities. Within the Commission, the spirit of collegial administration prevents commissioners of the same political family from forming lasting alliances. Within the Council framework, the detailed rules for the balancing of votes and sharing of leadership functions prompt governments to make unanimous decisions. The European Parliament is no exception: its political configuration, combined with voting rules, favours compromises between the main groups.

This makes an extreme form of 'consensus democracy' out of the Union. Unlike the parliamentary regimes which stem from the Westminster matrix, the Union has not experienced any predominant concentration of power. It remains distinguished by the interdependence of the three poles. Unlike majority democracies, conflicts in the Union are not polarized around a major split either. In this respect, the Union presents a configuration close to that of the small 'consociative' democracies studied by Arendt Lijphart thirty years ago: there, political cleavages intersect more than they are superimposed. Opposition between a left and a right wing is not absent, but it is encumbered by divisions which are just as visible if not more so. Clashes of interests between states, which bring into conflict the biggest and the smallest powers, the richest and the poorest, military powers and neutral states, punctuate many negotiations within the Council, but also in the ranks of the Commission and Parliament. Moreover, from the outset, a more or less explicit confrontation between those advocating and those opposing integration penetrates all the interests involved. If, at times, European divisions seem to predominate (as during institutional discussions), they become of secondary importance in other matters where an ideological (market regulation) or national (budgetary issues) polarization occurs. Still, this presentation is excessively schematic. Depending on the case, British Labour Party members can find themselves closer to German Conservatives than to their socialist friends, while English Liberals may get on more easily with the Social Democrats or the Greens than with their Belgian counterparts. These examples of complex alignments, crossing the cleavages, could carry on indefinitely.

The relationships of partisan forces and decision-making mechanisms conceived with the aim of avoiding confrontations only convey and consolidate this major characteristic of European political society. Consequently, it is difficult to imagine that the Union's institutional system could move in the direction of a classic federation in the medium term. With time, the President of the Commission might manage to establish a certain leadership; political parties within the Parliament and Council might more clearly assert their support or opposition to the College. But all this depends on very hypothetical scenarios. If Belgium, Switzerland or the Netherlands have never managed to reduce the diversity of their internal tensions to a bipolar split, it is difficult to see how the European Union (which is permeated by still more intense conflicts and which has more firmly institutionalized the practices of compromise) can escape governing by consensus.

Chapter 7

In the Shadow of the Law: Politics and the Court

Alongside 'political actors', judges now play a major role in contemporary democratic regimes. This chapter will show that the European Union is no exception. Built by states, it reproduces their most striking features. Moreover, being a complex regime, based on a plurality of power levels and subtle institutional balances, it offers a framework particularly favourable to the development of judicial arbitration. No doubt the Court of Justice is still barely known to the general public: geographically remote, austere and grave, it stays away from daily political games. And yet, its functions and position in the Union's regime give it an essential role. The long-term dynamics of European integration, and its contemporary balances, are closely linked to the status and actions of the Court.

Why a Court?

At the time when the Court was founded, the practice of constitutional justice was still largely foreign to European political culture. Among the six founding members of the European Communities, only two states, which had just recovered from authoritarianism, Italy and Germany, had established a constitutional court in their new fundamental law. The predominant legal doctrines on the continent remained hostile to the unwarrantable interference of legal instruments in the highest political spheres. In Europe (with Montesquieu), it was generally still considered that of the three areas of power, 'judging is, in some fashion, null', because the magistrate can only be 'the mouthpiece of the law'.

However, aware that the treaty could not anticipate every-thing, and knowing that conflicts setting governments against each other or setting them against institutions were inevitable, the initiators of the treaties of Paris and Rome had immediately detected the need to establish the Communities' own court. They do not seem to have had a clear idea of the role that it would play in the medium term. The evidence on this part of the negotiations is rare (Pescatore 1981), but it confirms what the economy of the texts indicates: government representatives knew that a Community of states would inevitably create tensions that would call for an arbitrator, without having, for all that, a precise idea of the nature of these conflicts, or of how they would be resolved.

Presumably, they intended above all to protect themselves, and protect their nationals and their enterprises, from the High Authority. As a supranational instrument, enjoying guarantees of independence and decision-making power, it might infringe the rights of states and private individuals; it was therefore necessary to establish means of recourse. In his famous speech of 9 May 1950, Robert Schuman had already mentioned 'arrange-ments which will ensure necessary ways of recourse against deci-sions from the High Authority'. In other words, the European court would first of all be an administrative jurisdiction, ensur-ing that the law was obeyed.

Its role does not end there, however. The treaty also gives it duties which relate to *international jurisdiction*. In the event of a conflict between states, due to one of them not respecting its obligations, the Court acts as an arbitrator. In the last instance at least: as was seen in Chapter 3, the governments established a mechanism for resolving conflicts which gave preference to amicable arrangements at the politico-administrative stage of the procedure, and only anticipated judicial arbitration in the rare cases where compromises and warnings from the Commission proved insufficient. In practice, the governments generally prefered non-judicial ways of resolving conflicts. This was also fortunate for the Court, which was anxious about fac-ing sensitive issues dealing with conflicts between governments.

These two functions did not seem to call the states' privileges into question: as an administrative jurisdiction, the Court would mainly control the supranational executive; as an international jurisdiction, it would defend their rights against their partners and (as an indispensable counterbalance) remind them of their obligations. There remained, however, a third, more original mission, which the governments apparently did not at first fully take into account: the power to interpret Community law. The mechanism of 'preliminary reference' established by the initial treaties simply aimed at allowing a national jurisdiction (in cases where it was hesitating over which direction to give a European norm that it needed to apply) to ask the Court to provide it with an interpretation. None of all that seemed to give much power to the Luxemburg judges: they would be required to reach a decision only on the basis of questions asked by national jurisdictions, would only have to interpret European law, and would not reach a verdict on the content of the case – the national jurisdiction remaining free to draw the implications of the norm as it was interpreted by the Court. In practice however, with the passing of time, this mechanism became a means open to private individuals to get the Court to compel national authorities to obey European law (Alter 2002). In other words, preliminary reference performs a role which makes the Court of Luxemburg similar to the *constitutional jurisdiction* of a federal order. Perhaps some of the initiators of the treaty had anticipated this evolution. The jurists who drew up these measures may have been influenced by the mechanisms of judicial review recently established in Italy and Germany (Pescatore 1981). But, at best, this was only a possibility. It was on its own, by using a deliberate strategy, that the Court asserted this constitutional dimension of its functions.

Judges facing political actors: prudent audacity

To begin with, the judges showed little audacity. The cases referred to them came from governments or economic operators contesting the High Authority. Until the early 1960s, the Court passed about twenty judgements a year, in which it checked that the rights of the *Usines à tube de la Jasse, des Compagnies des Hauts Fourneaux de Chasse* and other economic operators with poetic names had not been harrassed by the supranational executive. In doing this, it perfectly accomplished its mission as guardian of the treaties, assigned to it by the governments.

From the early 1960s, the Court grew bolder. Exercising its power to ensure uniform application of Community law, it specified and consolidated the significance of the legal obligations accepted by the states. To do so, it has developed a relationship of fruitful cooperation with national jurisdictions. The Luxemburg judges, in fact, depend on their national counterparts: they are only able to accomplish their interpretative work if cases are referred to them. On their side, the national jurisdictions were able to find a way to consolidate their own power in this mechanism. By referring to the Court of Luxemburg's interpretations, they were able to set aside national standards on the grounds that they did not conform to treaty rules, which amounted to exerting a kind of judicial review. In other words, the preliminary reference mechanism gave them a power that, more often than not, they had not obtained from their own constitution. The two parties, European and national, found an almost natural interest in cooperating (Weiler 1991). Besides, the Court did a lot to convince the national magistrates of the qualities of this mechanism. While giving very precise interpretations, and in fact providing solutions, it made sure that it was not seen to interfere with the actual decision-making. While reserving the right to draw conclusions from the interpretation of the Luxemburg judges, the national magistrates are not under their authority. Officially, it is more about a dialogue between equals than a hierarchical relationship, which is not only reassuring but also flattering for ordinary jurisdictions. Moreover, the servants of the Court frequently organize seminars and conferences to which national magistrates are invited, and attach a great importance to communication.

As regards the states' constitutional courts, they have long been more hesitant about going into this cooperative relationship. Enjoying the power to control the constitutionality of laws, for a long time they were highly suspicious of a European jurisdiction seen as a rival and, moreover, giving ordinary jurisdictions a power of control which used to be their own monopoly. The German and Italian constitutional courts, and the French civil and administrative high courts, were the most hesitant to accept the supremacy of European law over their national legislation and constitution (Slaughter, Stone Sweet and Weiler 1998). Today, however, no supreme court openly calls into question the fundamental principles of the direct application and primacy of European law as set out by the Court, and the Convention has suggested putting these principles down in black and white in the new treaty.

The judicial collaboration formed around the mechanism of preliminary reference was, historically, the main way of asserting European law in national areas. Let us consider the first major judgement made by the Court, for the following reasons. First, by asserting the 'direct effect' of European law, this judgement profoundly altered the nature of the European legal order. Next, the balance of power which was established in this first case illustrates very well the singular relationship maintained since then by judges, politicians and private individuals within the Union.

In December 1962, having been referred to by a Dutch fiscal court, the Court made the first of its famous judgements. The Dutch transport company *Van Gend en Loos* (whose name is now known by all law students across Europe) had asked the national jurisdiction to appeal to the Court of Luxemburg, in order to determine whether an article of the treaty could be invoked by individual litigants before a national court. Apparently a technical issue, this question was eminently political. If the Luxemburg judges gave a negative response, this would confirm the international nature of the Community Treaty, whose obligations would mainly be imposed at the state level. If, on the other hand, they responded positively, they would show that, like a federal legal order, the treaty creates rights which the citizens can invoke, even when the states have not explicitly anticipated it. The then protagonists clearly perceived what was at stake (Stein 1981). Three of the six governments, the Netherlands, Belgium and the Federal Republic of Germany, although reputed to be those mainly in favour of integration, submitted observations to the Court and raised objections: in substance they argued that the article referred to could not have a direct effect, because this had not been their intention when they drafted the treaty, and that the Court was not entitled to make such a decision, where the members of the Court were, effectively, in an arbitrating position between the governments on the one hand and the supranational executive on the other, over an issue of interpretation essential for the future of the European legal order. Faced with this configuration of forces, the judges chose to show both audacity and prudence.

First, audacity in choosing the method of interpretation: according to the principles of international law, the Court should have restricted itself to the 'intentions of the High contracting parties' such as they emerge from the terms, content and context of the treaty. Following the Commission's argument, the Court dismissed this method of interpretation of the treaty, and established that it had to envisage the 'spirit, the general scheme and the wording' of the treaty (*Van Gend en Loos*). It thus favoured a teleological reading of the treaty – that is to say, an interpretation based on the eventual aims of integration rather than on a literal analysis of the text. According to this logic, the Court set down an essential principle (not without a certain semantic provocation, however): the 'Community constitutes a new legal order of international law, for the benefit of which the States have limited their sovereign rights, albeit within limited fields, and the subjects of which comprise not only the member States but also their nationals'. Using political vocabulary brandished by government representatives to defend their interests ('international law', 'sovereignty', 'states', etc.), it presented a profoundly innovative interpretation of European integration. From this *petitio principii*, it then deduced that 'independently of the legislation of member states, community law not only imposes obligations on individuals but is also intended to confer upon them rights which become part of their legal heritage'. In other words, where the governments asserted that the treaty pertained to classic international law, the Court upheld that it set up a legal order of a federal type, directly imposed on the citizens. Incidentally, it openly encouraged them to defend these rights, by arguing that 'the vigilance of individuals concerned to protect their rights amounts to an effective supervision', in addition to the control exerted by the governments and the Commission. By doing so, it set preliminary reference up as a means of controlling the governments' actions, while the latter had only conceived it to interpret European law.

It was a bold statement. The Court had restructured the European legal and judicial order as a whole. In the enthusiastic terms of one of its distinguished members, the aim of this decision was 'to withdraw community law from the hands of the politicans and bureaucrats, to place it into the hands of the people' (Mancini and Keeling 1994:183). In its very audacity, however, the Court showed prudence. First, it bound up the assertion of the direct effect principle of Community law with a series of conditions, so that the practical significance of this decision might, in the short term, seem limited. This is a well-known tactic, and widely used by the American Supreme Court: setting down a principle while declaring it inapplicable in the case in point, or surrounding it with limitations in order to reduce its impact in the short term, which allows for the anticipation of hostile reactions from governments. The Court's caution is also shown in the gradualism of its action. In this first case, it had not completely followed the Commission's reasoning, which encouraged it to draw the inferences of affirming the direct application by laying down the principle of the primacy of Community law over national law. No doubt concerned with not offending the governments more than was necessary, the Court had contented itself with getting things started. With the passing of time, however, it would reconsider, little by little, each of these limitations, to give full force to European law: the principle of the primacy of Community law was set down the very next year; the later jurisprudence was to spread its scope by lifting each of the initial conditions (Stein 1981).

The importance of this decision is linked not only to its content, but also to the legal dynamics which it introduced. The relations then established between the courts of law, governments and private individuals became a classic configuration of forces. First, it may be noted that, afterwards, members of the Court continued to favour their role of interpretation. We have seen that control over the national authorities' respect for their obligations is achieved essentially through administrative procedures set in motion by the Commission. These controls rarely reach the Court. Today, these types of cases correspond to a little less than 40 per cent of the judgements made. The other function of the Court – in its capacity as an international jurisdiction – therefore appears to be less important. At the same time, the Court discouraged private individuals from addressing it directly. It always stuck to a very strict interpretation of the conditions of admissibility for appeals introduced by private individuals, so as to avoid over-burdening in this respect. This also allowed it not to consider the facts (quite often complex and demanding long investigations), and to concentrate on the legal aspects (Rasmussen 1980; Costa 2001b). In fact, the Court suggested, and obtained, the setting-up of a lower court (the Court of First Instance) to receive the cases brought by individual litigants, particularly the very absorbing litigations of the EU civil service, competition law as well as state aid. Where these are concerned, the Court no longer acts except on appeal from the Court of First Instance, to specify points of law. Consequently, its role as administrative court is also relegated to a position of secondary importance. Therefore, to assert their rights, private individuals are more willing to resort to the preliminary reference mechanism. Of the cases on which the Court is led to make a decision now, more than half reach it through this indirect means, which strengthens the constitutional profile of the European jurisdiction.

Here too, in the continuity of founding judgements, this strategy was to prompt the mobilization of 'interested parties'. By inviting private individuals to be 'vigilant', the Court encouraged sectors of European civil societies concerned with community policies to use judicial proceedings to promote their interests. Many studies have shown the role of these organized networks. Statistical analyses were able to demonstrate that the flow of preliminary references closely follows that of trade: most of the plaintiffs come from countries and economic sectors most involved in the circulation of goods and services on the European market (Stone Sweet and Brunell 1998). More commonly, and not surprisingly, the characteristics of the litigants reflect the intensity of community action. The most active plaintiffs deal with areas where European law is the most developed, like agriculture, competition or the environment (Harding 1992). Thus, following the evolution of European legislation, fishermen, manufacturers of tomato purée, hypermarkets, dairy producers or customs officers can be seen pouring into Luxemburg. Some of the plaintiffs have a clearly militant profile. 'European social law' has thus been established, for the most part, in national contexts, through judgements made by the Court on the request of organized groups.

The principles of the free movement of workers and the transfer of social security benefits, and the struggle against discrimination due to nationality and sex, have been at the heart of such deliberate strategies (Harlow 1992). The famous 'Defrenne' judgements, which gave direct effect to the article of the treaty related to equal treatment of men and women, were made at the request of a Belgian jurisdiction, which itself was referred to by a lawyer and feminist academic who had recruited the plaintiff through classified-ads, according to the technique described in the United States as 'test-cases'. Associations defending the rights of migrant workers, feminist groups, and more generally movements promoting basic rights, quickly learnt how to integrate legal disputes into their repertoire of action. Various studies have also highlighted the mobilization of pressure groups around the Court, aiming not just at protecting their acquired rights, but at getting European integration to progress through the law. Having become aware of the opportunities offered by judicial means, a series of pressure groups have systematically resorted to them in order to erode national regulations by referring to the principles of European law. The large industrial groups quickly understood that the Court could be used to get restrictive norms and practices invalidated, in the name of European market principles. The saga of the British tradesmen trying to obtain authorization for shops to be opened on Sundays is one among many cases of the use of legal channels as a tool (Rawlings 1993).

This obvious, even undeniable, complicity between certain organized sectors (aiming to defend their commercial interests or rights) and the Luxemburg judges (making sure that European law is applied) have revived the concern of some governments. Caught in a pincer movement between European judges and pressure groups, the governments might seem to be losing control of the political agenda. This also raised renewed interest in functionalist theories on integration, which advance the hypothesis of an alliance between organized groups and supranational institutions aimed at speeding up integration in spite of resistance from the governments (Burley and Mattli 1993). In retrospect, this tactical alliance seems to have been a particularly favourable 'moment' in a generally more complex dynamic of legal integration (Mattli and Slaughter 1998), because if they were not always able to control it, the governments nevertheless watched this legal mobilization more attentively, which compelled the Court to remain prudent.

Politicians vs. judges: voluntary servitude

Why did the governments let themselves be persuaded? Why did they accept that a Court which they themselves had established, should change the meaning of the European legal order and interpret the system of settlement procedures in such a way that private individuals might be armed with the power to control their own actions? There are several answers to this apparent mystery (Weiler 1993).

First, it may be recalled that Court action often protected the interests of the governments themselves. If they established it, and strengthened its powers with the passing of time, it is because they know that they often need it. In the absence of jurisdictional control, governments would be strongly tempted to dodge their obligations and to surrender to unfair competition. Each of the governments could in turn suffer because of this, and the regime as a whole would be weakened. In their clashes with the Commission, more often than not, the governments also found in the Court an impartial arbitrator. This requirement explains why they themselves had consolidated the Court on several occasions. The establishment of the Court of First Instance in 1989, as well as the possibility opened up by the Treaty of Nice in December 2000 to create more limited 'panels', meeting the demands of the Court itself, have the aim of avoiding cluttering up the Court, which could harm the efficiency of its work. The power granted to the Court by the Maastricht Treaty to penalize states not abiding by its decisions falls under this same logic.

The formalism nourishing our political cultures is also frequently put forward to explain the rulers' docility. Coming into open conflict with a Court, criticizing the very bases of its action, would be perceived as a demagogic or anachronistic action in present-day Europe. In fact, the examples of such rebellions are extremely rare. In May 1980, during the Dublin Summit, President Giscard d'Estaing declared that 'something needed to be done about this Court and its unlawful decisions' and suggested that each of the big governments appoint one more judge to counter the Court's 'integrationist' majority (Rasmussen 1986:654). He was thus following the example of President Franklin D. Roosevelt, who had threatened the US Supreme Court with appointing additional judges to counter the conservative members' opposition at the time of the New Deal. But this is an extremely rare phenomenon, still more complicated within the Union by the fact that the number of judges is set by the treaty itself. The proposal was, indeed, not discussed by the governments.

The politicians' docility is also facilitated by the formalist attitude of the Court itself. The strict rigour it imposes on itself in conducting its legal arguments prevents anyone from accusing it of political bias. Even when its decisions are particularly innovative, and clash with the interests and ideas of certain governments, it takes care to express itself only in the language of lawyers and using legal terms and arguments. Sometimes accused of being esoteric, this discursive strategy contributes to making the political significance of its judgements less obvious, and to facilitating the governments' obedience. Moreover, the cooperative logic of preliminary reference avoids confrontations. It is no doubt the Court of Luxemburg which gives EU law its meaning, but it is the national courts which formally draw conclusions from this. It is even more difficult for a government to rebel against its own courts than it is for it to subject a distant and 'foreign' Court to public stricture.

Finally, and perhaps above all, the structure of the Union's regime itself explains the national rulers' submissiveness. Relations between the governments and the Court are defined in such a way that the judges can profit from a wide margin of independence, while the governments are deprived of any power of reply. This fundamental asymmetry – due to the governments themselves as originators of the treaties – is the main source of the particular relations established between judges and politicians in the Union (Weiler 1985; Shapiro 1999). The formal guarantees of independence enjoyed by the judges are of a more classic style, and governments even seem to be still entitled to a certain say. The judges and public prosecutors must be 'chosen from persons whose independence is beyond doubt and who possess the qualifications required for appointment to the highest judicial offices in their respective countries or who are jurisconsults of recognised competence' (TCE, article 223). This is a flexible condition as it refers to national criteria which, for example, allowed Belgium to send a former minister of justice, who had reached the end of a long political career, to the Court in 1999. Moreover, while the treaty states that the judges and Advocates-General are appointed 'by common accord' by the governments, according to an implicit rule each state has 'its' judge, which it appoints. Furthermore, the five biggest states each appoint an Advocate-General, the other three being attributed, in turn, to the other states (Kenney 2000). The six-year mandate is relatively short, compared with that of the national constitutional judges; since terms can be renewed, one wonders whether the governments did not originally have the intention of controlling 'their' judges in this way. In practice, however, the members of the Court have been safe from political pressure. The governments have for a long time mainly appointed academics and it has often been thought that the Court's jurisprudence was partly indebted to the 'systematic mind' of law professors. A drop in this trend has nevertheless been noted in recent years. The judges and Advocates-General are more and more often professional magistrates or civil servants from ministries of justice, with academics only accounting for a quarter of the members.

Although the temptation must have been recurrent, 'one was not aware of situations where these audacities would have cost the post of one judge or another' (Dehousse 1998). The rules for the internal functioning of the Court explain this independence. According to a tacit principle, a case concerning a state is not entrusted to a judge of the same nationality. The decisions are collegial and publishing dissident opinions is not authorized. In these conditions, it is very difficult for a government to know 'its' judge's policy. In the long run, members of the Court have shown themselves not to be very receptive to messages sent by governments, either in their anticipated observations or through more informal means.

No doubt the main strength of the Court lies in the political incapacity of governments to take retaliatory measures. Formally, they are still free to change the treaties and therefore the powers of the Court. In practice, the need to achieve unanimity to do so makes the threat unconvincing: since the jurisprudence of Luxemburg affects the governments' interests differently, there will always be at least one of them to veto a revision of the treaty. If theoretically the judges can undergo individual sanctions by their governments, collectively they are safe from any threat.

The fact remains that, since the end of the 1970s at least, governments have become more vigilant. There are two indications of this. First, we see more and more of them submitting observations before the Court and thus trying to affect its judgement. The French government, for example, took this opportunity in only 2 to 3 per cent of cases in the early 1970s, but now does it in one case out of four. Similar tendencies can be observed in Germany and in the United Kingdom. The governments intervene even more frequently when the cases originate in their own countries. France and the United Kingdom set down their observations in almost all cases, the Federal Republic of Germany and Italy in nearly half (de la Mare 1999). This shows that today the work of the Court is closely followed by national administrations.

Then, if the governments have never managed to force the Court to go back on what was said or to annul its judicial precedents, they have frequently made sure they contained its effects. At the time of the adoption of the 1986 Single European Act, two new articles had set limits for the range of the free circulation of goods; these limits went back on recent jurisprudence. An additional declaration prevented new measures being too boldly interpreted by the Court. In the same way, two protocols annexed to the Maastricht Treaty aimed at containing the effect of recent jurisprudence which might have weighty consequences for public finance or the criminal law of member states. (The *Barber* protocol aimed at limiting the retroactive effect of the decision regarding equal pension rights for men and women. The protocol relating to the *Grogan* judgement aimed at preventing a later judgement from preventing Ireland from maintaining the ban on abortion.) In both these cases, instead of reconsidering the jurisprudence, the governments aimed at limiting its later effects (Stone Sweet 2000). Finally, the governments also made sure that they kept the Court out of sensitive new areas of cooperation, where they feared jurisprudence could help European law progress beyond what they were willing to accept. This explains why the actions pertaining to foreign policy and common security are not justiciable, and why the law produced in the area of cooperation concerning police and criminal matters, is only so in very restrictive conditions. More generally, governments are now extremely careful when they add new clauses to the treaties. If recent articles have tended to become longer and more precise, sometimes to the point of being superfluous, it is because the negotiators intend to limit the judges' margin of interpretation as much as possible. Dependence is therefore reciprocal: the governments have no means of eluding the judges' jurisprudence, but the latter know that they cannot ignore the politicians' instructions.

The Court and the future of EU politics

In retrospect, the jurisprudence of the Court seems to have gone through three major periods (Lenaerts 1992; Shapiro 1999). At the beginning, the Luxemburg judges laid the foundations for European legal order. The assertion of direct effect and primacy principles, as well as the role given to the mechanism of preliminary reference, transformed the treaty into a 'constitutional charter' and established the authority of the jurisdiction which is in charge of it. Perhaps the first generation of judges (some of whom appear among the negotiators of the treaty) was driven on by an ethos of integration. Perhaps they benefited from the 'blocking' of political decision, due to the unanimous vote rule

(Weiler 1981). But perhaps this first jurisprudence was also fore-seeable. Could the Court have done otherwise, being in charge of the very general task of ensuring 'that in their interpretation and application of this treaty, the law is observed' (TEC, article 220), and faced with a very ambiguous text? If it had not asserted the direct effect of Community law, and its primacy over national law, each state could have given its own interpretation of its obligations, or even circumvented them by adopting different national legislation. In these circumstances, European law would have gone unheeded. It would have been but a vague reference, for which people could give their own versions. With the benefit of hindsight, it may be thought that this first phase of legal integration was not as bold as it appeared at first glance, or even that the governments must have known that such an evolution was inevitable (Shapiro 1999).

With these principles laid down, the Court interpreted the fundamental rules of the Community legal order (free movement and equal treatment) to contribute to the construction of the Common Market. By doing this, it mainly supported the dynamics of negative integration, which consisted in dropping national regulations that could have limited the circulation of goods and services, and the movement of labour. Prompted by interested parties in favour of the formation of a single market, it gave a wide interpretation of the 'import restrictions' and thus limited the states' capacity for regulation. From the end of the 1970s, it also understood how to recognize the limits to this logic. Insofar as the European legislative process was kept in check by the unanimous vote rule, there was a considerable risk of a widening 'regulation deficit'. National standards were invalidated in the name of common market principles, while governments often failed to establish European regulations. So, on many occasions, the Court accepted that the states could maintain import restrictions when it meant preserving other general objectives, such as environmental protection and public health. By doing this, it set itself up as an arbitrator of conflicts which set market objectives against other aims. In order to maintain national regulations which control imports, a government must show that the rules it sets down are necessary to the pursuance of such an objective, and it is up to the Court to judge this. Generally speaking, in the long run the jurisprudence of the Court seems to reflect the evolution of political preferences (Maduro 1998). Favouring deregulation in the late 1970s and early 1980s, in a very liberal political climate, it would become more sensitive to regulation demands regarding environmental protection, the consumer and public health in the 1990s. When recently forced to give an opinion on applying competition principles in areas linked to social welfare, it has proved cautious – underlining the specificity of this sector and the need to preserve its financial stability.

Market formation also enabled the Court to contribute to a more positive dynamic of integration. Beyond the abolition of national regulations, it sometimes promoted the adoption of common standards. For example, it set down a general principle which was to have a profound influence over the conception of the market: mutual recognition. In substance, the Court asserted that a product authorized in the state where it was manufactured should also be authorized in the other member states. The Commission immediately relied on this jurisprudence to promote a new approach to market integration. Rather than seeking to harmonize all national regulations, an immensely painstaking task, it was better to lay down the general principle of mutual recognition of these rules. In this way states could retain the power to regulate products manufactured on their own territory, but without hindering the circulation of goods. In making this principle one of the keys to completing the single market, the governments went along with the Court's argument.

On the whole, the very nature of the Court's powers tends to favour a system of negative integration (Scharpf 1998). When it prohibits a national standard, in the name of the market or of competition rules, it is only acting as a 'negative power' imposing respect for the treaty. As soon as it wants to suggest the adoption of positive standards, it seems to be acting as a substitute legislator, and abusing its functions. The Court can therefore only support positive regulations insofar as it can find a basis of an action in the treaty itself. After lengthy hesitation, it thus encouraged, for example, the equalization of the social rights of men and women, by enforcing the principle of equal treatment. But we are dealing here more or less with the exception proving the rule. The essentially negative nature of judicial power, combined with the asymmetry of the treaty itself, tends to strengthen market principles at the expense of other collective ends.

Many observers consider that, in the last few years, the Court has entered a third stage of its history. The integration period which was opened with the Maastricht Treaty has transformed the political climate and generated a new wave of constitutional issues. Public debates raised by the ratification of the treaty put an end to the long period of 'benign neglect'. The Court now knows that its most sensitive judgements are expected in the capitals, and sometimes even in the newspaper offices. Its *Bosmans* judgement, applying the principles of the free movement of workers in the enclosed world of football, sparked off a wave of reactions (hostile more often than not) in the media and national political environments. The judgement by which it cancelled a directive relating to the ban on tobacco advertising in October 2000 also received wide-reaching public feedback. Leaving aside its opinion on the content of the directive, the Court's grounds for cancelling it were that it had been adopted on an inadequate legal basis. Although its reasoning is strictly procedural, the Court has sometimes been presented in the press as being hostile to objectives for the protection of public health. This case is a good illustration of how difficult it is for a jurisdiction to explain its legally complex reasoning to opinion-makers, and the risk it takes when it is led to express an opinion on politically sensitive matters.

This new context has created a new constraint on the Court. It not only needs to convince the leaders and national magistrates, it must also persuade public opinion that its decisions are well-founded. As the Union's sphere of activity expands, the Court is led into more and more sensitive areas. Moreover, the growing politicization of integration is creating new disputes, which also compel the Court to advance into sensitive areas. We can note at least four major open issues where political conflicts are frequent and sometimes brought before the court.

First, inter-institutional relations. This matter is not new: procedures established in the founding treaties already aimed at settling such tensions. Nevertheless, for a decade, conflicts of this type have tended to increase. Throughout the 1980s, the European Parliament relied on the Court to defend its rights against the Council and the Commission (Bradley 1987). Over the same period, governments were seen clashing with the Council when they had been defeated in a vote. Even within the European Parliament, certain political groups brought their disputes before the Luxemburg judges. Whether this suits it or not (and its attitude leads one to think that this does not suit it very well), the Court is now forced to resolve these purely political disputes hidden behind legal arguments.

At the same time, vertical conflicts are intensifying. Far from attenuating disputes over competence between the states and the Union, the assertion of the principle of subsidiarity has provided a concept which polarizes them. There too, the Court balks at expressing its opinion. Until now, it has preferred not to meddle in the Council's business. Yet, the Convention has suggested that it may receive a complaint at the instigation of national parliaments, if they consider that the principle of subsidiarity has been violated by the Union's institutions. The dynamics of integration, here too, could push the Court into sensitive areas.

Incorporating the charter of basic rights into the treaty will place the Court even more at the centre of public attention. Admittedly, it has been enforcing respect for these rights for over thirty years; but since they now appear in writing, they could gain more visibility. Civic associations until now looking more towards Strasbourg than Luxemburg, might be tempted to test the exact impact of these rights in the Union. This is why the government of the United Kingdom has insisted (within the Convention and the intergovernmental conference in 2002–4) that the 'explanations' of the charter be included in the treaty, so as to narrow the Court's margin of interpretation.

Finally, over recent years, we have seen the development of a degree of movement around issues pertaining to the construction of 'European public law'. Putting transparency at the forefront of the Union's principles, and granting private individuals a right of access to the institutions' documents, have already generated political strategies: journalists, researchers, activists, lawyers and MEPs have taken up conflicts with the Commission and the Council and taken them before the Court of First

Instance. This Court has proved to be receptive to their demands, and has laid the foundations of a demanding doctrine of transparency, causing concern or even angry reactions from a certain number of governments preoccupied with preserving the privacy of their deliberations. The setting up of regulatory agencies and the increase in committees will also call for a definition of the principles of public law, which could be laid down by jurisprudence.

The Union's jurisdiction remains infinitely more discreet than that of the American Supreme Court. The appointment of its members is done in the capital cities and, despite repeated demands, the European Parliament has never obtained the right to question the candidates in public hearings. The judges continue to avoid parliamentary tempers and attention from public opinion. Moreover, the collegial administration of decisions, as well as a ban on the publication of dissident opinions or minority reports, limit the development of political debates about the Court's jurisprudence. Yet, at the mercy of the constitutionalization of treaties that it has itself encouraged, the Court sees itself being drawn towards more and more political litigations. As a victim of its own success, the Court must now deal with the reactions of its citizens, whom it formerly asked to be vigilant.

Chapter 8

Politics and the People: a Fragmented Public Sphere

So far in this book, we have seen how the European Union's regime manages Europe's diversity. Without losing their independence and their identity, the member states and their officials are involved in a complex set of mechanisms designed to help them coordinate their policies and settle their conflicts. These last two chapters focus on the way the citizens are affected by this new framework. To what extent are they aware of the EU's impact on their own lives, and how deeply do they manage to be committed in EU politics? Is the 'European public sphere', called for by a wide range of academics and activists, taking shape or does it remain an unfulfilled promise? Does the idea of a 'continental democracy' make sense in such a diverse area?

This chapter first examines the evolution of collective action in the EU. We have seen that national officials have become ever more involved in the EU: ministers meet in the framework of the Council; diplomats bargain in COREPER; civil servants take part in the negotiations of a wide network of committees and agencies coordinated by the Commission; national magistrates often come into contact with the EU's Court. Can we observe a similar pattern of 'horizontal integration' in the civic sphere, or is it confined to the domestic arena?

Some recent events might induce us to think that, after some delay, private individuals are following the path set by the officials. On 16 March 1997, nearly 100,000 people took to the streets of Brussels to protest at the closure of the Renault factory in Vilvoorde a month earlier. In the demonstration, French trade unionists' banners were mixed with those of their Belgian counterparts. Here and there, one was able to catch a glimpse of Spanish, British or Dutch trade union groups. Intermingling with the crowd, the main representatives of the Belgian and French left-wing political parties stressed the symbolic impact of the event. Indeed, it was not the first time that a social movement had crossed the Union's internal boundaries. Since the mid-1950s, miners, farmers, fishermen and other 'European workers' affected by community policies had come to Brussels to express their discontent, and the inhabitants of the Cinquantenaire, the district where the Union's main institutions were established, had become accustomed to these occasional marches, following the arrival of European civil servants a few years earlier. The stir caused by the Renault group's brutal action, which forced Belgian, French and Spanish political rulers, and the main Commission members concerned, to demonstrate their indignation, would, however, give this movement an unprecedented media impact. A multinational company closing down one of its main production sites, coinciding with new investments elsewhere on the Union's territory and in countries applying for membership, illustrated how weak the governments and community institutions were in the face of the evolution of the European market. Vilvoorde will remain an important moment in the history of European social mobilization (Imig and Tarrow 2000; Lefébure and Lagneau 2002).

Some weeks later, in Amsterdam, some 50,000 protesters from all over Europe marched against unemployment, precariousness and social exclusion (Chabanet 2002), just when government representatives had finished negotiating a new treaty bearing the name of that very town. Since then, every or almost every European Summit has been flanked by a counter-Summit protest. In the streets, the protests of a colourful 'civil society' respond to the muffled exchanges of leaders meeting in the corridors of power.

The symbolic impact of these events must not conceal their exceptional nature. These multinational demonstrations, more or less targeting the Union and its policies, show an awareness of power dynamics in Europe (an awareness that they accentuate, moreover), but these demonstrations are still rare. More often than not, the protests are the result of strictly national groups set against the European 'constraint' and prove to be in competition with each other as much as they cooperate (Imig and Tarrow 2001). Apart from these few movements, which are all the more spectacular as they are so infrequent, political life remains deeply segmented in Europe.

With hindsight, the functionalist theories of the 1950s seem naively optimistic. Those who thought that the gradual shift in power centres would go hand in hand with a recomposition of forms of collective mobilization; or that the increase in communication between nations would bring their points of view closer, had to realize that, following a seldomly refuted historical logic, power can change more quickly than the public's opinions and attitudes do. National officials have now become accustomed to negotiating an increasing part of their public policies with their European partners. But collective actors structuring national political life, such as parties, trade unions, associations, interest groups and the media, have largely remained confined within national boundaries. The gap has continually widened between the more and more Europeanized decision-making spheres and the public spheres of debate and deliberation still implanted in the states. Since the areas where opinions are formed remain a state stronghold, collective representation cannot become Europeanized. Today, the EU is still very much a place of 'policies without political life'.

True, the shifting of decision-making centres has affected the strategies of some collective actors. From the very beginning, the interests most affected by community policies have been coordinated and focused on 'Brussels'. But the generalist actors animating political life at the national level, especially political parties, were late in following suit. Consequently, the 'European public space' shows a physiognomy almost the exact opposite of that of the states. In the national arenas, parties continue to enjoy a near-monopoly in structuring political life, which has only been partially eroded by the growth of civic movements and interest groups. In the Union, the balance of power is reversed: interest groups and associations take up the main part of a public space where parties are struggling to find their bearings.

The polyphony of interests

Since the mid-1980s, it has become almost banal to see Brussels as a form of 'European Washington'. The large building sites have slowly given the Schuman district the appearance of a

'European district' bristling with glass towers. At the same time, lobbyists and interest groups with varied intentions have followed in the footsteps of the bureaucracies. In this active core of European negotiation, MEPs, lobbyists, civil servants working for the Commission or the Council, journalists and activists intermingle and sometimes become confused in the eyes of the visitor from outside.

Fluctuating relations

Figures confirm what superficial observation tends to show. More than 3,000 interest groups are represented in Brussels today, employing about 10,000 people (Greenwood 2003). This vast sector alone accounts for three times more human resources than the Parliament and the Council combined, and almost half of the Commission's workforce.

Rallying interests around European institutions, and the Commission in particular, is nothing new. But over recent decades, it has undergone a double transformation, reflecting the change in the impact of European integration itself. On the one hand, the increase in community responsibilities has continually enlarged the circle of organized groups around European institutions. In addition to miners, metallurgists and farmers, one finds industrial firms and trade unions, associations for environmental protection and public health, private and public service providers, feminist movements and movements promoting migrant rights, regions and Churches – so that no single section of national 'civil society' escapes the ongoing dynamics of Europeanization. On the other hand, these groups have adapted their strategies to correspond to changes in the Union's methods of intervention. A more and more flexible logic of consultation between ever more numerous and varied groups has gradually been substituted for the original set-up of a closely associated, very organized and limited number of actors. In other words, the 'corporatist' matrix of the first few years has faded away to leave room for more 'pluralist' relations between institutions and interests.

The development of the farming sector is a good illustration of this change (Delorme 2002). The first Commissioner in charge of this matter – Sicco Mansholt of the Netherlands, the former Dutch minister of agriculture, who has been a commissioner for almost fifteen years – managed to build an 'agricultural corporatism' at the outset, reproducing at the European level, dialogue mechanisms between producers and authorities which already existed at the state level. Organizations representing farmers (trade unions, cooperatives, the different sectors) had been strongly encouraged to form a single transnational committee suited to the Community, which would be regarded by the Commission as its privileged partner. Through a typically corporatist transaction, the Commission gave this committee almost all of the consultation rights, in exchange for its support for the common agricultural policy (CAP). For almost twenty years, this central policy, accounting for the major part of the community budget, was thus the subject of a real joint management between the interested parties and the Commission. This connivance was facilitated by the close ideologies of both private and public participants, tied to Christian democracy and to a lesser extent social democracy, and by the very structure of the CAP, which had the aim of protecting the producers.

From the mid-1980s, this arrangement was gradually called into question. Reflecting the ideological evolution of European governments, the Commission gradually abandoned the interventionist conception of the agricultural policy, in favour of a logic based on giving the market free rein. At the same time, the CAP reforms increased the governments' room for manoeuvre and decreased the Commission's power accordingly. In this new context the corporatist logic of the early decades no longer seemed appropriate. The Commission extended its talks to cover new interests – other confederations of farmers, trading sectors and the food-processing industry. For their part, the original committees contacted the Council directly. The special relationship between the Commission and organized groups was increasingly threatened by other relationships. At the same time, the forms of dialogue also tended to be relaxed: advisory committees now rival more informal meetings – seminars, hearings, talks etc. – organized by the Commission. While the number of interested parties involved is increasing, consultation is spreading beyond the Commission and taking on ever more fluid and varied forms. From a 'government' arrangement between a public authority and a highly concentrated sector, the agricultural policy is moving towards a form of fluid governance. The case of the agricultural policy exemplifies the general evolution of relationships between interested parties and institutions. To a large extent, it reflects how an initially interventionist doctrine can move towards a logic based on the more self-governing arbitration of the market.

Beyond the shifts in paradigm, one may indeed wonder why the change in relationship between interested parties and the Commission does not also pertain to a more general dynamic. In the long run, it actually seems that the relationships between the 'lobbies' and the Commission follow two stages. In the initial phase of a European policy, the interests of the sectors concerned and those of the Commission seem to converge in favour of forms of structured joint management. The Commission needs the support of organized sectors to promote its projects with the governments and to collect technical information necessary for its proposals. On the other hand, the Commission's policies provide interest groups and associations with an opportunity to promote their cause, and sometimes to circumvent the governments' reservations. This explains why, in the 1970s, the Commission encouraged the formation of coordinating platforms for organizations actively involved in the field of environmental and consumer protection or equal rights for men and women. In the 1980s, according to the same set-up, the Commission favoured supporting manufacturers and service providers interested in the project of completing the single market, and made contact with the regional authorities engaged in reforming policies of economic cohesion. When new policies are conceived and launched, the Commission is able to get interest groups to enter into a stable and structured dialogue in exchange for its support.

With the passing of time, however, relations tend to relax – first of all because the Union's policies become more diversified and adaptable. In the spirit of subsidiarity, the general trend of recent years consists in allowing governments more leeway to implement policies; interest groups are consequently prompted to reinvest some of their resources at the national level. In addition, the growth of the European Parliament's legislative powers commits them to getting out of an over-exclusive relationship with the Commission and striking up direct links with the MEPs. For its part, when the foundations of a policy are laid, the Commission may judge it useful to diversify its contacts. A strict network of stable representatives could become a constraint limiting its autonomy. Enlarging its circle of representatives and making forms of consultation more flexible enable the Commission to avoid being held prisoner to the interests it has itself established. In other words, everything contributes to the erosion of the most structured forms of concerted action.

Filtering interests

The amount of influence interested parties have over European policies varies a lot. It goes without saying that a large industrial group, with imposing material resources and means of applying pressure linked to its economic influence, carries more weight than an association representing a diffuse interest, such as the protection of minority languages or the defence of people with autism. It is just as obvious that a group able to organize a media campaign around its actions and heighten public awareness, like large environmental and humanitarian NGOs, is more efficient than an association whose object is confidential and only affects a tiny section of public opinion.

The Commission is concerned with, and to some extent capable of correcting, these imbalances. The links it has established with organizations in the farming sector, then with manufacturers, have given rise to numerous criticisms: in academic literature, as well as in political speeches, the Commission is often presented as 'the friend of lobbies', favouring the interests of particular sectors. Commission members are concerned to correct this image, and to avoid being accused of bias. For almost thirty years, in conducting deliberate policies to promote 'diffuse interests', they have made sure that they corrected inequalities inherent in the lobbying phenomenon. By giving financial support to some associations useful for the development of its market regulation policies, and by giving them almost a monopoly on consultation, the Commission aims at restoring a balance between the interests. So it has encouraged the formation of groups for consumer protection, environmental protection or womens' rights, for example. But other sources of inequality persist, which stem from the very nature of the Union. Generally speaking, it may be said that the strength of action groups depends on three structural factors of European policies.

Not surprisingly, sectorial interests are internally affected by tensions between their national components. The result of the diversity of socio-economic situations is that group motivation varies considerably according to which part of Europe they come from. Multinational companies often have an immediate interest in gathering their forces and taking concerted action against the Commission, while other economic operators, more dependent on national markets and public resources, tend to be split along state lines. Among trade unions, clashes related to ideological traditions limit their capacity for joint action. Among local authorities, the most powerful and richest regions might be tempted to exploit competition where the least well-off would plead for solidarity. Groups for the protection of diffuse interests are not spared these internecine quarrels; those promoting the environment, public health and womens' rights also come up against misunderstandings and clashes of strategy connected to the persistence of national visions.

The extent of the Union's competence constitutes a second filter. In areas where the main part of politics continues to be organized on a national or regional scale – like education, for example – pressure groups have virtually no reason to be organized beyond their borders. If, for example, environmental NGOs or groups for consumer protection coordinate their action at the European level more efficiently than do groups of unemployed people, it is not only because they are supported by the Commission, but also and above all because the Union's capacity to act in these matters is much wider. By definition, a specialized 'civil society' corresponds to a functional Union. Beyond legal constraints, the groups' strength also very largely depends on their capacity to formulate their demands in a language that complies with the fundamental principles of community action (Kohler-Koch 1997; Surel 2000; Saurugger 2002). This is a phenomenon which is in no way only characteristic of the Union: the more distant the priorities of a group are from the main paradigm of public action, the more difficulties it will meet with in putting them forward.

Within the European context, the specialization of public policies around market regulation accentuates this phenomenon of conceptual guidelines. Diffuse interests can only make themselves heard insofar as they manage to put their claims forward in the context of market regulation. Levelling out salaries between men and women, for example, could be promoted if it was justified less by matters of principle than by the need to avoid distortions of competition within the single market. Environmental, public health and consumer protection on the Union scale are justified in the same way. The spirit of subsidiarity strengthens this filtering. The Commission must be careful to explain how the measures it proposes fall within the Union's objectives, and what legal basis they rest on. With the Union's most clearly established objectives, and means pertaining to the market's organization, policies that can be said to fall within this framework are considered favourably.

Modes of action and decision-making procedures within each area of competence are a third factor influencing the actors' strategies. Where the Union can only coordinate national policies, and where decisions are made unanimously, the sectors concerned know that direct pressure on the governments remains the most efficient channel. By contrast, where a normative power exists at the European level, and where voting by a qualified majority is in force within the Council, it becomes more advantageous to act on the Union scale. When they realized in the 1980s that the new rules of the game gave the College a wider capacity of constraint and compromise, many large companies which until then had focused their pressure on the governments turned to the Commission.

The hazards of the so-called 'social Europe' are a good illustration of the weight of these three constraints. Until the mid-1980s, these policies were left on the sidelines of the European agenda: trade unions and employers' representatives tried to act on the Community's different sectorial policies, but without investing much in cross-disciplinary social issues. The project for the completion of the single market registered by the Single European Act changed views and strategies. Perceiving the vast movement of company mergers and acquisitions and the forthcoming increase in the circulation of capital, trade union circles were worried about the risks of 'social dumping'. The Single Act threatened to widen the gap between an ever more Europeanized economic area, and social spheres which were still mainly national. The European Commission then undertook to include the social question on the European agenda. According to the wishes of the President of the Commission, Jacques Delors, who is attached to the tradition of mutual consultation, social dialogue had to go hand in hand with the formation of the Single Market, so as to guarantee market regulation upon its inauguration. It must nevertheless be admitted that, twenty years later, the rate of economic integration has been much faster than that of social integration. The establishment of mechanisms of dialogue between social partners at the Union level came up against the three constraints referred to above.

First, the two sides had to counter their own internal heterogeneity. Workers' representatives, organized around the European Trade Union Confederation (ETUC), do not form a united front. Trade unions from countries where social dialogue is strongest have always been wary of European initiatives for fear they might lead to the erosion of national acquisitions. Between social democrats, communists and Christian democrats, differences in analysis and points of view regarding the purposes of a European 'social dialogue' remain strong (Gobin 2000). For the employers' part, tensions are just as marked.

Furthermore, European dialogue is limited by the strict definition of the EU's sphere of activity. Even if the Treaty of Amsterdam re-incorporated a social agreement which had remained on the sidelines because of British hostility, the impact of social dialogue remains limited. The Union's actions can only complement those of the states. They are only directed at some specific areas (such as working conditions, consultation of workers, the integration of the excluded, equality between men and women) and are confined to 'minimum requirements for gradual implementation', which must avoid 'imposing administrative, financial and legal constraints in a way which would hold back the creation and development of small and medium-sized undertakings' (TCE, article 137.2). In these conditions, social partners only agreed when it came to organizing the dialogue itself, or to setting down some minimal principles for the labour market. Even then the elements for social dialogue established at the European level, such as the European Workers' Councils, have only been accepted slowly, and under strong pressure from the governments (Branch 2002).

The method set out for social dialogue has finished by tracing its limits. Decisions can be adopted by standard legislative procedures or by conventional agreements between social partners – agreements that the aforesaid partners can ask the Council to endorse. But in the most sensitive matters (social welfare and social security, collective protection of workers), unanimity is still required. Consequently social dialogue has been deprived of what makes it work in national contexts: political pressure. Partners are disinclined to negotiate and come to agreements, knowing that, in the event of failure, the Commission cannot act in their stead. These structural barriers account for social regulation remaining uncoordinated. So long as distributive policies are still confined in national areas, and while social redistribution policies are confined to the national sphere, and the modalities of European action are subject to difficult conditions, they have no incentive to try to overstep their national and/or sectorial divergences.

The Union, as a public policy-creating framework, is not neutral. The specialization of its competencies, and the resulting specificities of its decision-making processes, affect the elements of European civil societies to varying degrees. Combining the results of many sectorial studies, Richard Balme and Didier Chabanet conclude that the Union plays 'more in favour of capital than labour, more in favour of urban consumers than agricultural producers, and by affecting centre–periphery relations rather in favour of the latter' (Balme and Chabanet 2002:82). These effects are all the more incisive since, so far, they are not really counterbalanced by any reconciliation of sectorial interests.

Embryonic parties

Among those who fashion political life at the Union level, parties today play only a minor role. As shown in Chapter 6, political groups were formed within the European Parliament at the very beginning of the 1950s, and they acquired considerable influence at the parliamentary level: although they still have national views, the elected members have got into the habit of coordinating their positions within cross-border groups.

As in the classic history of parliamentarism, these groups were the core from which European parties emerged. In the mid-1970s, when it was established that the European Parliament would be elected by direct suffrage, the national parties undertook to formalize their relations more within real European political parties. Yet, integration only took place with caution, so that the elected members chose to form only adaptable party confederations, on the model of international organizations established for decades in the Socialist, Christian Democrat and Liberal families. The objective was simply to coordinate electoral campaigns, which would take place on the same day in the nine member states. Like their American counterparts, at this stage the European parties remained electoral machines, to be mobilized during the poll, but becoming inoperative the very next day.

It was only at the end of the 1980s that they began to have a larger role and consolidated structure. The multiplication of European Summits, meant to 'kickstart' integration, gave rise to an increase in occasional meetings between the leaders of the big political families. On the eve of meetings between heads of state and government, the Socialists and Christian Democrats took to meeting to try and coordinate their points of view. The frequency of these congresses of leaders grew with the passing of the 1990s, and today there are three or four meetings annually. They rally most of the high officials from member parties of the same political family. Since the early 1990s, such meetings have taken place before each of the European Council's main meetings (Hix and Lord 1997).

Over the same period, European parties began to formalize their organizations. Under the pressure of these embryonic party networks, the negotiators of the Maastricht Treaty inserted an article giving them a legal foundation and defining their shape: 'Political parties at European level are important as a factor for integration within the Union. They contribute to forming a European awareness and to expressing the political will of the citizens of the Union' (TEC, article 191). The use of the simple present tense pertains more to its performative than to its descriptive register: in reality, the contribution these parties make to developing an awareness and to forming a common will remains modest. This 'constitutional' establishment nevertheless shows the European leaders' increasing desire to formalize their collaboration. Following the adoption of this article, the European parties changed their statuses, names and organizations. Since then, they have generally been described as 'parties' and no longer simply as 'party federations'. All of them have adopted statutes which are very close to one another's: each of them has endowed itself with the classic array of partisan structures – congresses, councils, office and secretariat – and with a small quota of officials made up of about fifteen people (Bell and Lord 1998; Delwit, Külahci and Van de Walle 2001).

The structural limits to the development of European parties

Institutional mimesis does not suffice, however, to make a central issue of European parties and place them at the heart of European decision-making. In spite of their efforts at organization, European parties remain flexible organs, whose activity is occasional and irregular. Three structural features of the Union's system of government put a brake on their development.

Like other collective actors present on the European scene – interest groups, associations and trade unions – the parties suffer first of all from the heterogeneity of their members' views and interests. Between French socialism, Tony Blair's third way and Gerhard Schröder's *Neue Mitte*, the differences are as clear as, and at times sharper than, those between two closely related parties from the same country. The other political families are even more divided ideologically. The European People's Party is paying the price for its enlargement strategy: reconciling the standpoints of Dutch Christian Democrats, federalists and centrists, and those of the Gaullists, British Conservatives and Mr Berlusconi's populist right wing, is often a seemingly impossible task (Delwit 2003). The enlargement to include ten new member states, bringing a dozen new parties into the EPP, can only increase the tensions. Being smaller, the Liberals, the Greens and the regionalists are relatively less torn apart but, like the others, they are experiencing divisions between rich and not so rich countries as soon as it is a question of public expenditure, between big and small states as soon as institutional issues are involved, between the left wing and the right wing, and between supporters of more or less integration. The Union's still highly intergovernmental nature nurtures these divides. Each of the constituent parties knows that, quite often, its preferences are defended better by its compatriots from other parties than by its political allies from other countries.

These centrifugal forces have nothing original in themselves. All political parties in all systems of government, even the most centralized ones, have been formed from local bases and conserve regional idiosyncrasies. Within the state framework, however, parties have been able to find vectors of centralization in the dynamics of the parliamentary system. The necessities linked to the organization of legislative elections and, through them, winning over the executive power, give the party leadership a means of structuring their organizations. Promises and threats made to the candidates by the party apparatus allow them to ensure a certain discipline in their ranks. In the Union, on the other hand, the system's 'headless' nature deprives the European parties of such instruments. The European elections do not determine the composition of the Commission. Consequently, they are deprived of this 'major choice' corresponding to a personification and simplification of the political offering (Mair 2000; Magnette 2001).

Theoretically, nothing prevents the European parties from naming their candidate to run for the Commission's presidency. The proposal put forward by the German social democrats had also been supported by Jacques Delors before the 1999 June elections. But it is a risky initiative. The heads of state and government, who alone have the right to name the President of

the Commission, did not want to abandon the margin of negotiation that the present system allows them. The MEPs themselves
seemed hesitant. They know that in the configuration of the
current forces, the party in the lead should negotiate a majority
with another party, which might not accept their candidate.
Besides, they fear that politicization of the Commission may
weaken it, depriving it of the neutrality it needs to fulfil its duties
of mediation and control. In a system where neither the Council,
nor the Parliament, nor the Commission are in a position to
impose their leadership on a long-term basis, European parties
are forced to exert pressure on the three poles of the institutional
triangle, rather than to concentrate on a dominant organ.

The functional nature and the segmentation of the Union's
competencies are a third factor hindering the parties' development. Since they are general actors, which conceive broad
'visions of society' by linking up interests and spheres of activity,
political parties constitute a form of organization that is poorly
adapted to the Union's functional nature. Devising a European
programme implies taking into account the scale of competencies and the variety of modes of action throughout Europe, and
obliges issues pertaining to national competencies to be left to
one side. Now, it is precisely there where the parties usually
concentrate their priorities and where citizens are the most
attentive, that the Union is the least active: the tax system,
social policies, criminal law, security, education and culture, all
these areas mainly or exclusively come under the control of the
individual states. It remains difficult to form a 'European programme' likely to generate citizen mobilization without evoking
any of these issues, and by focusing exclusively on the single
market and its regulation.

These limitations explain why European parties exercise
practically none of the central functions of political parties in a
parliamentary system. They have no role in selecting the elite:
the Council members come from national elections, MEPs are
pre-selected by the national parties, and Commission members
are nominated by the governments. The composition of the
European parties' apparatus also depends on negotiations
between national delegations. Deprived of members and militants
(if one disregards national members' indirect adherence to

European parties that most of them are not aware of), they are not instrumental in the mobilization and political socialization of voters either. They only just manage to fulfil the typical party function consisting of coordinating institutions. As we have seen, the MEPs agree to coordinate their actions within transnational political groups, and widely follow the commonly agreed-upon line at the time of voting. But coordination ends there. The Commission's asserted neutrality, and the social norm that it imposes on its members, prevents them from determining a stable political course. In the rare cases where Commissioners and MEPs seem to have a certain solidarity, they tend to deny it rather than display it. As for the Council and the European Council, the members sometimes try to coordinate their points of view, at least on major commitments, but they know that they are accountable to their national electorate first.

Outline of an ideological polarization

Finally, only the programming function is partially fulfilled by the European parties. Since the mid-1990s, they have all done their best to establish joint 'electoral manifestos' when European elections are coming up. A long internal negotiation process between national parties has allowed them to bring out the guidelines that each is committed to defend within its national context. Most of the time this remains a formal commitment. Observation forces one to acknowledge that transnational parties and their manifestos are barely present at the time of European polls, which, in the eyes of the voters, bring national parties (whose lists of candidates are strictly national) into competition – driven by domestic concerns, and whose media coverage stops at the state boundaries (Gerstlé et al. 2000). European political life is still today a sum of fifteen national political lives (Seiler 1998).

Empirical studies show, however, that in the last few years, a clearer polarization of the European political arena has begun to take shape. National positions remain the main determining factors for representative action, in both the Parliament and the Council, but a left–right split has also tended to assert itself. Analysis of the European parties' electoral manifestos shows that the ideological opposition between political groupings in favour of market regulation and those defending a less regulated market has tended to be strengthened (Gabel and Hix 2002). The split does not directly set the 'wealthy classes' against the 'workers', it does not concern tax levies and wealth redistribution in the classic left–right configuration of the twentieth century, but in some manner it constitutes a functional equivalent for it. Insofar as the Union's policies are more 'regulatory' than 'redistributive', it is logical that polarization concerns the issue of regulation. Beyond party manifestos, a voting analysis in the European Parliament confirms that the opposition between the 'regulators' and the advocates of the open market determines the outcome of a large number of the debates (Noury 2002; Hix, Noury and Roland 2003).

The intensification of the Union's action in the fields of asylum, immigration, justice and policing is likely to increase polarization. In debates relating to what is known as 'the area of freedom, security and justice', right-wing parties emphasize the law-and-order part of their policies whereas the left-wing parties put more stress on promoting public liberties (Hoogh, Marks and Wilson 2002). The cross-check is not perfect, but it could result in an increase in ideological demarcations.

In a federal system, the left–right division never totally dominates political life. The clashes setting supporters of increased centralization against those defending states' rights remain a permanent feature of political debates in the United States, as they do in Germany, Switzerland and Belgium. The European Union is also governed by disputes relating to the distribution of competencies. The divide placing 'federalists' and 'sovereignists' face to face is omnipresent.

This being the case, we must ask ourselves how these two forms of political polarization are linked. Will the EU evolve towards more frequent left–right oppositions, will it remain dominated by pro-European vs. anti-European tensions, or will these two major divisions continue to interact? Three hypotheses have been formulated in this respect. For a long time, it seemed that these two divisions crossed each other. Some on the left were openly federalist, but others remained attached to national social benefits and were wary of European policies.

On the right wing, there were also federalist movements and sovereignist factions. All the political families are more or less divided by this pro-European and anti-European divide (Hix and Lord 1997). A second hypothesis considers that this configuration of forces is typical of the system's formation phase, but that as it stabilizes, the two divisions will tend to become aligned (Hoogh and Marks 1999). Most of the left-wing political forces, in favour of market regulation, tend to request more integration – in order to control the market. The right-wing forces, hostile to regulation, would, in these circumstances, be more reluctant to consolidate the Union's institutions and policies. From another point of view, we can consider that this alignment (which is far from complete) is perhaps more circumstantial than structural. So long as the Union continues to promote the principles of free competition, the right wing can find support for its aspirations within European policies, while the left wing may be tempted to defend national public services and social systems. Besides, comparative history teaches us that the relationship between these two sides is changing in federal systems. In the United States, the Democratic Party had for a long time been the advocate of states' rights against a federal administration packed with Republicans. Starting in the 1930s, the Democrats would identify more and more with the federal government, defending social policies and promoting individual rights. The Republicans then sided with the states, until the Reagan administration rediscovered the power of the federal government to reduce the policies which controlled the market. Commitment to the central government thus slides from left to right, following ideological shifts and strategic necessities.

Unstructured opinions

The intermingling of sides is finally only a reflection of the state of public opinion in Europe. Except for a few exceptional circumstances, such as the mobilization against the war in Iraq in the Spring of 2003 (Reynié 2004), public opinions are still chiefly determined by a national agenda, whose themes and pace profoundly differ from one state to the next. The perceptions of the Union, and the attitudes generated, depend on references firmly fixed in political cultures and histories characteristic of each state or even of each region. For most Germans, Italians, Spaniards and Portuguese, European integration has a strong symbolic dimension, in that it was contemporary with the establishment of democracy and economic reconstruction. On the other hand, for the British, the Danes or the Swedes, who only joined later and with no experience of an authoritarian regime, the European project is mainly that of a market whose value is proportional to the commercial benefits it obtains.

Beyond national variations, general trends crossing state boundaries can be observed which seem to show a certain Europeanization of opinions. It is striking to note, in particular, that (according to surveys) support for European integration experienced a clear decline in all European states (with the exception of Ireland and the Netherlands) around 1991. The parallel evolution of public opinion shows that EU membership, as much as the identification with Europe, depends on socio-cultural factors which can be found, almost identically, in each of the states. In other words, the sociology of opinions with regard to Europe does not depend exclusively on national contexts. For example, it has been known for a long time that, in every state, people in higher socio-cultural categories support the European project more widely than the others (Percheron 1991; Cautrès 1998). A survey of 'top leaders' conducted in 1996 had confirmed that, among the economic, political and social elite, support for the European project is over 40 per cent greater than the average support of the population. All studies show that, in all member countries, integration is more appreciated among the richest and more educated fractions of the population. Adherence to the Union is conditioned by sociological determinants, at least as much as it is by national trajectories. If, in every state, socio-culturally privileged groups support the European project more widely than the other social categories, it is because they are 'confident as to their ability to understand and even to control social innovation, and that for this reason they feel they have their place and role to play within the future European Union' (Belot 2002). In the same way, identification with Europe seems conditioned as much by general sociological factors as it is by the singular history of each nation (Duchesne and Frognier 2002).

All in all, the divisions within European public opinion are not an inevitable result of the persistence of national identities. In many respects, the opinions of the Union's different member states are going through parallel changes, and are structured by identical determinants. Tastes, ways of life and values tend to converge in the entire western world, and all the more so among these adjacent nations. Opinion surveys conducted on the scale of the Union also show that, beyond (sometimes very clear) differences from one country to the next, citizens are mainly defined along a left–right axis, both at the socio-economic level and as regards security and public liberties (Van Der Eijck and Franklin 1996; Gabel and Anderson 2002). The citizens' perceptions and attitudes therefore do not fundamentally vary from one state to the next. But they are filtered through national contexts, which are the only ones in which they can really be expressed today – the European elections still being, in actual fact, a juxtaposition of national polls.

In this respect, the European Union's political system is profoundly conservative. The central role it gives governments and national actors, and the impediments it places on the emergence of cross-border political parties, tend to consolidate the historical forms of opinion-making. The system maintains the sociology it derives from. Concerned with protecting their particularities and national interests, governments have placed themselves at the heart of the Union's institutional system. The latter, in return, encourages citizens and collective actors to join forces mainly within the national area. Like 'consociative democracies', the Union's regime protects the 'segments' which it stems from against majority temptations that could marginalize them.

It is not unlikely that transnational mobilizations will become more frequent in the future. At the instigation of MEPs, the European Convention has suggested that citizens be given a form of legislative initiative: a petition signed by at least a million citizens, coming from a significant number of states, could invite the Commission to submit a proposal for a European Act. If formalized by the governments, this mechanism could act as a powerful incentive to transnational mobilization.

Already, many organized groups have resorted to the use of a petition (addressed to the European Parliament) in order to make themselves heard. Such an instrument would provide trade unions, lobbyists, groups defending public interests, and so on with an ideal way of generating a public debate on their concerns, and of getting them on the European legislative agenda. The Commission would still be free not to respond, while the Council and the Parliament could choose not to adopt these proposals. But Swiss, Italian or Californian experience shows, here too, that this kind of mechanism strongly encourages civic mobilization, in particular for single-issue associations and groups with no institutional relays or means of putting pressure on the parties (Papadopoulos 1998). Putting such a mechanism in the paragraph of the constitution project relating to the 'Union's democratic life' shows that the aspiration to develop transnational political movements is becoming widespread in European political circles. But at present it remains an aspiration more than an actual civic practice.

Chapter 9

Participation and Citizenship: Towards a Transnational Democracy?

For over thirty years, the European Union has had the reputation of suffering from a 'democratic deficit' which undermines its legitimacy. According to these platitudes, which are solidly established in the political imagination, a distant, opaque, technocratic and arrogant Europe eludes the prevailing canons of democracy as it is experienced in this part of the world at the beginning of the twenty-first century. Opinion polls, showing that a large majority of citizens questioned find Europe less satisfactory than their state as far as democratic functioning is concerned, confirm the strength of this impression. The continuous growth in abstention on the occasion of European elections both reveals and increases this state of civic disarray. This chapter will examine the debate raised by these issues. It will first argue that, even if the EU's democratic deficit is often exaggerated, it cannot be ignored. The widespread belief that the EU lacks popular legitimacy weakens its capacity for action and nurtures its constant reform; it is a social fact that observers must examine as such. We will then see that the 'parliamentary path' followed so far by European leaders to democratize the EU falls short of offering a solution. We will finally look at recent proposals to conceive an original form of 'democratic governance' fitting the EU's regime, and analyse their potential as well as their limits.

The EU's democratic deficit: a powerful myth

Political scientist Andrew Moravcsik is right when he considers that the Union's democratic deficit is a myth, due to the Europeans' fascination with abstract concepts (Moravcsik 2002).

To a large extent the discredit the EU is suffering from is due to an ignorance of its institutions and functioning.

First, the European Union does relatively few things. Insofar as it does not levy taxes, and its budget is almost forty times less than that of the member states, its capacity to affect the distribution of wealth is very limited. And furthermore, since the states remain largely in control of their foreign and defence policies, as well as their criminal policies, the Union is just about deprived of coercive power. A political body of this nature does not have the same need for legitimation as a state whose fiscal, social and security missions heavily affect the citizens' lives. This fact should not, however, be overestimated. The relation between the states' powers and the Union's competencies is not as simple as it seems at first glance. Indeed, the Union has no, or virtually no, competence as regards public health, social security, employment or education. But these essential public policies, which appear at the top of the list of citizens' concerns, are nevertheless affected by the formation of the European market. With no common social and fiscal policies, the integration of markets encourages competition between the national systems, and thus 'dumping' weighs heavily on the states' solidarity mechanisms. In some cases, European pressure is still more direct. The jurisprudence of the Court in relation to the free movement of workers, or to free provisions of services, based on single market principles, affects areas as sensitive as organizing football or funding health care. The 'European constraint' felt by the citizens is therefore not unfounded. If there are many denouncing the Union's 'democratic deficit', it is because they feel that the political choices they have clearly made at the national level clash with European orientations. Furthermore, they do not see how the latter were formed, nor how they could modify them.

The second argument made by those who understand the EU's democratic deficit as a myth is based on an institutional analysis. They remind us that the Union's institutions are the most controlled in the world. The three poles of the decision-making triangle, the Council, the Commission and the Parliament, are not autonomous powers occupied by stateless 'European leaders', but places of negotiation for ministers, civil servants and MPs, who are all, more or less directly, derived from the states.

The governments, omnipresent in the European decision-making sphere, and whose rights are carefully protected by very strict voting procedures, retain a very large margin of control and influence over the Union's institutions. It must not be forgotten that the Union's delicate institutional balances nurture intense activities of reciprocal control. The Commission is at the centre of all the attention, both in the Parliament and in the Council. Ministers keep a tight control over the activity of MEPs, who, for their part, closely follow the actions of governments and national administrations. The strict division of tasks between the institutions guarantees a vigilance without respite, consolidated by the Court in its role as arbiter.

Keeping the main elements of its regime in mind, it could be thought that, compared with the United States' regime, the EU is not undemocratic. Like the North American Republic, the Union guarantees a sound rivalry between the states and the Union on a vertical level, and continuous competition between 'branches of the government' on a horizontal level. This double division of powers is to avoid both the 'tyranny of the majority' and the 'rule of factions' feared by Madison.

The virtue of a revisionist analysis of this nature, à la Schumpeter, is to rid the debate on the Union's democratic nature of the many biases affecting it. We cannot consider, for all that, that the Union's democratic deficit is only an imaginary problem, which would disappear on its own if 'reasonable criteria to assess democratic governance' (Moravcsik 2002:605) were adopted. The conception of democracy which is the basis of this revisionist analysis indeed falls within a very liberal philosophy: 'The classic justification for democracy is to check and channel the arbitrary and potentially corrupt power of the state' (Moravcsik 2002:606). If the Union does not appear as a fully democratic system, it is precisely because, according to present political culture, democracy does not boil down to the idea that the government is essentially corruptible and that it must be controlled by all possible means.

This liberal view of politics is only one of the normative foundations of democracy. In today's Europe, as in large fringes of the American civic body, the idea of democracy also covers two other ambitions. First it evokes a feeling of control over the collective future: voting is not only giving a verdict on a ruling party, it is also choosing a 'vision of society' and vesting a political majority with the power to transform it into facts (Schmidt 1997; Gustavsson 1999). Moreover, democracy consists of an ideal of civic training and of the equalization of political conditions, which is declining but has not disappeared. Robert Dahl, one of the most respected theoreticians of democracy in recent decades, reminds us of this basic foundation of democratic politics, and it is on this basis that he casts doubts on the EU's democratic quality: 'In practice, delegation might be so extensive as to move a political system beyond the democratic threshold', he argues, adding that this implies that 'an international organization is not and probably cannot be a democracy' (Dahl 1999:19). In Dahl's book, democracy requires political institutions that 'provide citizens with opportunities for political participation, influence and control' and this in turn implies that citizens need to be 'concerned and informed about the policy decisions' and that 'political and communication elites ... need to engage in public debate and discussion of the alternative in ways that ... engage the attention and emotions of the public'. Viewed through this lens, the EU is not democratic, because accountability remains confined to institutional actors and elitist stakeholders, and it will not be, as long as it is deprived of an 'international equivalent to national political competition by parties and individuals seeking office' (ibid.:31). In more optimistic accents, German sociologist Jürgen Habermas follows this line of thought when he argues that the Union could become more legitimate if it managed to forge redistributive policies that would provide the EU with 'normative goals' and if it adopted a constitution inspired by federal and parliamentary principles so as to politicize its policies (Habermas 2001). Whether we agree with these arguments or not, they bear witness to the persistence of a 'democratic ambition' in the EU, which is not content with the revisionist account of the EU's legitimacy.

Now, from this point of view, the EU is far short of the target. As has been seen over the previous chapters, its regime is conceived in such a way that political issues are fragmented, and its decisions are compromises based on fluctuating coalitions of minority interests. Under these conditions, it remains extremely difficult to present European stakes as clear choices between a limited number of collective projects. This in turn explains why the citizens have only a very partial perception of European issues, and are offered little encouragement to take an interest in them. This is what the discourse of 'democratic deficit' reveals: a feeling of being dispossessed when facing a political process whose ideological tendencies and the way in which they are formed are not clearly perceived. And even if it lacks objectivity, this feeling must be taken seriously because it conveys the current state of opinions, and because it nurtures reform projects acting upon the evolution of the Union's regime.

Parliamentary tropism

For a long time, the issue of the Union's democratic deficit was not raised. The Economic Communities, as they were then called, formed an international organization, among many others, whose objective seemed limited and which rarely drew the attention of public opinion. The decision-making power remained in the hands of the governments, which enjoyed a right of veto. Insofar as the Union was made up of governments subject to voter control, it seemed to be indirectly democratic (Wallace 1993).

Some national rulers sometimes resorted to a rhetoric tinged with democratic concerns in order to oppose European institutions, like de Gaulle in the 1960s, denouncing the manoeuvres of a Commission described as a 'stateless Areopagus' or as a 'mostly foreign technocracy, intended to encroach upon French democracy' (de Gaulle 1970:930). But the force of the rhetoric must not make us forget the exceptional nature of these criticisms. It could also be thought that, paradoxically, this type of discourse rather contributed to making the Union legitimate. By minimizing the role of supranational institutions, and by showing that they remained under the governments' vigilant control, these declarations led us to think that the Europe of Brussels was a classic international organization, no more or less democratic than any other.

The issue of 'democratic deficit' only appeared after twenty years of European integration, at the time of the first enlargement. In the early 1970s, in the countries applying for membership, which had seen the Union growing without being able to influence its development, the concerns were much greater than among the founding members. In the United Kingdom, as in Denmark, many academics and political leaders considered that European integration tended to strengthen the executives at the parliaments' expense: by secretly negotiating in Brussels, behind the Council doors, the ministers could evade parliamentary scrutiny (Allott 1974). Consequently, EU membership might alter essential internal balances both politically and symbolically.

This very institutional diagnosis opened the way for a simple view of democratization. Since the integration movement tended to shift the place for decision-making to Brussels, it was also there that the capacity for control had to be strengthened. In other words, the democratic deficit would be absorbed if the European Parliament was elected by direct suffrage and if it was granted control in the form of legislative and budgetary powers equivalent to those of the national parliaments (Marquand 1979). This discourse (which most MEPs enthusiastically adopted and have steadfastly supported ever since) rapidly became a commonplace for debates on European institutions (Dehousse 1995). We have seen that many institutional reforms have been inspired by this desire to absorb the 'democratic deficit' by reproducing on a European scale, mechanisms characteristic of national parliamentarism.

This very structural analysis nevertheless proved to be incomplete. The constant reinforcement of the European Parliament was not enough to convince citizens that the Union had become fully democratic. Quite the reverse: since 1979, the date of the first European elections, turnout has constantly decreased. Brutally invalidating the optimistic scenarios of the 1960s and the 1970s, the rate of abstention has continued to grow while the Parliament has continually gained new powers. Furthermore, institutional reforms conceived through imitating others have revealed their limitations. The Union's regime is such that parliamentary balances cannot be easily transferred to it. MEPs themselves show this when, preoccupied with not jeopardizing the Commission's impartiality, they refuse to follow through with the logic of nomination and control of the executive that they themselves promoted (Magnette 2001).

The acknowledgement of these impasses explains why, since the early 1990s, other channels have been explored so as to give the Union a more 'democratic' profile. Political leaders first shifted their hopes to national parliaments. Continuing to reason in classic institutional terms, but becoming aware of the limits of 'European parliamentarism', they sought to re-establish the National Assemblies' capacity of control over governments. Within the 2002–3 European Convention, many representatives from national parliaments considered that, after over ten years of inter-parliamentary cooperation, the Union's method of organization was continuing to make their work difficult, and demanded that European decision-making procedures be adapted so as to allow them to monitor affairs more closely. Some of the measures to this effect are: to make Council meetings public where their government sits, to make it compulsory for the Commission to inform the national parliaments directly of its projects, and to establish deadlines allowing them to express their views in time. Experience shows that, where their governments have given them the opportunity to do so, national parliaments have been able to recover margins of control they had lost following integration (Bergman 1997; Raunio and Hix 2000; Rozenberg and Surel 2003). So far, this does not seem to have noticeably improved European awareness of the citizens and their elected representatives. Except for the close circles of MPs specializing in European issues, the Union's policies are not debated in the national arenas any more than they were in the past. Despite their constraints upon the states' political orientations, European norms generally only appear at the bottom of the lists of rulers' priorities and citizens' preoccupations. The national parliaments' involvement has perhaps allowed the elected members to monitor the actions of the executive members better. To date, however, it has not contributed to Europeanizing political agendas.

This form of decentralized democratization, moreover, includes the basic disadvantage of confining the debate within the state framework. Even if each parliament were to keep a close and constant watch on its government's European activities, this would only produce a series of widely compartmentalized national debates on Europe. The governments would be under control individually but the Council would, as a collective organ, remain safe from coordinated pressures.

Since the early 1990s, the MPs have tried to collaborate (and to this end, they have established a Conference of parliamentary organs specializing in community affairs, which meets four times a year) but they refuse to set themselves up as a collective institution, and their cooperation is confined to the exchange of experience, and to thoughts on what parliamentary cooperation could be (Costa and Latek 2001). The claims they put forward within the European Convention, like their reluctance to form themselves into a permanent Congress, have shown that national MPs remain more concerned about strengthening their capacity for individual control, than about having a collective influence over the definition of European orientations.

From parliamentary government to democratic governance

Beyond institutional analyses, focusing on the formal dimensions of the 'democratic deficit' and trying to provide answers inspired by national constitutional organizations, other reflections intend to further highlight the Union's original structures, and seek forms of democratization adapted to it. Such is the ambition of those in the academic circles and around the Commission, defending a more innovative conception structured around the notion of 'democratic governance'.

This approach is based on a double observation. It comes first from the idea that the Union is not, and does not have a vocation to become, a state, and that because of the diverse societies it is made up of, it would be unrealistic to envisage the formation of something like a European people. The citizens are mainly defined by their national identity, and the Union has neither the ambition nor the means to form a nation embodying them. In these circumstances, institutional copying is of only relative assistance. To mimic parliamentarism, in the absence of a feeling of political unity and basic loyalty towards the Union, leads to a dead-end. We see a formally parliamentary political regime, but deprived of the social bases that constitute the substratum of parliamentarism. The majority government and the alternation between parties, which are the golden rules of the parliamentary regime, presuppose that the actors and citizens accept that they may be in a minority or be relegated to the opposition, which in turn requires a community feeling stronger than the political divisions. In the Union's present regime, the rules protecting and consolidating the states' identity are opposed to this majority evolution and oblige one to look for another form of political structuring (Lord 2004). The chief ambition of those advocating 'governance' is precisely to provide the concept of a method of political decision-making which does not presuppose the previous existence of a strong civic identity.

Moreover, many authors stress the difference in nature between the missions taken on by the Union and those incumbent upon the state. European policies, they argue, essentially pertain to a logic of market regulation, whereas national public action mainly focuses on distributive policies (Majone 1996). The regulation norms, they add, are in essence different from national laws. Applying to subjects such as the environment, public health, consumers' protection, or the definition of working conditions, they correspond to a more flexible rationality than the one underlying legislative action. In these matters, a decision should ideally take into account the geographical diversity, the technical complexity, the dispersion of tasks, and rapid and incessant technological developments (De Schutter et al. 2001). In order to adapt to this volatile context, it would be necessary to set up more complex and more flexible forms of 'governance' than those of 'democratic government' based on governmental initiative and parliamentary debate.

From this double observation (the absence of a European people and the regulating nature of European decisions), the authors diverge as to the Union's future democratization. Accordng to a first trend of thought, European governance should basically depend on the action of independent 'agencies', made up of experts capable of meeting the fluctuating needs for regulation (Majone 2001b). We have seen that this form of centralized regulation already constitutes one of the ways in which the Union works. Some recommend that its sphere of activity be extended, beyond monetary policy or competition, to other matters which also offer an advanced technicality and which are subject to market or government pressure. By virtue of their technical competence, these new agencies would be able to provide an objective analysis of the situation and to put forward the 'right' measures that are called for. Because of their independence, they would, moreover, escape the broken rhythm of electoral cycles, and could consequently take into account both rapid contextual fluctuations and long-term needs.

Such an institutional set-up makes classic parliamentary forms of political control inapplicable: regulatory agencies, such as the European Central Bank or the recent Agency for Food Security, in fact draw their legitimacy from their autonomy vis-à-vis political majorities. They may nevertheless be subject to other mechanisms of responsibility. The governments that establish them can impose a set of procedural conditions on these agencies, forcing them to account for their actions. Their granting to private individuals of a right of access to their documents, their obligation to justify their decisions by indicating which facts they based their judgements on, and how they balanced them – all this already exists in the Union's constitution and is supposed to make an *a posteriori* control possible. The 'interested parties' should be in a position to assess, and if need be to criticize, the way in which an agency has made its decisions. Insofar as jurisdictional and extra-jurisdictional channels are open to them, private individuals should also be able to have sanctions imposed on agencies guilty of abusing their powers or of not acting impartially. The said agencies, anticipating a possible sanction, would be prompted to respect the terms of their mandate. Political responsibility is no longer demonstrated so much before MPs, but is practised before a diffuse and well-informed public. There are no more sanctions (generally these agencies cannot be censured by the elected members) but control is shown through the continuous influence that the environment of 'interested parties' exerts over the regulating organ (Héritier 1999). According to some authors, this would actually correspond to a more general development of democratic forms within the Union, characterized by 'a political differentiation, between a critical function which would be assumed by a public space for confrontation, and a technical function of regulation, naturally falling to the EU decision-making authorities' (Ferry 1995:98). In other words, the democratic problem is to ensure not that the rulers 'represent' the governed, but that they are subject to their vigilance and criticism. Governance can rely on technocracy, provided that it is an 'open technocracy'.

Other authors have tried their best to develop a more radical variant of democratic governance, based less on regulation by experts than on the active and diffuse participation of 'interested parties' in decision-making (Cohen and Sabel 1997; Gerstenberg and Sabel 2002). The initial report is the same: the decisions incumbent upon the Union's organs often pertain to such volatile, complex and varied matters that it is impossible to adopt them as general and lasting laws. Rather than entrusting the task of regulating these areas to experts, opting for open and participative forms of decision-making might be considered. These two forms of 'governance' – by expertise or by the partici-pation of interested parties – can also be combined: adopting standards in relation to working conditions may involve the participation of experts alongside trade unions and employers; the decisions related to public health can result from a con-frontation between the experts' points of view and those of local actors or functional groups.

Within the context of general tendencies defined by the legislative organs, certain measures (which should be able to be adapted to local or specific contexts) would be entrusted to such private actors. Decentralizing the creation of norms to the places to which they apply, and involving in their conception the people for which they are intended, would allow one to gather the partial and dispersed knowledge that each of the parties has, and to make decisions more in phase with real contexts (accord-ing to these authors). This logic already governs some areas of community action, such as 'social dialogue' being entrusted to employer and trade union representatives, or the co-regulation of certain products being left to producers and organs for consumer protection (Smismans 2004).

By delegating these matters to the private sector, European actors are not totally ridding themselves of their duties. The 'deliberative polyarchy' formed by the entente between these decentralized processes requires the intervention (before and afterwards) of institutions in order to ensure a degree of coordination. It is up to the 'legislative' organs, the Council and the Parliament, to determine which issues can be dealt with in this way, which principles should guide the regulation standards, and what procedures the actors to whom these missions are entrusted must follow. As for the Commission, its task is to support this process by providing the parties involved with useful information; while the Court can be called on to check that the actors to whom decisions have been delegated are respecting their mandate.

Long reticent, for fear of weakening its functions and sharing its prerogatives, the European Commission has recently pleaded in favour of these new decision-making methods. In a white paper on 'European Governance' published during the summer of 2001, it supported these proposals and suggested broadening their scope. According to the Commission, this was supposed to make European decision-making more efficient, because it would be better adapted to the relevant contexts, and would also be more legitimate. Echoing the discourse spread by institutional representatives of local authorities and organized interests, it maintained that a stronger involvement of the 'civil society' in decision-making would make the Union more democratic. Alongside a democratic logic based on the equal representation of citizens within the legislative organs, a more fluid form of democracy (through direct and open participation of interested parties and civic organizations) was to develop. This revisionist approach to the discourse on the Union's 'democratic deficit' also falls within an evolution common to the entire western world. The 'economic and social affairs committees' established in the postwar years in every European country had already aimed at nurturing the elected members' reflection through their experience of 'real-life worlds'. Today, the invocation of civil society aims, in its turn, to enrich public deliberation by diversifying channels of expression.

This sudden passion for civil society and governance raises a few doubts. At first, one wonders how far these practices (conceivable within the context of adopting certain executive measures) provide an answer to the more general problem of 'democratic deficit'. If it is true that many of the Union's areas of competence pertain to a logic of regulation which is likely to be governed by decentralized agencies or participatory cooperation, other modes of action call for more conventional forms of public intervention. When it is a question of coordinating economic policies, nobody expects the governments to delegate their duties to private agencies. Police and judicial cooperation naturally appears to elude regulations negotiated in public by private actors. What is more, the decentralizing of decisions calls for coordination mechanisms in order to guarantee a certain coherence in joint action and to avoid discrimination.

The paradox of this new fancy for civil society is that, conceived in order to make up for the deficiencies in public action, it in fact entails new forms of public regulation and creates new institutional strategies. Civil society cannot manage without the state. The European Commission, continuing the reflections of the Economic and Social Committee, is well aware of the dilemmas it is confronted with when it envisages extending its relations to private actors, beyond the conventional forms of 'consultation' (Armstrong 2002). It must avoid being accused of partiality: considering that the organizations of civil society are, by definition, non-representative, it is extremely difficult to determine which groups must be consulted or involved. There is always the risk of accentuating inequalities by favouring the more powerful or better organized, or by neglecting those who, because of the confidentiality of their objective or the dispersal of their support, lack visibility. The Commission is aware of these dangers, but has experienced some difficulty in defining reliable criteria which allow for group representation and balanced consultation. Consequently, it hesitates to embark on a process of accrediting associations and further formalizing its relations with them. On the one hand, the lack of norms feeds suspicions of arbitrariness. By keeping its discretion to consult or not, and to choose its interlocutors freely, the Commission preserves its room for manoeuvre but lays itself open to accusations of bias. On the other hand, codifying relations between the institutions and civil society can cause the latter to lose its spontaneity and its autonomy, and institutionalize the advantages gained by privileged groups. Moreover, any form of 'proceduralization' gives it extra work. Setting out principles and criteria for the civil society's involvement would oblige the institutions to show that they respect these norms and would open up new contentious issues that would be for the courts to arbitrate. Far from relieving the institutions, the 'civil society's' arrival on the scene gives it new responsibilities and makes procedures more onerous.

Furthermore, for some years, this issue has been the subject of intense rivalries between the Union's institutions (Smismans 2003). Frightened of seeing its monopoly of representation weakened, the European Parliament in turn embarked on processes of dialogue with the civil society, organizing vast hearings and establishing special relations with transnational associations (through its topical committees). For its part, the Economic and Social Committee, whose *raison d'être* is precisely to make the voices of the civil society's organs heard, has tried its best to broaden its contacts with non-economic actors, and to appear as the mainstay of 'civil dialogue'. These internecine quarrels have accentuated the associations' distrust – they are afraid of being absorbed by the institutional game and losing their independence; the discourse on civil society seemed to be a simple alibi.

More so, the experiences conducted so far do not enable one to show that making available a third type (belonging to neither the public nor the market sphere) really contributes to reducing the Union's democratic deficit. In practice, all studies show that these forms of participation remain very elitist (Wallace and Young, 1997). Movements and interest groups consulted by the institutions are ever more numerous and varied, but they constitute only a tiny part of the European societies' rich network of associations. Some of these transnational groups claim to represent hundreds of movements established in the member states, which themselves have thousands or tens of thousands of affiliated members, but in reality, only a few officials installed in Brussels, who have the financial and conceptual resources needed for a useful involvement, are really able to join the game of 'deliberative polyarchy' (Weisbein 2002). Civil society cannot escape the phenomena of professionalization and bureaucratization previously experienced by parties and trade unions.

In itself, this is not characteristic of the Union alone. In all western societies, a very large majority of citizens remain passive. However, this does not mean that European decisions would systematically be biased in favour of a social elite. As Kant has already noted, the mobilization of an elite promoting the defence of 'common interests' benefits all citizens, be they active or not. When, for example, academics and journalists commit themselves to making the functioning of the institutions more transparent, and win their case before European courts, the entire 'civic body' enjoys these democratic advances.

But what is peculiar to the Union, and which 'democratic governance' does not allow to be corrected, is the citizens' lack of subjective participation. In all democracies, the citizens follow the major events of political life and are occasionally able to express a choice. Their passivity is not structural: in times of strong political polarization or crisis, citizens manage to come out of the state of lethargy they seemed to have fallen into. The Union, on the other hand, tends to produce a lastingly depoliticized civil society: because the public only perceive European issues, and the way in which things could be changed, in a confused way, citizens do not follow European political life, and, to a much wider extent than can be observed within the states, claim to be incapable of forming an opinion.

This state of civic apathy is due to the fundamental structures of the Union's political regime, only reinforced by the logic of 'governance' (Magnette 2003). Political sociology in fact shows that public arousal, even when subjective or virtual, necessitates cognitive and motivational resources that only the regime can provide. The public only get involved when they feel they are 'politically competent' (Millner 2002). This implies that they have the impression they understand the essential mechanisms of the regime. Participation also requires motivation, which the citizens obtain from a clear perception of the issues at stake. Competition between a limited number of parties allows (often by personifying them) for the simplification of the terms of political choice (Przeworski et al. 1999). But the Union does not provide these civic resources. Its institutional system, based on a balance, and continuous competition, between the three poles of the decision-making triangle, makes it impossible for a 'power centre', able to attract attention, to emerge. To understand the logic of European decisions, it is not enough to know the colour of the ruling majority. Rivalries between 25 governments must be taken into account, as well as debates between about a hundred parties assembled into half a dozen groups in the European Parliament, and the Commission's ability to find a compromise incorporating these divided interests. Insofar as it extends the spectrum of participants in decision-making, blurs the boundaries between public and private spheres, disperses areas of negotiation and makes standards more fluid, 'governance' does nothing but accentuate the complexity of the political game. In this respect, the EU resembles the pre-New Deal United States, described in the following terms by the philosopher John Dewey:

> The ramification of the issues before the public is so wide and intricate, the technical matters involved are so specialised, the details are so many and so shifting, that the public cannot for any length of time identify and hold itself. It is not that there is no public, no large body of persons having a common interest in the consequences of social transactions. There is too much public, a public too diffuse and scattered, and too intricate in composition. And there are too many publics, for conjoint actions which have indirect, serious and enduring consequences are multitudinous beyond comparison, and each one of them crosses the others and generates its own group of persons especially affected with little to hold these different publics together in an integrated whole.   (Dewey 1927:187)

Aware of this limitation, some of the most ardent defenders of governance claim to be guided by a concern to revitalize the educational ambition of democracy (Cohen and Sabel 1997). Paraphrasing the Tocquevillian argument so often brought up, they assert that citizens involved in decentralized forms of deliberation will be more civically competent, and that the diffuse participation channels constitute many learning experiences for 'democratic governance'. But nothing confirms this intuition. As widespread as it may be, the notion that the membership of associations and local participation nurture a feeling of civic competence has never been proved (Putnam 1994). There are good reasons to doubt that a citizen participating in a local meeting aimed at assessing (in accordance with a European directive) the consequences of building a road or a rubbish dump, becomes more sensitive to European issues than any other citizen. On the contrary, experience shows that involvement in local or thematic debates can make it more difficult to perceive wider issues. Until the civic virtues of 'deliberative polyarchy' are proven, there is still a need to consider ways of structuring European political life to favour political learning for the great majority.

Beyond pluralism

All theoreticians on democracy, even those most open to pluralism, acknowledge that such a regime must be able to offer the citizens clear options to structure their opinions. Robert Dahl, who was the most ardent defender of pluralist democracy, maintains that such a regime implies that the citizens should have a certain degree of 'enlightened understanding', which in turn calls for a clear structuring of the issues at stake. In the same spirit, John Rawls asserts that a 'just society' cannot content itself with bargaining between sectorial groups, and that it therefore calls for the training of those who can help bring out alternative conceptions of the common good. Joshua Cohen, while speaking in favour of a governance based on the active role of decentralized associations, concedes that democracy cannot do without parties, because they provide grounds whereby 'debate is not reduced as it is in local, sectorial or thematic organizations', and by doing so compensate for the inequalities in civic competence (Cohen 1997:86). In other words, political theory has rediscovered what has never been forgotten by political science, which is that the parties are the backbone of democracies. They concentrate political attention, compensating for the insurmountable complexity of the decision-making machine, and they shape ideologies, making the socialization of citizens possible.

If this obvious fact is being brought to our attention again, it is precisely because in debates on the Union's democratization, it has ceased to be so obvious. The fascination with new forms of governance and with the civil society (and the care taken by the Commission to remove parties from the so-called 'civil' organization list) have made reflection on the roles of conventional actors of the political game of secondary importance. It must be acknowledged that arguments deployed to show that the Union cannot content itself with mimicking forms of political life typical of states do not lack cogency. The Union's competencies often pertain to technical matters, or issues (such as environmental or consumer protection) which cut across established political cleavages. In these conditions, it remains difficult to politicize European agendas. Moreover, the European institutional system, based on competing channels of representation and on the mediation of an 'impartial' Commission, does not facilitate the polarization of debates.

These arguments must be taken seriously, but they do not constitute obstacles, as insurmountable as they may seem at first sight. Analyses of the European parties' programmes and their attitudes in the parliamentary arena show that a certain polarization is taking shape. Regulatory measures are not in essence a-political. In many cases, the demarcation line separates those insisting on preserving or even increasing market flexibility from those wanting to impose limits on it in the name of 'the common good'. The contrast between advocates of the open market and supporters of the regulated market is not fundamentally different from the left–right split which dominated European political life during the twentieth century. The mobilizations of trade unions and associations around issues linked to the regulation of the European market and world trade, confirm that there is nothing to stop them from politicizing these issues and clarifying the alternatives.

For their part, the institutional balances of the Union's regime do not preclude the simplification of European political life either. Proposals formulated by the convention on Europe's future follow these lines. Distinguishing legislative and executive functions more clearly, and specifying the Council's role in adopting norms; reducing the number of decision-making procedures; establishing a link between the coordination of economic policies and that of employment; focusing public debates on legislative programmes: all this is likely to put some order into European agendas and emphasize the need to specify times and places.

What seems to be primordial, and is crucially lacking in the Union, is particularly the structuring of political debates. In the national arena, clashes of extremely complex interests are conveyed as simpler ideological oppositions by the competitive game between the parties. In Dahl's words:

> Thanks to political parties and interest organizations, the amount of information that citizens need in order to be adequately informed, actively engaged in politics, and politically effective is actually reduced to more easily attainable levels. A political party usually has a history known in a general way to voters, a present direction that is ordinarily an extension of its past, and a rather predictable future. Consequently, voters have less need to understand every important public issue. Instead, they can simply vote for the candidate of the party of their choice with some confidence that, if elected, their representatives will generally pursue policies that accord broadly with their interest. (Dahl 1998:185)

On the scale of the Union, this mediatization does not yet exist, because the political actors who are the most likely to deal with this, that is the parties, remain weakly structured.

The strengthening of European parties and the polarization of issues which would ensue, would not inevitably lead to politicizing the Commission and making it lose the impartiality it cannot do without in order to fulfil its duties of mediation and control. It is incorrect to reduce, as is often done, the possible evolution of the Union to the terms of the following alternative: either the Commission clearly issues from a parliamentary majority, and it will lose its singular position, or it preserves its autonomy and prevents clear political debates from emerging. This platitude is strongly rooted in political representations. The former commissioner Pascal Lamy and some of his friends have recently written:

> A 'reshaped' Commission should be politically homogeneous for its action to be clear and understood, and enjoys the presence of a very visible opposition. In order to ensure both the coherence of its action and the interest of public opinion, it will be necessary to go beyond the principle of a Swiss-style executive, where all moderate parties are represented and, relentlessly keeping a check on each other, often paralyze each other. So let us stop advocating in Brussels the baneful effects that our unfortunate cohabitation causes in France. (Lamy et al. 2001)

As widespread as it may be, this impression is not justified. To reduce the possible scenarios to such an alternative means misunderstanding the way in which conflict and compromise coexist in complex democracies. For a Belgian, Dutch, Finnish or Austrian citizen, the presence of an executive body representing the greater part of the parliamentary forces, and not just a majority, is in no way unusual, and does not prevent clear debates. When the party arena is not too fragmented, the public have no difficulty understanding the projects and ideas of the four or five parties dominating political life. The fact that most of them are associated with exercising power and that the decisions are the fruit of compromise rather than the expression of monolithic majorities, changes nothing. The citizens of the beginning of this century are capable of understanding that political choices are not reduced to binary oppositions (Milner 2002), and that a balanced compromise between the opposing camps is possible and desirable.

Such a set-up is perfectly conceivable in the present Union, without postulating a constitutional disruption, nor a radical conversion of mindsets. The Commission (in accordance with its monopoly on initiative) will continue to put forward proposals which attempt to reconcile governments' viewpoints to those of political families, and which by definition can only be compromises. The debate would, however, gain clarity if the organs for legislative decision-making, the Parliament and the Council, explained their support or their criticisms in more distinct and definite terms. The logic of European decision-making and the lasting influence of national divisions would continue to make big compromises necessary, but at the end of a more clearly staged debate, its terms would be better understood.

Furthermore, polarizing political discussions around parties does not exclude an increased participation of associations from within civil society. The French philosopher Paul Ricoeur, interpreting Karl Mannheim, has recalled that democracy is nurtured by the constant opposition between ideologies and utopias, as two different representations of reality. Ideologies play an essential role of socialization and social integration, but at the price of a certain confinement of debate; whereas utopias combat 'the fossilization of ideologies' (Ricoeur 1987:409), but tend to encourage a certain withdrawal from reality as well as political secession. The continuous opposition between these two visions of the world, through parties and civil associations, can increase their virtues while at the same time lessening their defects. In a 'European public space', better structured by parties representing the great tendencies of the citizens on a formal and egalitarian basis, the problems of the representativeness of civil society's organizations would also be less acute. Strengthening parties would facilitate the acknowledgement of the civil society's political role.

The European Union's political life will probably never be as majestically simple as Westminster's parliamentarism. In the absence of a cabinet dominating political games, and faces personifying choices, and in a context where national identities and sectorial interests are strong, the stakes will remain more confused than they are in national arenas. De Tocqueville saw the future of federalism in this:

> The Union is a vast body, which presents no definite object to patriotic feeling. The forms and limits of the state are distinct and circumscribed, since it represents a certain number of objects that are familiar to the citizens and dear to them all. It is identified with the soil; with the right of property and domestic affections; with the recollections of the past, the labors of the present and the hopes of the future. Patriotism,

then, which is frequently a mere extension of individual selfishness, is still directed to the State and has not passed over to the Union. Thus the tendency of the interests, the habits, and the feelings of the people is to center political activity in the states in preference to the Union.   (de Tocqueville 1985)

Observing the present-day United States, de Tocqueville would probably add some reservations to his remarks, which must remind us that the European Union's future has not yet been written.

Chapter 10

Conclusion: the Union, its Nature and Value

More than a half-century after its foundation, the European Union still remains a contested polity. The number of its resolute opponents has declined over recent decades, but it still arouses more indifference than enthusiasm. A survey published in autumn 2002 revealed that if the undertaking had to be abandoned, less than half of those Europeans questioned (44%) would feel 'great regret'; one-third (34%) proclaimed themselves indifferent, whilst 11 per cent stated that if the Union disappeared they would be 'relieved' (Eurobarometer 57). Other surveys confirm the indifference of European affections: only 45 per cent of those questioned claim to be 'very attached or rather attached' to the Union, compared with 90 per cent expressing their attachment to their country, 87 per cent to their town or village and 86 per cent to their region (Eurobarometer 58). The EU has become institutionalized; it now interferes in all or almost all areas of politics, but it remains poorly rooted in collective sentiments. No wonder: comparative history teaches that representation evolves more slowly than power (Elias 1978).

Latent Euroscepticism may often be understood as the expression of fears and worries prompted by major power changes. Integrating national markets also affects the interests of a wide range of constituencies, resulting in disappointment and bitterness. Miners, farmers, fishermen, migrant workers and others have experienced the consequences of European policies in their everyday lives. As consumers, students, tourists, patients, producers or service providers, Europeans also perceive the impact of European integration on different aspects of their lives, at least indirectly. As citizens, we realize that our historical state is now part of a broader 'thing', without understanding precisely what this means. In other words, the contested nature of the EU is not

189

only due to the cost of 'adjustments', it is also the consequence of the difficulty European citizens and leaders have in conceiving the 'nature' of this new framework.

Rethinking sovereignty

In the preceding chapters, we have seen that what makes it difficult to understand the EU's regime and politics is partly the persistence of a political grammar constructed on the conception of state sovereignty. Although we have the vague feeling that the idea of a powerful and autonomous state is increasingly at odds with an ever more globalized world, we have not yet found another language to conceptualize contemporary politics. When we think of the EU, we therefore tend to see it either as a simple and rather innocuous confederation of sovereign states or, conversely, as an emerging federal state. This dichotomy remains so powerful that we are at pains to accept the EU's 'in-betweenness'.

This is the reason some scholars suggest that we will never understand the Union unless we do away with these classical concepts, inherited from seventeenth-century political theory. We should accept that the world has changed so much that we need a paradigm shift (Rosenau 1997). In their opinion, we should substitute a more realistic concept of 'multi-level governance' for the old-fashioned idea of 'government' (Marks et al. 1996). It is indeed tempting to insist on the uniqueness of the EU, to see it as a *sui generis* polity or, as Jacques Delors once called it, an 'unidentified political object'.

This book has not followed this line of thought, first and foremost because it underestimates the persistent strength of historical states. Each government is not one actor among many others, participating in a complex and fluid negotiation in which it is forced to adapt its interests. By looking at the interaction between the national governments and the European institutions, examining the role given to national leaders and officials in the EU's decision-making machinery, and analysing EU 'politics', we have shown that state interests and national visions remain the major structures of the EU's regime. Considered over the long term, European integration is merely a new stage in the plurisecular movement bringing European markets together. Through this integration, Europe has resumed a very long tradition of the circulation of goods and capital, the movement of people and the free flow of ideas, which was interrupted, but never stopped, by virulent nationalism and wars. As the historian Fernand Braudel (1963) and the sociologist Norbert Elias (1978) understood, the formation of the Union constitutes a new stage in the continuous dynamics of integration which has characterized the western world since the eve of modernity. The states are affected by it, but are not meant to be dissolved into it. Quite the contrary. With the historian Alan Milward, we can recall that European integration, to some degree, 'rescued' the state from collapse.

Never have the European states been more prosperous, more stable and more peaceful than they were in the thirty years after the Second World War, which was also the period of the creation of the EU. The formation of appeased democracies and modern welfare states, with their massive turnout at the polls, their strong fiscal capacity, their broad solidarity policies and their heavy bureaucratic apparatus, is contemporary with the construction of the European Union. This does not authorize us to see European integration as the cause of these changes, but it shows that, contrary to what the classic dichotomy might induce us to think, strengthening the Union does not amount to undermining its member states. Still today, the states only allow the Union's institutions to have a small share of their prerogatives. In other matters, they exercise their sovereignty jointly and only accept the constraints of the majority vote and supranational control with caution. The state remains the Union's cornerstone, and the successive enlargements have always made the perspective of the states' absorption by a centralized Europe more unlikely.

Now, this argument requires a caveat. Putting the accent on the EU's intergovernmental nature does not mean that the EU is a banal international organization. To understand the EU, we must accept that it is primarily an intergovernmental order, but we should also acknowledge that what makes it so fascinating – and sometimes misleading – is precisely the fact that it is in many respects an original international organization. Or, to put it in more academic terms: in a typology opposing 'states' and 'inter-state regimes', the EU would clearly fall within the second category, but sub-categories would be needed to distinguish it from other, much less sophisticated, international regimes.

Scholars have endeavoured to forge new concepts in order to make sense of the EU. Following those who argue that the EU is 'less than a federation, more than a regime' (Wallace 1983), constitutional scholars have labelled it a 'federation of states' (Beaud 1995) to distinguish it from the classic notions of the federal state and confederal union. Highlighting its dynamics more than its legal nature, political scientists have seen it as a form of 'intergovernmental federalism' (Quermonne 2004) or of 'institutionalised intergovernmentalism' (Menon 2003). The semantic reflection is only in its early phases. It will probably take time for scholars, leaders and citizens to agree on a 'concept' encapsulating the EU's nature. In the meantime, these are very useful working definitions, which help us understand the primarily intergovernmental nature of the EU, while acknowledging that it is more institutionalized and more entrenched in domestic contexts than other international regimes. What makes the EU so original is the fact that, unlike other federations, it does not shift sovereignty from one place to another (Weiler 1999); nor does it 'disperse' sovereignty in the way the Founding Fathers of the American Republic hoped their Constitution would (Bellamy and Castiglione 1998). In the EU, the member states remain the major source of authority: they remain 'sovereign' but they are forced to *exercise* their sovereignty differently.

First, it involves a much wider set of participants in the negotiations between states. The EU is not the realm of diplomats and members of the executive. Beneath the tip of the iceberg – the European Council and the Council of Ministers – the EU assembles thousands of civil servants, regulators, judges, MPs, civil society activists – who form horizontal networks, and constitute the basis of the EU's pyramid of negotiation. The EU is still primarily an intergovernmental forum, but one where states are much more linked than in other international regimes (Keothone 2002; Slaughter 2004).

Moreover, European integration also alters the states' and the nations' self-perceptions, and thereby their behaviour. Through the effect of the circulation of people, goods and capital, national identities are slowly being transformed. European citizens remain proud of their nations, as is confirmed by all opinion polls, but this attachment has been losing its exclusiveness and aggression. Opening up the boundaries, increased travel, the ever more intense flow of communications: all this produces a certain homogenization of ways of life and a related standardization of customs. But this does not imply that national civic ties will dissolve, as Rousseau feared. By discovering other ways to be European, the citizens are becoming aware of their own particularities. When they re-examine their history, they distance themselves more from national mythologies (Ferry 2000). Attachment to the nation, to tastes, to the ideas and habits it epitomizes remains, while at the same time ridding itself of its most arrogant aspects. Identities are becoming less exclusive and more reflexive. This movement first took shape in the field of law. The fundamental principle of 'non-discrimination', the keystone of European law, compelled the states to adapt their legislations and administrative practices, so as to relieve them of the national restrictions which sullied them (Magnette 1999). The same goes for representation. Citizens who cross boundaries, live and work in a member state other than their own, now enjoy full civil and social rights as well as some political rights. In very concrete terms, they are thus experiencing the life of nations which remain proud of their singularity, but are becoming more hospitable to citizens from other member states.

Indeed, the coexistence of the Union and the nations produces rivalries and tension. The EU is not a haven of peace governed by people of good will, looking impartially for the common good. But these clashes are politically more virtuous than is often thought. The constraints that European law and cooperation between governments impose on the states, like those with which social life burdens the individual, paradoxically make the states more stable. Having been prevented from engaging in overly rough competition and encouraged to settle their clashes of interest through negotiation or legal arbitration, the states are less inclined to be aggressive. The fact that they have been obliged to purge their laws of discriminatory practices, and prompted to revisit their history, makes them more tolerant. Since the states are forced to respect the principles of democracy and the rule of law under the watchful eye of their partners, there is less risk of their slipping into authoritarianism (Weiler 1997). European construction makes the relations between the nations more civil and 'tames' these states.

The opposition also plays in the other direction. Cut off from the nations, the Union would be a cold and anonymous bureaucracy, a huge forum for diplomatic negotiations and interest bargaining. This fear, widespread in Europe, is shared by all those who value Europe's cultural diversity, like the American philosopher John Rawls:

> Isn't there a conflict between a large free and open market comprising all of Europe and the individual nation-states, each with its separate political and social institutions, historical memories, and forms and traditions of social policy? Surely these are of great value to the citizens of these countries and give meaning to their life.   (Rawls 2003:9)

Abstract and distant, the EU might threaten to lapse into bureaucratic high-handedness, market competition and legal dogmatism. But critics of European integration, provided with more or less explicit national references, protect it from these excesses. Trade unions denouncing the ravages of social dumping, farmers protesting against the tyranny of productivity, football enthusiasts refusing to subject sport to market rules, all draw motives and motivations for their criticisms in real worlds which are deeply rooted in the nations. They all force the Union's actors to take into account the solidarity and affection which emanate from historical communities. The civilized opposition between national sentiments and European principles prevents technocratic deviation at the EU level as well as nationalist violence at the level of the state (Magnette 2000). This is what makes it so valuable: the EU does not create a perfect order, but it channels tensions in order to make them useful to all parties.

Why the EU cannot become a state

These dynamics are an essential dimension of European politics, and leave their mark on each of the components of the Union's regime. The vertical confrontation between the states and the supranational institutions is a permanent feature of the Union's political life. It punctuates the conflicts over the distribution of competencies, and respect for the law. It is the mainspring of the EU's singular institutional arrangements. The governments' omnipresence in decision-making, the extreme precision of the system of vote allocation and distribution of seats, the increasing number of opportunities for negotiation and arbitration, opt-outs and flexibility clauses all convey the spirit of civilized confrontation between states. The same logic applies to public opinions and political forces: interests have organized on a European scale, parties have federated, opinions have converged; yet the Union still remains marked by the primacy of national entities. Each of the successive waves of enlargement, bringing in new members preoccupied with not relinquishing their sovereignty and autonomy (recently acquired for many of them), has, at regular intervals, revitalized this aspiration to consolidate national identity in European cooperation.

This basic feature of the Union's regime also explains its 'limits'. Europe is not and cannot be a welfare state. Its meagre budget prevents it from conducting real policies of redistribution – even if the agricultural policy and the 'cohesion funds' constitute means of distribution of wealth among professional groups and regions. Its states' passionate attachment to their fiscal prerogatives and to a belief in the economy and the solidarity they embody makes the implementation of broad solidarity mechanisms beyond boundaries impossible for the foreseeable future. The EU has formed and regulates a single market, but it leaves to its member states policies specifying the relations between social groups and generations. The analogy with other federal experiences might lead one to think that this limit is not necessarily fixed. After all, the formation of a common market preceded the establishment of social policies in the United States as well as in Germany or Switzerland. But the EU reveals an essential particularity which distinguishes it from those other examples. If redistribution policies are long in coming, it is not just because of decision-making rules which hinder the formation of political majorities, but because such policies already exist within the member states. Forming a European welfare state would not be to create such policies but to shift them. Every fiscal and social security regime epitomizes a conception of equality that is deep-rooted in the nation's substratum. Harmonizing these rules or shifting wealth-redistribution mechanisms to Europe would require a preliminary convergence of the nations' social ideologies, which remains highly unlikely. In the current phase of European integration, there is more a spirit of recognition, and protection, of 'legitimate diversity' (Scharpf 2003).

The EU is not, and will not become, a majoritarian democracy. Reducing political choices to only two alternatives would imply a mutilation of distinctive identities. The acceptance of alternation would demand prime loyalty towards the Union and there is no indication of this happening. The European institutional mechanisms tend more to perpetuate divisions than to over-ride them, while at the same time making compromise possible. The political game loses in clarity what it gains in flexibility. In theory, there is nothing to prevent the adaptation of political deliberation to European diversity in a way that would make the stakes clearer without marginalizing minorities. And no doubt it is here that the Union's scope for evolution is at its broadest, and changes most desirable. Unless the political possibilities are clarified and simplified, the public will remain unaware of the Union's political life. In the long run, the legitimacy of this so fragile European project is likely to be affected.

Clarifying EU issues does not necessarily mean reducing them to classic left–right oppositions. European decisions are often different from national choices, because the EU performs different functions through different institutions. But they are the source of a new form of politics; they are 'politics among nations', focusing on the interaction between domestic and international contexts. As de Gaulle remarked in 1962:

We are in politics when we jointly handle tariffs, when we convert the Coal Board, when we make sure that salaries and social security contributions are the same in the six states, when each state allows workers from the five others to come and settle within it, when we consequently make decrees, when we ask the Parliament to pass laws, grant credits, impose necessary sanctions. ... We are in politics when we deal with the association of Greece, or African states, or the Malagasy Republic. ... We are still in politics when we consider the candidacies put forward by other states concerning their participation or association. We are still in politics when we are led to envisage the demands announced by the United States with regard to their economic relations with the Community. (De Gaulle 1970)

These issues, linked to the relations between the domestic and international spheres, are probably the core of future politics, and Europe is in this respect a laboratory of broader evolutions.

The Union is also not, and cannot be, a military power in the short term. The procrastinations of its governments in the turmoil of the Iraq crisis of Spring 2003 recalled all the frailty of earlier ententes among European states. And even if this crisis may also be seen as a 'catharsis' – inducing European leaders to strengthen their cooperation in the field of defence and armaments – the EU will not become a unified military actor in the short or medium term. The views of national leaders on many issues remain in such profound conflict that the cooperation mechanisms have proved incapable of – or have not even tried – reconciling them. Outside of such situations of crisis, however, the EU manages to maintain an international profile and to influence world affairs. As the world's leading commercial power, it is represented in international arenas where commercial agreements are negotiated by the commissioner in charge of trade, who acts on the governments' mandate and under their control, without his negotiating capacity suffering on account of it.

The EU is also the biggest provider of aid for development in the world, and the political entity most present in operations for upholding peace and supervising democratic transition. Next to the dollar, its currency is becoming a world currency. Europeans manage to maintain a united front wherever international agreements on environmental protection, development, public health and social rights are being prepared. In international negotiations related to cross-border crime and penal cooperation, the Union asserts its values and its conception of fundamental rights.

Europe is not a military, but a 'civilian power'; it aspires to be a 'quiet superpower' (Manners 2002; Moravcsik 2002; Telò 2004). In a world still dominated by the balance of power, this Kantian idealism can appear naive or hypocritical. By presenting themselves as a civilian power, might the Europeans not have simply theorized their weakness? After all, two centuries earlier, this pacifist discourse, based on peaceful trading and legal arbitration, belonged to the Americans, confronted by the great European monarchies (Kagan 2003). Circumstances no doubt make doctrine; but it would be wrong to underestimate the force of this aspiration. Behind justificatory rhetoric, is found the strength of experience. More than any other region in the world, the Europeans have experienced the effects of the containment of violence, by both constraint and weaponry. For half a century, they have tried cooperation, legal arbitration and commercial interdependence. Without their always being aware of it, European integration has left its mark on the rulers' minds. The habit of 'negotiating in the shadow of the law' has changed attitudes. In keeping with their history – while trying to be less imperialistic – Europeans have continued to export what they consider to be their 'model', first to closely associated territories, later integrated into the Union following the collapse of authoritarian regimes and empires; then to more distant regions, where the European experience is meticulously studied (Telò 2000; Nicolaïdis and Howse 2002). It will be some time before regional integration shapes the international order; but the idea is part of the current climate (Slaughter 2004). And comparative history teaches us that political forms are never fixed and that at times minority models finish by coming to the forefront.

Towards a regime change?

But what if this rather optimistic interpretation of the EU has underestimated the structural changes it has been going through in recent years? Might the admission of ten new states (mostly originating from the former Soviet bloc) not be liable to upset patiently acquired balances and habits? How can the Union resist this revolution in number now that it has been enlarged to encompass almost all of the continent, from the Atlantic to the Mediterranean, and from the Baltic to the Black Sea, grouping together half a billion inhabitants? Will the successive reforms accomplished since the beginning of the decade (to prepare the Union for these new measures) not change the very structure of the regime?

The impact of this still very recent event is difficult to measure. Even if strong pro-federalists generally refrain from saying it in public, they fear that the Union will dissolve. The way they see it, Europe has enlarged too quickly and is preparing to enlarge even more to the Balkans and Turkey. They think that the Union should have been reformed thoroughly before enlargement took place. What is more, the new states – infinitely less wealthy, lacking in experience as regards European cooperation, and where liberal institutions have not yet had the time to become established – could undermine the Union's foundations. During the crisis provoked by the war in Iraq, most of them contributed to intra-EU conflicts by taking sides with the Anglo-American coalition, and thereby going against the Franco-German axis. At the same time, they have attracted companies long-established in western European countries, by playing on fiscal and social competition. In the course of the first budget negotiations, they showed their determination by openly defending their national interests. And although the citizens of these countries overwhelmingly approved their admission to the Union, the first European elections in central and eastern Europe were marked by a low turnout and successes for populist parties and Eurosceptics. Do these few realities not constitute a range of convergent facts, showing us that the days of a Europe driven by the Franco-German axis are over? This is a widespread concern in the most pro-European circles. Enlargement seems to announce victory for those who see the Union only as a huge open market, devoid of solidarity mechanisms, regulations and ambitions for power, and where EU authorities play only a marginal role.

Others fear, on the contrary, that recently accomplished reforms will bring about an increase in regulations, which will weigh heavily on the states. The paradox of enlargement is that by increasing the Union's heterogeneity, it is inclined to increase European constraints. The 'constitutional treaty' established by the Convention, and renegotiated by government representatives of the 25 members, has caused the spectre of a European super-state to re-surface in Eurosceptic circles. As from the very beginning, disappointed federalists and concerned sovereignists are once again polarizing opinions.

Analysing the evolution of the Union's political regime is complicated by the fact that, in a union of states, mental frameworks through which the power structure is examined are numerous and often competing. Any observer, just like any political actor, reads the circumstances through his own 'pattern of thought'. As has been said, the opposition between those supporting a federal interpretation of the Union and those defending an intergovernmental reading has been a permanent feature of the history of European integration from the very beginning, recalling the rivalries between federalists and anti-federalists in the early history of the United States. Each group tends to understand reforms in the context of its own mental world.

Beyond these divergences, European leaders share a common concern. They all tend to focus their attention on the executive's status and prerogatives. In this respect, the Union is nothing special. The 'leadership issue' – knowing who leads and represents political dynamics – has been at the heart of debates since political science came into being (Mansfield 1989). Throughout the European Convention in 2002–3 and the intergovernmental conference which followed, the liveliest discussions turned on the two poles of the European executive: the Council and the Commission. Heated controversies over state representation and the balance between the biggest and the smallest in these two institutions have already been described in Chapter 5 (should the Council's rotating presidency be preserved; how should the mechanism of voting by a qualified majority be reviewed; and must each state be given a Commission member?). Beyond these basic questions, dominated by the states' desire to maximize their influence in the machine, constitutional discussion mainly concerns the balance between the two heads of the European executive duopoly.

By establishing the election of the Commission's President by the European Parliament, the constitutional treaty in fact seems to extend the 'parliamentarization' of the Union's regime. The paradox of enlargement would be that, by increasing European diversity, it strengthens the central institutions – as in the United States, where the conquest of the West attenuated the North–South cleavage and therefore further nationalized American politics. But by establishing a permanent presidency for the European Council, the constitutional treaty also confirms intergovernmental leadership. Having decided not to choose between two competing models, the governments have left all possibilities open.

Three scenarios can be envisaged. Either the parliamentary component will be asserted, leading the Union to a German-style federal-type regime; or the intergovernmental element will gain ascendancy; or finally and most likely, the Union will remain halfway between these two ideal types.

Although theoretically feasible, the parliamentary option is politically unlikely. It may indeed be imagined that the Council would be gradually weakened to the benefit of the directly elected chamber – the European Parliament. The governments would appoint a President for the Commission close to the party which won the European elections – as is stipulated in the constitutional treaty, which sets out that the European Council should make its choice 'taking into account the elections to the European Parliament'. Enjoying a parliamentary legitimacy and the power to organize the work within his College, the President of the Commission would be similar to a head of government. If the President succeeded in embodying the Union and leaving his or her mark on policies, this would condemn the 'European Council Chair' to gradual oblivion, reducing it to a function of protocol similar to that of the heads of state in Germany and Italy. Since the treaty does not preclude it, it might even be envisaged that the President of the Commission could be the 'chair' of the European Council, thus assuming unrivalled leadership, like that of the British prime minister.

At first sight, the Barraso Commission seems to fall within this perspective. Close to the main group in the European Parliament (the EPP–ED), in charge of a Commission two-thirds of whom are conservatives and liberals, having himself shared out the responsibilities within his team, the President of the European Commission should be able usually to rely on the support of the conservative and liberal groups of the European Parliament, just as a centre-right German government would do. In such a set-up, the Council of Ministers would seem to be the European equivalent of the Bundesrat, ensuring that the primacy of European laws over state prerogatives was limited.

However, this scenario underestimates the governments' capacity for resistance, which is clearly greater than that of the German *Länder*. It must first be recalled that the constitutional treaty still grants important powers to the Council, not only as regards foreign policy and security, where it is still the dominant institution, but also in the broad area covered by the Economic and Monetary Union and by the 'open coordination' of social and employment policies. Here, the President of the Commission will have to reckon with another 'chair' attentive to messages from the various governments. In addition, the dangers which threaten a Commission President who politicizes his or her team should be taken into account. By choosing to favour his Italian, British, Spanish and Polish allies at the expense of the Franco-German axis, President Barroso has risked revenge: feeling marginalized within the Commission and continuing to see themselves as the driving force of European integration, the two governments might be tempted to increase their cooperation and to form alliances within the European Council, or even outside the framework of treaties, as they have sometimes done in the past.

On the other hand, the scenario of a rampant renationalization of the European Union is not really plausible. Once again, it may be imagined *in abstracto* that the President of the European Council, enjoying the governments' trust, might assert himself or herself as the main leader. Embodying the Union on the international scene; working on good terms with the Union's minister for foreign affairs, also designated by the governments; appearing as the orchestrator of the European summit meetings, he or she could be perceived by public opinion as the 'President of the Union'. In this perspective, the President of the Commission would be reduced to following the lead of the European Council, like the Secretary-General of an international organization. At the same time, we can also imagine the governments using 'their' commissioner more and more as a representative of national interests in Brussels, and stepping up their control over MEPs, thus contributing to renationalizing the three poles of the institutional triangle.

Even if this picture is not unfounded, it is just as caricatural as the parliamentary scenario. Practising European negotiation makes a complete renationalization difficult. Even if the member states – both old and new – display their national priorities more openly than in the past, they will continue to be subjected to the constraints of collective action. Within the Commission, all members know that they must avoid appearing to be loyal emissaries of the governments that appointed them if they want to keep the trust and support of their colleagues, without whom they can do little. In Parliament, MEPs know that they will be powerless if they do not follow the logic of collective action with the colleagues of their group, which often compels them to deviate from their own countries' national interests. Similar logics apply to the Council and the European Council. Governments which are unable to form alliances – which inevitably force them to make concessions – find themselves marginalized.

If the Union can become neither a parliamentary regime nor a classic international organization, it is forced to keep this mixture of 'supranationalism' and 'intergovernmentalism' which has been its hallmark from the beginning. No doubt, as it does in French dualism, the balance of power will vary according to political circumstances. When national and European electoral cycles converge, as was the case with the appointment of Jose Manuel Durrao Barroso in June 2004, the President of the Commission can rely on the support of both a wide parliamentary majority and a large number of governments. In these circumstances, his chances of identifying political lines likely to form the subject of a consensus – and therefore asserting his leadership – will be high. But while national political life is still very widely dissociated from European stakes, this convergence remains uncertain.

Thus, Europe's political heterogeneity, combined with the rules of the constitutional treaty guaranteeing representation by the governments, makes simple scenarios unlikely. After all, the history of the United States reminds us that a civil war, a dramatic economic crisis and two world wars did not suffice to impose a monistic regime against the subtle balances of the 1787 Constitution. More recent and diverse, further protecting the rights of its member states, and not yet having determined its eastern boundary, Europe has more chances of conserving a political life made up of complex and oscillating compromises – to the federalists' deep disappointment and to the researchers' great pleasure.

References

Ackerman, B. (1991) *We, the People: Foundations*, Cambridge, MA: Harvard University Press.

Allott, P. (1974) 'The Democratic Basis of the European Communities, the European Parliament and the Westminster Parliament', *Common Market Law Review*, 11(2): 298–326.

Alter, K. (1998) 'Who are the "Masters of the Treaty"? European Governments and the European Court of Justice', *International Organization*, 52(1): 121–47.

Alter, K. (2002) *Establishing the Supremacy of European Law: The Making of an International Rule of Law in Europe*, Oxford: Oxford University Press.

Armstrong, K. A. (2002) 'Rediscovering Civil Society: the European Union and the White Paper on Governance', *European Law Journal*, 8(1): 102–32.

Axline, J. (1969) 'Legal Integration through Judicial Fiat', *Journal of Common Market Studies*, 7(3): 240–59.

Balme, R. and Chabanet, D. (2002) 'Action collective et gouvernance de l'Union européenne', in R. Balme, D. Chabanet and Vincent Wright (eds), *L'Action collective en Europe*, Paris: Presses de sciences-po.

Beaud, O. (1993) 'La souveraineté de l'Etat, le pouvoir constituant et le Traité de Maastricht', *Revue française de Droit administratif*, 9(1): 1045–68.

Beaud, O. (1995) 'La Fédération entre l'Etat et l'Empire', in B. Théret (ed.), *L'Etat, la finance et le social, Souveraineté nationale et construction européenne*, Paris: La Découverte.

Bell, D. and Lord, C. (eds) (1998) *Transnational Parties in the European Union*, Aldershot: Ashgate.

Bellamy, R. and Castiglione, D. (1998) 'Between Cosmopolis and Community: Three Models of Rights and Democracy within the European Union', in D. Archibugi, D. Held and M. Kölher (eds), *Re-Imagining Political Community*, Cambridge: Polity.

Belot, C. (2002) 'Les logiques sociologiques de soutien au processus d'intégration européenne: éléments d'interprétation', *Revue internationale de politique comparée*, 9(1): 11–30.

Bergman, T. (1997) 'National Parliaments and EU Affairs Committees: Notes on Empirical Variation and Competing Explanations', *Journal of European Public Policy*, 4(3): 373–87.

Bestock, D. (2002), 'Coreper revisited', *Journal of Common Market Studies*, 40(2): 215–34.

Bobbio, N. (1995) 'Democracy and the International System', in D. Archibugi and D. Held (eds), *Cosmopolitan Democracy*, Cambridge: Polity.

Bradley, K. St C. (1987) 'Maintaining the Balance: the Role of the Court of Justice in Defining the Institutional Position of the European Parliament', *Common Market Law Review*, 24(1): 41–67.

Branch, A. P. (2002) 'The Impact of the European Union on the Trade Union Movement', in R. Balme, D. Chabanet and Vincent Wright (eds), *L'Action collective en Europe*, Paris: Presses de sciences-po.

Braudel, F. (1963) *Grammaire des civilisations*, Paris: Flammarion.

Burley, A.-M. and Mattli, W. (1993) 'Europe before the Court: a Political Theory of Legal Integration', *International Organization*, 47(1): 41–76.

Cautrès, B. (1998) 'Les Attitudes vis-à-vis de l'Europe', in P. Bréchon and B. Cautrès (ed.), *Les Enquêtes Eurobaromètre, Analyse comparée des données socio-politiques*, Paris: L'Harmattan.

Chabanet, D. (2002) 'Les Marches européennes contre le chômage, la précarité et l'exclusion', in R. Balme, D. Chabanet and Vincent Wright (eds), *L'Action collective en Europe*, Paris: Presses de sciences-po.

Christiansen, T. and Kirchner, E. (eds) (2000) *Committee Governance in the European Union*, Manchester: Manchester University Press.

Cini, M. (1996) *The European Commission, Leadership, Organisation and Culture in the EU Administration*, Manchester: Manchester University Press.

Closa Montero, C. (1997) *Sistema político de la Unión europea*, Madrid: Editorial Complutense.

Cohen, J. (1997) 'Deliberation and Democratic Legitimacy', in J. Bohman and W. Rehg (eds), *Deliberative Democracy, Essays on Reason and Politics*, Cambridge, MA: MIT Press.

Cohen, J. and Sabel, C. (1997) 'Directly Deliberative Polyarchy', *European Law Journal*, 3(4): 313–40.

Committee of Independent Experts (1999a) *First Report on Allegations regarding Fraud, Mismanagement and Nepotism in the European Commission*, 15 March 1999.

Committee of Independent Experts (1999b) *Second Report on the Reform of the Commission, Analysis of Current Practice and*

Proposals for Tackling Mismanagement, Irregularities and Fraud, 10 September 1999.

Constantinesco, V. (2000) 'La Responsabilité de la Commission européenne. La crise de 1999', *Pouvoirs*, 92: 117–31.

Corbett, R. (1998) *The European Parliament's Role in Closer European Integration*, Basingstoke: Palgrave Macmillan.

Costa, O. (2001a) *Le Parlement européen, assemblée délibérante*, Brussels: Editions de l'Université de Bruxelles.

Costa, O. (2001b) 'La Cour de justice et le contrôle démocratique de l'Union européenne', *Revue française de science politique*, 51(6): 881–902.

Costa, O. and Latek, M. (2001) 'Paradoxes et limites de la coopération parlementaire dans l'Union européenne', *Revue d'intégration européenne/Journal of European Integration*, 24(2): 139–64.

Costa, O. and Magnette, P. (2003) 'The European Union as a Consociation: A Methodological Assessment', *West European Politics*, 26(3): 1–18.

Costa, O. and Magnette, P. (2004) 'La Société civile européenne entre contestation et cooptation', in B. Frydman (ed.), *La Société civile et ses droits*, Brussels: Bruylant.

Curtin, D. (1993) 'The Constitutional Structure of the European Union: a Europe of Bits and Pieces', *Common Market Law Review*, 30(1): 17–69.

Dahl, R. (1998) *On Democracy*, New Haven, CT: Yale University Press.

Dahl, R. (1999) 'Can International Organizations be Democratic? A Skeptic's View', in I. Shapiro and C. Hacker-Cordon (eds), *Democracy's Edges*, Cambridge: Cambridge University Press.

de Bùrca, G. (1998), 'The Principle of Subsidiarity and the Court of Justice as an Institutional Actor', *Journal of Common Market Studies*, 36(2): 217–35.

de Bùrca, G. (1999) 'The Institutional Development of the EU: a Constitutional Analysis', in P. Craig and G. de Bùrca (eds), *The Evolution of EU Law*, Oxford: Oxford University Press.

de Gaulle, C. (1970) 'Conférence de presse du 09 septembre 1965', in *Mémoires d'espoir, allocutions et messages*, Paris: Plon, 1970.

Dehousse, R. (1994) 'Community Competences: Are there Limits to Growth?', in R. Dehousse (ed.), *Europe After Maastricht*, Munich: Law Books in Europe.

Dehousse, R. (1995) 'Constitutional Reform in the European Community: Are there Alternatives to the Majoritarian Avenue?', *West European Politics*, 18(1): 118–36.

Dehousse, R. (1998) *The European Court of Justice: The Politics of Judicial Integration*, Basingstoke: Palgrave Macmillan.

De la Mare, T. (1999) 'Article 177 in Social and Political Context', in P. Craig and G. de Bùrca (eds), *The Evolution of EU Law*, Oxford: Oxford University Press.

Delorme, H. (2002), 'Les Agriculteurs et les institutions communautaires: du corporatisme agricole au lobbyisme agro-alimentaire', in R. Balme, D. Chabanet and Vincent Wright (eds), *L'Action collective en Europe*, Paris: Presses de sciences-po.

Delwit, P. (ed.) (2003) *Démocraties chrétiennes et conservatismes en Europe. Une nouvelle convergence?* Brussels: Editions de l'Université de Bruxelles.

Delwit, P., De Waele, J.-M. and Magnette, P. (eds) (1999) *A quoi sert le Parlement européen? Pouvoirs et stratégies d'une assemblée transnationale*, Brussels: Complexe.

Delwit, P., Külahci, E. and Van de Walle, C. (eds) (2001) *Les Fédérations européennes de partis. Organisation et influence*, Brussels: Editions de l'Université de Bruxelles.

De Schutter, O., Lebessis, N. and Paterson, J. (eds) (2001) *La Gouvernance dans l'Union européenne*, Luxemburg: Office des publications officielles.

Dewey, J. (1927) *The Public and its Problems*, New York: H. Holt (reprint: Ohio University Press).

de Zwaan, J. (1995) *The Permanent Representatives Committee: Its Role in European Decision-making*, Amsterdam: Elsevier.

Dinan, D. (2004) *Europe Recast: A History of European Union*, Basingstoke: Palgrave Macmillan.

Dubois, V. and Dulong, D. (ed.) (1999) *La Question technocratique. De l'invention d'une figure aux transformations de l'action publique*, Strasbourg: Presses universitaires de Strasbourg.

Duchesne, S. and Frognier, P.-A. (2002) 'Sur les dynamiques sociologiques et politiques de l'identification à l'Europe', *Revue française de science politique*, 52(4): 355–74.

Elias, N. (1978) *The Civilizing Process: The History of Manners*, Oxford: Blackwell; New York: Urizen Books.

European Commission (2001) *Report to the European Council: Better Lawmaking*, 7 December 2001, COM(2001) 728 final.

European Commission (2003) *XXth Report on the Implementation of EU Law*.

Featherstone, K. (1994) 'Jean Moment and the "Democratic Deficit" in the European Union', *Journal of Common Market Studies*, 32(2): 149–70.

Featherstone, K. and Radaelli, C. (eds) (2004) *The Politics of Europeanization*, Oxford: Oxford University Press.

Ferry, J.-M. (1995) 'Souveraineté et représentation', in M. Telo (ed.), *Démocratie et construction européenne,* Brussels: Editions de l'Université de Bruxelles.

Ferry, J.-M. (2000) *La Question de l'Etat européen*, Paris: Gallimard.

Forêt, François (2003) 'L'Europe comme tout. La représentation symbolique de l'Union dans le discours institutionnel', in S. Saurugger (ed.), *Les Modes de représentation dans l'Union européenne*, Paris: L'Harmattan.

Gabel, M. G. and Anderson, C. J. (2002) 'The Structure of Citizen Attitude and the European Political Space', *Comparative Political Studies*, 35(8): 893–913.

Gabel, M. G. and Hix, S. (2002) 'Defining the EU Political Space, an Empirical Study of the European Elections Manifestos 1979–1999', *Comparative Political Studies*, 35(8): 934–64.

Gellner, E. (1997) *Nationalism*, New York: New York University Press.

Gerstenberg, O. and Sabel, C. (2002) 'Directly Deliberative Polyarchy: an Institutional Ideal for Europe', in C. Joerges and R. Dehousse (eds), *Good Governance in Europe's Integrated Market*, Oxford: Oxford University Press.

Gerstlé, J., Semetko, J., Schoenbach, K. and Villa, M. (2000) 'L'Européanisation défaillante des campagnes nationales', in G. Grunberg, P. Perrineau and C. Ysmal (eds), *Le Vote des Quinze. Les élections européennes du 13 juin 1999*, Paris: Presses de sciences-po.

Gobin, C. (2000) 'L'Europe syndicale au risque de la mondialisation', *Les Temps Modernes*, 607: 159–77.

Gobin, C. (2002) 'De l'Union européenne à … l'européanisation des mouvements sociaux?', *Revue internationale de politique comparée*, 9(1): 119–38.

Grabbe, H. (2001) 'How does Europeanization Affect CEE Governance? Conditionality, Diffusion and Diversity', *Journal of European Public Policy*, 8(6): 1013–30.

Greenwood, J. (2003) *Representing Interests in the European Union*, 2nd edn, Basingstoke: Palgrave Macmillan.

Grewe, C. and Ruiz-Fabri, H. (1995) *Droits constitutionnels européens*, Paris: Presses Universitaires de France.

Gustavsson, S. (1999) 'Reconciling Suprastatism and Democratic Accountability', *Harvard Jean Monnet Working Paper*, 11/99.

Habermas, J. (2001) 'Why Europe Needs a Constitution', *New Left Review*, 11: 5–26.

Hall, P. (ed.) (1998) *The Political Power of Ideas: Keynesianism Accross Nations*, Princeton, NJ: Princeton University Press.

Harding, C. (1992) 'Who Goes to Court in Europe? An Analysis of Litigation against the European Community', *European Law Review*, 17(2): 105–25.

Harlow, C. (1992), 'Towards a Theory of Access for the European Court of Justice', *Yearbook of European Law*, 12(2): 213–48.

Hass, E. (1958) *The Uniting of Europe: Political, Economic and Social Forces, 1950–57*, Stanford, CA: Stanford University Press.

Hayes-Renshaw, F. and Wallace, H. (1997) *The Council of Ministers*, Basingstoke: Macmillan.

Héritier, A. (1999) 'Elements of Democratic Legitimation in Europe: an Alternative Perspective', *Journal of European Public Policy*, 6(2): 269–82.

Hix, S. (1999) *The Political System of the European Union*, Basingstoke: Palgrave Macmillan.

Hix, S. (2000) 'How MEPs vote', *ESRC: One Europe or Several*, Briefing Note 1/00.

Hix, S. (2002) 'Constitutional Agenda-Setting through Discretion in Rule Interpretation: Why the European Parliament Won at Amsterdam', *British Journal of Political Science*, 32(3): 259–80.

Hix, S. and Lord, C. (1997) *Political Parties in the European Union*, Basingstoke: Macmillan.

Hix, S., Kreppel, A. and Noury, A. (2003) 'The Party System in the European Parliament: Collusive or Competitive?', *Journal of Common Market Studies*, 41(2): 309–31.

Hix, S., Noury, A. and Roland, G. (2003) 'Power to the Parties: Competition and Cohesion in the European Parliament, 1997–2001', *British Journal of Political Sciences*, 34(4): 767–93.

Hobsbawm, E. (1994) *The Age of Extremes: The Short Twentieth Century, 1914–1991*, London: Michael Joseph.

Hobsbawm, E. and Ranger, T. (eds) (1983) *The Invention of Tradition*, Cambridge: Cambridge University Press.

Hoffman, S. (1966) 'Obstinate or Obsolete? The Fate of the Nation State and the Case of Western Europe', *Daedalus*, 95.

Hoogh, L. and Marks, G. (1999) 'Making a Polity: the Struggle over European Integration', in H. Kitschelt, P. Lang, G. Marks and J. Stephens (eds), *Continuity and Change in Contemporary Capitalism*, Cambridge: Cambridge University Press.

Hoogh, L., Marks, G. and Wilson, C. J. (2002) 'Does Left/Right Structure Party Positions in European Integration?', *Comparative Political Studies*, 35(8): 965–89.

Imig, D. and Tarrow, S. (2000) 'Political Contention in a Europeanising Polity', *West European Politics*, 23(4): 73–93.

Imig, D. and Tarrow, S. (eds) (2001), *Contentious Europeans, Protest and Politics in an Emerging Polity*, Lanham/Boulder/New York/ Oxford: Rowman & Littlefield.

Joana, J. and Smith, A. (2002) *Les commissaires européens. Technocrates, diplomates ou politiques?* Paris: Presses de sciences-po.

Kagan, R. (2003) *Of Paradise and Power: America and Europe in the New World Order*, New York: Knopf.

Kassim, K., Menon, A., Peters, B. G. and Wright, V. (eds) (2001) *The National Co-ordination of EU Policy*, Oxford: Oxford University Press.

Keating, M. (1998) *The New Regionalism in Western Europe: Territorial Restructuring and Political Change*, Cheltenham: Edward Elgar.

Kenney, S. J. (2000) 'The Judges of the Court of Justice of the European Communities', in S. J. Kenney, W. M. Resinger and J. C. Reitz (eds), *Constitutional Dialogues in Comparative Perspective*, Basingstoke: Palgrave Macmillan.

Keohane, R. (2002) 'Ironies of Sovereignty, the European Union and the United States', *Journal of Common Market Statistics*, 3: 743–65.

Kohler-Koch, B. (1997) 'Organized Interests in European Integration: the Evolution of a New Type of Governance?', in H. Wallace and A. R. Young (eds), *Participation and Policy-Making in the European Union*, Oxford: Clarendon Press.

Kohler-Koch, B. (2000) 'Framing: the Bottleneck of Constructing Legitimate Institutions', *Journal of European Public Policy*, 7(4): 513–31.

Kreppel, A. (2002) *The European Parliament and Supranational Party System: a Study in Institutional Development*, Cambridge: Cambridge University Press.

Lacroix, J. (2002a) 'Le "national-souverainisme" en France et en Grande-Bretagne', *Revue internationale de politique comparée*, 9(3): 391–408.

Lacroix, J. (2002b) 'For a European Constitutional Patriotism', *Political Studies*, 50: 944–58.

Laffan, B., O'Donnell, R. and Smith, M. (2000) *Europe's Experimental Union: Rethinking Integration*, London: Routledge.

Lamy, P., Jeanneney, J.-N., Nallet, H. and Strauss-Kahn, D. (2001) 'Europe: pour aller plus loin', *Le Monde*, 20 June 2001.

Leben, C. (1991) 'A propos de la nature juridique des Communautés européennes', *Droits*, 14: 61–72.

Lefébure, P. and Lagneau, E. (2002) 'Le Moment Vilvoorde: action protestataire et espace public européen', in R. Balme, D. Chabanet and Vincent Wright (eds), *L'Action collective en Europe*, Paris: Presses de sciences-po.

Le Galès, P. and Lequesne, C. (eds) (1998) *Regions in Europe*, London: Routledge.

Leibfried, S. and Pierson, P. (2000) 'Social Policy, Left to Courts and Markets?', in H. Wallace and William Wallace (eds), *Policy-making in the European Union*, Oxford: Oxford University Press.

Lenaerts, K. (1992) 'Some Thoughts about the Interaction between Judges and Politicians in the European Community', *Yearbook of European Law*, 1–34.

Lequesne, C. and Rivaud, P. (2001) 'Les Comités d'experts indépendants: l'expertise au service d'une démocratie supranationale?', *Revue française de science politique*, 51(6): 867–80.

Lewis, J. (2002) 'National Interests: Coreper', in J. Peterson and M. Schackleton (eds), *The Institutions of the European Union*, Oxford: Oxford University Press.

Lijphart, A. (1999) *Patterns of Democracy*, New Haven, CT: Yale University Press.

Lippert, B., Umbach, G. and Wessels, W. (2001) 'Europeanization of CEE Executives: EU Membership Negotiations as a Shaping Power', *Journal of European Public Policy*, 8(6): 980–1012.

Lord, C. (1998) *Democracy in the European Union*, Sheffield: Sheffield Academic Press.

Lord, C. (2004) *A Democratic Audit of the European Union*, Basingstoke: Palgrave Macmillan.

Lowi, T. (1979) *The End of Liberalism: The Second Republic of the United States*, New York: Norton.

MacGowan, F. (2000) 'Competition Policy: the Limits of the European Regulatory State', in H. Wallace and W. Wallace (eds), *Policy-making in the European Union*, Oxford: Oxford University Press.

MacKay, D. (2001) *Designing Europe: Comparative Lessons from the Federal Experience*, Oxford: Oxford University Press.

MacMullen, A. (1997) 'European Commissioners: National Routes to a European Elite', in N. Nugent (ed.), *At the Heart of the Union*, Basingstoke: Macmillan.

MacRae, K. (1997) 'Contrasting Styles of Democratic Decision-making: Adversarial versus Consensual Politics', *International Political Science Review/Revue Internationale de science politique*, 18(3): 279–96.

Maduro, M. P. (1998) *We the Court: The European Court of Justice and the European Economic Constitution*, Oxford: Hart.

Maduro, M. P. (2001) 'L'Équilibre insaisissable entre la liberté économique et les droits sociaux dans l'Union européenne', in

P. Alston et al. (eds), *L'Union européenne et les droits de l'homme*, Brussels: Bruylant.

Magnette, P. (1999) *La Citoyenneté européenne: Droits, politiques, institutions*, Brussels: Editions de l'Université de Bruxelles.

Magnette, P. (2000) *L'Europe, l'état et la démocratie. Le Souverain apprivoisé*, Brussels: Complexe.

Magnette, P. (2001) 'Appointing and Censuring the Commission: the Adaptation of Parliamentary Institutions to the Community Context', *European Law Journal*, 7(2): 292–310.

Magnette, P. (2003) 'European Governance and Civic Participation: Beyond Elitist Citizenship?', *Political Studies*, 52(1): 144–61.

Magnette, P. and Nicolaïdis, K. (2004) 'The European Convention: Bargaining in the Shadow of Rhetoric', *West European Politics*, 27(3): 381–404.

Mair, P. (2000) 'The Limited Impact of Europe on National Party Systems', *West European Politics*, 23(4): 27–51.

Majone, G. (ed.) (1996) *Regulating Europe*, London: Routledge.

Majone, G. (1997) *La Communauté européenne: un Etat régulateur*, Paris: Montchrestien.

Majone, G. (2001a) 'Two Logics of Delegation', *European Union Politics*, 2(1): 103–22.

Majone, G. (2001b) 'Nonmajoritarian Institutions and the Limits of Democratic Governance: a Political Transaction-Cost Approach', *Journal of Institutional and Theoretical Economics*, 157(1): 57–78.

Malova, D. and Haughton, T. (2002) 'Making Institutions in Central and Eastern Europe, and the Impact of Europe', *West European Politics*, 25(2): 101–20.

Mancini, G. and Kelling, R. (1994) 'Democracy and the European Court of Justice', *Modern Law Review*, 57(1): 175–93.

Manners, I. (2002) 'Normative Power Europe: a Contradiction in Terms?', *Journal of Common Market Studies*, 40(2): 235–58.

Mansfield, H. C. Jr (1989) *Taming the Prince: The Ambivalence of Modern Executive Power*, New York: Free Press.

Marcussen, M., Risse, T., Engelmann-Martin, D., Knopf, H. J. and Roscher, K. (1999) 'Constructing Europe? The Evolution of French, British and German Nation State Identities', *European Journal of Public Policy*, 6(4): 614–33.

Marks, G., Scharpf, F., Schmitter, P. and Streeck, W. (2003) *Governance in the European Union*, London: Sage.

Marks, G. and Steenbergen, M. (eds) (2004) *European Integration and Political Conflict*, Oxford: Oxford University Press.

Marquand, D. (1979) *Parliament for Europe*, London: Jonathan Cape.

Mattila, M. (2003) 'Contested Decisions: Empirical Analysis of Voting in the EU Council of Ministers', *European Journal of Political Research*.

Mattila, M. and Lane, J.-E. (2001) 'Why Unanimity in the Council? A Roll Call Analysis of Council Voting', *European Union Politics*, 2(1): 31–52.

Mattli, W. and Slaughter, A.-M. (1998) 'Revisiting the European Court of Justice', *International Organization*, 52(1): 177–209.

McNamara, K. (2002) 'Rational Fictions: Central Bank Independence and the Social Logic of Delegation', *West European Politics*, 25(1): 47–76.

Menon, A. (2003) 'Member States and International Institutions: Institutionalizing Intergovernmentalism in the European Union', *Comparative European Politics*, 1(2): 171–202.

Meynaud, J. (1964) *La technocratie, Mythe ou réalité?* Paris: Payot.

Millon-Delsol, C. (1992) *L'Etat subsidiaire: le principe de subsidiarité aux fondements de l'histoire européenne*, Paris: Presses universitaires de France.

Milner, H. (2002) *Civic Literacy: How Informed Citizens Make Democracy Work*, Hanover, NH: University Press of New England.

Milward, A. (1992) *The European Rescue of the Nation State*, London: Routledge.

Milward, A. and Sørensen, V. (1993) 'Interdependence or Integration? A National Choice', in A. Milward et al., *The Frontier of National Sovereignty: History and Theory, 1945–1992*, London: Routledge.

Monnet, J. (1976) *Mémoires*, Paris: Fayard.

Moravcsik, A. (1998) *The Choice for Europe: Social Purpose and State Power from Messina to Maastricht*, Ithaca, NY: Cornell University Press.

Moravcsik, A. (2002) 'In Defence of the "Democratic Deficit": Reassessing Legitimacy in the European Union', *Journal of Common Market Studies*, 40(4): 603–24.

Muller, P. (2000) 'L' Analyse cognitive des politiques publiques: vers une sociologie politique de l'action publique', *Revue française de science politique*, 50(2).

Muller, P., Mény, Y. and Quermonne, J.-Q. (eds) (1996) *Adjusting to Europe: The Impact of the EU on National Institutions and Policies*, London: Routledge.

Nicolaïdis, K. and Howse, R. (eds) (2001) *The Federal Vision: Legitimacy and Levels of Governance in the United States and the European Union*, Oxford: Oxford University Press.

Nicolaïdis, K. and Howse, R. (2002) ' "This is my Utopia ...": Narrative as Power', *Journal of Common Market Studies*, 40(4): 767–92.

Noury, A. (2002) 'Ideology, Nationality and Euro-parliamentarians', *European Union Politics*, 3(1): 33–58.

Nugent, N. (ed.) (1997) *At the Heart of the Union: Studies of the European Commission*, Basingstoke: Macmillan.

Nugent, N. (2001) *The European Commission*, Basingstoke: Palgrave Macmillan.

Olsen, J. (2002a) 'Reforming European Institutions of Governance', *Journal of Common Market Studies*, 40(4): 581–602.

Olsen, J. (2002b) 'The Many Faces of Europeanisation', *Journal of Common Market Studies*, 40(5): 921–52.

Papadopoulos, Y. (1998) *Démocratie directe*, Paris: Economica.

Percheron, A. (1991) 'Les Français et l'Europe. Acquiescement de façade ou adhésion véritable?', *Revue française de science politique*, 41(3): 382–406.

Pescatore, P. (1981) 'Les Travaux du "groupe juridique" dans la négociation des traités de Rome', *Studia Diplomatica*, 34: 159–78.

Peterson, J. and Bomberg, E. (1999) *Decision-making in the European Union*, Basingstoke: Macmillan.

Pierson, P. (1996) 'The Path to European Integration: a Historical Institutionalist Analysis', *Comparative Political Studies*, 29(2): 123–63.

Pollack, M. (1997) 'Delegation, Agency and Agenda Setting in the European Community', *International Organisation*, 51(1): 99–134.

Pollack, M. (2002) *The Engines of European integration: Delegation, Agency and Agenda Setting in the European Union*, Oxford: Oxford University Press.

Przeworski, A., Stokes, S. C. and Manin, B. (eds) (1999) *Democracy, Accountability and Representation*, Cambridge: Cambridge University Press.

Putnam, R. D. (1994) *Making Democracy Work: Civic Traditions in Modern Italy*, Princeton, NJ: Princeton University Press.

Quermonne, J.-L. (2002) *L'Europe en quête de légitimité*, Paris: Presses de sciences-po.

Quermonne, J.-L. (2004) *Le Système politique de l'Union européenne*, 5th edn, Paris: Montchrestien.

Radaelli, C. (1999) *Technocracy in the European Union*, London: Longman.

Rasmussen, H. (1980) 'Why is Article 173 Interpreted against Private Plaintiffs?', *European Law Review*, 5(2): 112–27.

Rasmussen, H. (1986) *On Law and Policy in the European Court of Justice: A Study in Comparative Judicial Policy-Making*, Leyden: Stijhoff.

Raunio, T. (1997) *The European Perspective: Transnational Party Groups in the 1989–94 European Parliament*, Aldershot: Ashgate.

Raunio, T. and Hix, S. (2000) 'Backbenchers Learn to Fight Back: European Integration and Parliamentary Government', *West European Politics*, 23(4): 142–68.

Rawlings, C. (1993) 'The Eurolaw Game: Some Deductions from a Saga', *Journal of Law and Society*, 20: 309–40.

Rawls, J. (2003), 'Three Letters on the Law of the Peoples and the European Union', *Revue de philosophie économique*, 7–20.

Reynié, D. (2004) *La Fracture occidentale*, Paris: La table ronde.

Ricoeur, P. (1987) *Ideology and Utopia*, New York: Columbia University Press.

Risse, T. and Engelmann-Martin, D. (2002) 'Identity Politics and European Integration: the Case of Germany', in A. Pagden (ed.), *The Idea of Europe: From Antiquity to the European Union*, Cambridge: Cambridge University Press.

Rittberger, B. (2001) 'Which Institutions for Post-war Europe? Explaining the Institutional Design of Europe's First Community', *Journal of European Public Policy*, 8(5): 673–708.

Roemetsch, D. and Wessels, W. (eds) (1996) *The European Union and Member States: Towards Institutional Fusion?* Manchester: Manchester University Press.

Rokkan, S. (1999) *State Formation, Nation-Building and Mass Politics in Europe: The Theory of Stein Rokkan*, ed. P. Flora, S. Kuhnle and D. Urwin, Oxford: Oxford University Press.

Rosenau, J. (1997) *Along the Domestic-Foreign Frontier: Exploring Governance in a Turbulent World*, Cambridge: Cambridge University Press.

Ross, G. (1995) *Jacques Delors and European Integration*, Cambridge: Polity Press.

Rousseau, J.-J. (1997a) *Discourse on the Origin and Foundations of Inequality Among Men* (1755), in *The Discourses and Other Early Political Writings*, ed. V. Gourevitch, Cambridge: Cambridge University Press.

Rousseau, J.-J. (1997b) *The Social Contract* (1762), in *The Social Contract and other Later Political Writings*, ed. V. Gourevitch, Cambridge: Cambridge University Press.

Rozenberg, O. and Surel, Y. (eds) (2003) *Parlementarismes et construction européenne*, *Politique européenne*, special issue (9).

Sandel, M. (1996) *Democracy's Discontent: America in Search of a Public Philosophy*, Cambridge, MA: Belknap Press of Harvard University Press.

Sartori, G. (1976) *Parties and Party Systems: A Framework for Analysis*, Cambridge: Cambridge University Press.

Sartori, G. (1994) *Comparative Constitutional Engineering: An Inquiry into Structures, Incentives and Outcomes*, Basingstoke: Macmillan.

Saurugger, S. (2002) 'L' Expertise: un mode de participation des groupes d'intérêt au processus décisionnel communautaire', *Revue française de science politique*, 52(4): 375–401.

Scharpf, F. (1988) 'The Joint Decision Trap: Lessons from German Federalism and European Integration', *Public Administration*, 66(3): 239–78.

Scharpf, F. (1998) *Governing in Europe: Efficient and Democratic*, Oxford: Oxford University Press.

Scharpf, F. (2000) *Notes Toward a Theory of Multilevel Governing in Europe*, Max-Planck-Institut für Gesellschaftsforschung, Discussion Paper 00(5).

Scharpf, F. (2003) 'Legitimate Diversity: the New Challenge of European Integration', *Zeitschrift für Staats- und Europawissenschaften*, 1(1): 32–60.

Schmidt, V. (1997) 'European Integration and Democracy: the Differences among Member States', *Journal of European Public Policy*, 4(1): 128–45.

Schmidt, V. (2002) *The Futures of European Capitalism*, Oxford: Oxford University Press.

Schmidt, V. (2004) 'The European Union: Democratic Legitimacy in a Regional State?', *Journal of Common Market Studies*, 42(4).

Schoutheete, P. de (2006) 'The European Council', in J. Peterson and M. Schackleton (eds), *The Institutions of the European Union*, 2nd edn, Oxford: Oxford University Press.

Seiler, D.-L. (1998) *La Vie politique des Européens*, Paris: Economica.

Shapiro, M. (1999) 'The European Court of Justice', in P. Craig and G. de Bùrca (eds), *The Evolution of EU Law*, Oxford: Oxford University Press.

Slaughter, A.-M. (2004) *A New World Order*, Princeton, NJ: Princeton University Press.

Slaughter, A.-M., Stone Sweet, A. and Weiler, J. (eds) (1998) *The European Court and National Courts, Doctrine and Jurisprudence: Legal Change in its Social Context*, Oxford: Hart.

Smismans, S. (2003) 'European Civil Society: Shaped by Discourses and Institutional Interests', *European Law Journal*, 9(4): 482–504.

Smismans, S. (2004) *Law, Legitimacy and European Governance: Functional Participation in Social Representation*, Oxford: Oxford University Press.

Spence, D. and Edwards, G. (eds) (1998) *The European Commission*, 2nd edn, London: Cartermill.

Stein, E. (1981) 'Lawyers, Judges and the Making of a Transnational Constitution', *American Journal of International Law*, 75(1): 1–27.

Stevens, A. and Stevens, H. (2001) *Brussels Bureaucrats? The Administration of the European Union*, Basingstoke: Macmillan.

Stone Sweet, A. (2000) *Governing with Judges: Constitutional Politics in Europe*, Oxford: Oxford University Press.

Stone Sweet, A. and Brunell, T. L. (1998) 'The European Court and the National Courts: a Statistical Analysis of Preliminary References, 1961–95', *Journal of European Public Policy*, 5(1): 66–97.

Stone Sweet, A., Sandholtz, W. and Fligstein, N. (eds) (2001) *The Institutionalization of Europe*, Oxford: Oxford University Press.

Surel, Y. (2000) 'L' Intégration européenne vue par l'approche cognitive et normative des politiques publiques', *Revue française de science politique*, 50(2): 235–54.

Tallberg, J. (2002) 'Delegation to Supranational Institutions: Why, How, and with What Consequences?', *West European Politics*, 25(1): 23–46.

Taulègne, B. (1993) *Le Conseil européen*, Paris: Presses Universitaires de France.

Telò, M. (ed.) (2000) *The European Union, Regionalism and Globalisation*, Aldershot: Ashgate.

Telò, M. (2004), *L'Europa, Potenza Civile*, Bari: Laterza.

Tilly, C. (1992) *Contrainte et capital dans la formation de l'Europe, 1990–1990*, Paris: Aubier.

Tocqueville, A. de (1985) *La Démocratie en Amérique*, Paris: Garnier-Flammarion.

Tushnet, M. (2003) *A New Constitutional Order*, Princeton, NJ: Princeton University Press.

Van Der Eijck, C. and Franklin, M. (1996) *Choosing Europe*, Ann Arbor, MI: University of Michigan Press.

Wallace, H. (1993), 'Deepening and Widening: Problems of Legitimacy for the EC', in S. Garcià (ed.), *European Identity and the Search for Legitimacy*, London: Pinter.

Wallace, H. and Wallace, W. (eds) (2000) *Policy-making in the European Union*, Oxford: Oxford University Press.

Wallace, H. and Young, A. R. (eds) (1997) *Participation and Policy-making in the European Union*, Oxford: Clarendon Press.

Wallace, W. (1983) 'Less than a Federation, More than a Regime: the Community as a political system', in H. Wallace, W. Wallace and

C. Webb (eds), *Policy-making in the European Community*, 2nd edn, New York: Wiley.

Weiler, J. H. H. (1981). 'The Dual Nature of the European Community', *Yearbook of European Law*.

Weiler, J. H. H. (1985) *Il sistema communitario*, Bologna: Il Mulino.

Weiler, J. H. H. (1991) 'The Transformation of Europe', *Yale Law Journal*, 100: 2403–83.

Weiler, J. H. H. (1993) 'Journey to an Unknown Destination: a Retrospective and Prospective of the European Court of Justice in the Arena of Political Integration', *Journal of Common Market Studies*, 31(4): 417–46.

Weiler, J. H. H. (1997) 'To Be a European Citizen: Eros and Civilization', *Journal of European Public Policy*, 4(4): 495–519.

Weiler, J. H. H. (1999) *The Constitution of Europe*, Cambridge: Cambridge University Press.

Weiler, J. H. H. (2001) 'Federalism without Constitutionalism: Europe's Sonderweg', in K. Nicolaïdis and R. Howse (eds), *The Federal Vision: Legitimacy and Levels of Governance in the United States and the European Union*, Oxford: Oxford University Press.

Weil, P. and Hansen, R. (eds) (2001) *Towards a European Nationality? Citizenship, Immigration and Nationality Law in the European Union*, Basingstoke: Palgrave Macmillan.

Weisbein, J. (2002) 'Le Lobbying associatif à Bruxelles, entre mobilisations unitaires et sectorielles', *Revue internationale de politique comparée*, 9(1).

Westlake, M. (1999), 'The European Parliament's Emerging Powers of Appointment', *Journal of Common Market Studies*, 36(3): 431–44.

Weyembergh, A. (2004) *L'harmonisation des législations: condition de l'espace pénal européen*, Brussels: Editions de l'Université de Bruxelles.

Wood, G. (1969) *The Creation of the American Republic, 1776–1787*, Chapel Hill: University of North Carolina Press.

Wood, G. (2002) *The American Revolution: A History*, New York: Modern Library.

Index